TRANSACTIONS
of the
American Philosophical Society
Held at Philadelphia for Promoting Useful Knowledge

VOLUME 78, Part 3, 1988

Texts and Their Traditions in the Medieval Library of Rochester Cathedral Priory

MARY P. RICHARDS
Auburn University

THE AMERICAN PHILOSOPHICAL SOCIETY

Independence Square, Philadelphia

1988

Copyright © 1988 by the American Philosophical Society

Library of Congress Catalog
Card Number 87-072869
International Standard Book Number 0-87169-783-1
US ISSN 0065-9746

CONTENTS

List of Tables	v
List of Abbreviations and Symbols	vii
Preface	ix
I. The Rochester Cathedral Library	1
II. The *Textus Roffensis*	43
III. The Medieval Vulgate Tradition at Rochester	61
IV. The Medieval Homiliary at Rochester	86
V. Conclusion	121
Index	124

LIST OF TABLES

1. The Medieval Catalogues of Rochester Cathedral Library 23
2. MSS. Royal 2 C. III, Lincoln Cathedral 158 and Cambridge U. L. Kk.IV.13 99
3. MSS. Harley 652, Cambridge U. L. Ii.II.19, and Edinburgh NL Adv.18.2.4 105
4. MS. Vatican Lat. 4951 112

LIST OF ABBREVIATIONS AND SYMBOLS

I. The following symbols in Table 1 are adopted from Ker, *MLGB*, to indicate evidence of provenance:
c evidence from contents
e evidence from an *ex libris* inscription or note of gift
g evidence from an inscription consisting of a title followed by a personal name in the genitive
i evidence from an inscription of ownership by an individual member of a religious house
m evidence from marginalia
s evidence from character of script or illumination

II. Other abbreviations are as follows:
A.A.S.S. *Acta Sanctorum Ordinis S. Benedicti*, ed. L. d'Achery and J. Mabillon. 9 vols. Paris, 1668-1701.
AF The homiliary attributed to Alan of Farfa, described in Grégoire 1: 1-70.
Amb. Autp. Ambrosius Autpertus.
Barré It. MS., described in H. Barré, *Les Homéliaires Carolingiens de l'Ecole d'Auxerre*.
BL British Library.
CCCM Corpus Christianorum. Continuatio Medievalis.
CCSL Corpus Christianorum. Series Latina.
Clavis *Clavis Patrum Latinorum*, ed. E. Dekkers and E. Gaar, *Sacris Erudiri* 3, 1961.
EETS Early English Text Society.
Fleury The homiliary of Fleury, described in Grégoire 2: 263-80.
Grégoire 1 Reginald Grégoire, *Les Homéliaires du Moyen Age*, Rerum Ecclesiasticarum Documenta Series Maior, Fontes 6 (Rome, 1966).
Grégoire 2 Reginald Grégoire, *Homéliaires Liturgiques Médiévaux: Analyse de Manuscrits*, Biblioteca degli "Studi Medievali" 12 (Spoleto, 1980).
Grenoble 32 One of the Carthusian homiliaries described in R. Etaix, "L'Homéliaire Cartusien."
Mai A. Mai, *Nova Patrum Bibliotheca*, 1 (1852).
Ottobeuren The homiliary of Ottobeuren, described in Grégoire 2:321-42.
PG J.-P. Migne, *Patrologiae Cursus completus. Series graeca*.
PL J.-P. Migne, *Patrologiae Cursus completus. Series latina*.
PLS A. Hamman, *Patrologiae latinae, Supplementum*.

Ps. Aug. Pseudo-Augustine.
Ps. Max. Pseudo-Maximus.
Rd'A The Roman homiliary attributed to the priest Agimundus, described in Grégoire 2: 343-92.
Rab. Maur. Hrabanus Maurus.
Toledo The homiliary of Toledo, described in Grégoire 2: 293-319.
Vienne The homiliary of Vienne, described in Grégoire 2: 281-91.
Wilmart Andre Wilmart, "La collection des 38 homélies latines de S. J. Chrysostom," *Journal of Theological Studies,* 19: 305-27.
Wolfenbüttel The homiliary of Wolfenbüttel, described in Grégoire 2: 281-91.

PREFACE

When, in the aftermath of the Conquest, Lanfranc was consecrated archbishop of Canterbury, one of his earliest acts was to inspect the neighboring see at Rochester. There he found a dispirited group of some four canons inhabiting a few decayed buildings, all that remained of a secular foundation dating from the time of Augustine's missionary activities in Kent.[1] Founded by Æthelberht, king of Kent, in 604, Rochester served from the beginning as a small secular community first under Bishop Justus, and later under such illustrious men as Romanus, Paulinus, and Ithamar. Unlike the ecclesiastical centers of Winchester and Canterbury, Rochester remained relatively small and poor. It was an urban foundation and the seat of a small diocese, but its absence from historical and ecclesiastical records after the seventh century indicates that it played little, if any, part in the developments of Anglo-Saxon Christianity over the next three hundred years. Its very poverty and insignificance during this period, however, make Rochester an ideal backdrop against which to view the accomplishments of post-Conquest, Norman-influenced monasticism in southeastern England.

Particularly striking is Rochester's sudden involvement in learning and book production after refoundation as a Benedictine monastery. Whereas its surviving pre-Conquest books are largely homiletic collections in Old English, as might befit an unlearned secular community with parochial responsibilities, the new library emerged with standard patristic texts copied from Canterbury and continued to draw on local resources throughout the twelfth century. Paradoxically, books remaining from Rochester are in many instances important, if not unique, witnesses to Latin and Old English textual traditions borrowed from Christ Church and St. Augustine's, Canterbury, owing to losses suffered by the latter foundations at the Dissolution. In addition to the many items borrowed, the Rochester library in time began to include a substantial number of records relating to its history and possessions, witnesses to a growing self-consciousness of its particular role in the establishment of Christianity in England and of the continuing need to document holdings acquired after refoundation.

The post-Conquest scriptorium and library of Rochester are accessible to us through a fortunate set of coincidences. Not only were two extensive catalogues made in c. 1124 and 1202, but at least half of the books recorded

---

[1] Reginald A. L. Smith quotes three accounts of Lanfranc's discovery in "The Early Community of St. Andrew at Rochester, 604-c.1080," *English Historical Review*, 60 (1945): 299.

there, and a number of books not mentioned, survived the Dissolution.[2] A large proportion of the extant volumes has been preserved in the Royal collection housed in the British Library. Additional help in identifying Rochester books has been provided by a series of fourteenth-century *ex libris* inscriptions on the flyleaves of many volumes and, in fewer cases, pressmarks. Aside from identification purposes, the medieval inventories provide a means for tracing the growth of the library and the productivity of the scriptorium. From 1124 to 1202 the list expands from 98 to 246 items, a number in multi-volume sets. These resources are supplemented by still other materials preserving records from Rochester, including lists of donations, chronicles, charters, and two additional fragmentary catalogues of the medieval library.

Using these materials, scholars have begun the work of editing, attributing, and analyzing manuscripts and texts from the Rochester library. Foremost among these is Neil R. Ker, whose second edition of *Medieval Libraries of Great Britain* is the place where any study of the subject must begin.[3] His subsequent treatment of the distinctive Rochester variant of the Christ Church, Canterbury, script style that flourished in the first half of the twelfth century is essential to understanding the development of the scriptorium.[4] Peter Sawyer's facsimile edition of the *Textus Roffensis* makes available the single most important book produced at Rochester accompanied by cogent paleographic analysis.[5] The editions of Alistair Campbell (charters), Felix Liebermann (laws), and Rodney Thomson (*Vita Gundulfi*), together with the second edition of Dorothy Whitelock's *English Historical Documents*, augment Ker and Sawyer. Texts and studies published through the years in *Archaeologia Cantiana* record a steady interest in all aspects of the Rochester Cathedral and Priory.[6] And the work of Reginald A. L. Smith, incomplete at his untimely death in the Second World War, remains indispensable for the early history of the Rochester see and its post-Conquest relationship to Canterbury.[7]

These and other scholars, whose work will be drawn upon in the course of this book, have demonstrated that the study of Rochester manuscripts contributes substantially to the history of post-Conquest Benedictine monasticism. But much remains to be done before the full extent of Rochester's role in copying, compiling, and preserving texts in the pre- and post-Con-

---

[2] Notice of the Dissolution is given in John Le Neve, *Fasti Ecclesiae Anglicanae 1541-1857*, comp. Joyce M. Horn, III. Canterbury, Rochester and Winchester Dioceses (London, 1974), 45.

[3] N. R. Ker, *Medieval Libraries of Great Britain*, 2nd ed. (London, 1964), xi and 160-64. The catalogues occur in the *Textus Roffensis*, fols. 224-30, and BL MS. Royal 5 B. XII, fol. 2. They are printed respectively by R. P. Coates in *Archaeologia Cantiana*, 6 (1864-65): 122-28, and by W. B. Rye, *Archaeologia Cantiana*, 3 (1861): 54-61.

[4] *English Manuscripts in the Century after the Norman Conquest* (Oxford: 1960), 25-32.

[5] Early English Manuscripts in Facsimile, vols. 7 and 11 (Copenhagen, 1957 and 1962).

[6] *Charters of Rochester*, Anglo-Saxon Charters, v. 1 (London, 1973); *Die Gesetze der Angelsachsen*, 3 vols. (Halle, 1903-16; rpt. 1960); *The Life of Gundulf Bishop of Rochester*, Toronto Mediaeval Latin Texts, v. 7 (Toronto, 1977); *English Historical Documents c. 500-1042*, 2nd ed. (London, 1979).

[7] In *Collected Papers*, ed. David Knowles (London, 1947).

quest periods can be known. Issues such as paleographic influences and innovations, selection of texts, textual transmission and modification, and the choice and use of vernacular materials must be pursued as far as possible. From there, conclusions regarding the sources and aims of manuscript production at Rochester, the relationship of its texts to those at Canterbury, and the particular features of certain southeastern textual traditions can be drawn. The present study proposes to address the issues outlined above and to suggest implications for the history of the Rochester scriptorium and library by a series of related investigations of carefully defined groups of texts.

Using evidence provided by medieval inventories of the library, donation lists, and the extant manuscript books, the first investigation will focus on the growth of the library at Rochester—the kinds of books acquired and copied there—and will identify those individual manuscripts and groups of manuscripts that can provide the greatest insights into the activities of the scriptorium. The ensuing investigations will pursue the areas of paleography, sources, and relationships of texts in great detail, from the *Textus Roffensis*, through the Gospel and Vulgate texts, to the homiliaries in Old English and Latin. The aim is to focus on those works of central significance to the life of the Benedictine foundation as keys to the development of the Rochester library and to a better understanding of the sources and range of important textual traditions in southeastern England. By defining textual traditions at Rochester and tracing them, in so far as possible, to Canterbury and beyond, we can bring new focus to a subject that thus far has been studied from limited perspectives.

This study was aided by the cooperation of many individuals and institutions. First among these are the staffs of the British Library, the Bodleian Library, the Corpus Christi College, Cambridge library, the Huntington Library, the Pierpont Morgan Library, the Edinburgh National Library, the Walters Art Gallery, the Bibliothèque Nationale and the Kent County Archives Office. I am grateful for their continued assistance in matters large and small. I also wish to express thanks to the supervisor of the Vatican Film Library at St. Louis University, and to the staff of the Interlibrary Services Department at the University of Tennessee. Support for research was provided by the Huntington Library and the Hodges Better English Fund at the University of Tennessee.

Special assistance through the years has been offered by Richard Ringler, Linda E. Voigts, Paul E. Szarmach, Thomas Cable, Robert E. Lewis, and Gordon Whatley. My colleagues Joseph B. Trahern, Jr., and John H. Fisher have extended encouragement and critical judgments unselfishly. David A. E. Pelteret has helped with the *Textus Roffensis*. My students Chadwick B. Hilton and B. Jane Stanfield developed an inspiring enthusiasm for the Old English laws that led me to consider more basic questions about the *Textus*. To these and other colleagues who have offered their questions and observations at professional meetings, or dropped a note with a helpful reference, I give sincere thanks.

I am indebted to Jean Lester, who typed and revised the manuscript cheerfully and accurately. C. W. Minkel lent support in the final stages of the study, not the least by allowing his Associate Dean to travel one more time to visit manuscript collections in Great Britain. To my husband Bob, and my friends Kay, Herbert, and Millicent I owe a special debt of thanks for their support.

Any errors of fact or interpretation are solely my responsibility.

M.P.R.

I. THE ROCHESTER CATHEDRAL LIBRARY

The history of the medieval library assembled at Rochester Cathedral Priory begins with the refoundation of the see as a Benedictine monastic cathedral in 1075.[1] Although it had been one of the earliest cathedral foundations in Kent, dating from the advent of Bishop Justus in 604, St. Andrew's, Rochester did not thrive continuously during the Anglo-Saxon period.[2] Neither its endowments, nor the size of community they could support, was sufficient for Rochester to become a center of learning and book production. The small group of secular canons established there probably lived a regular life "centered in the Mass, the Divine Office, and the common duties of the episcopal household,"[3] but they were removed from the tenth-century monastic revival that brought, among other developments, the excitement of continental scholarship and texts to England.[4] The canons possessed a Bible, service-books, charters and other records, homilies in Old English and a copy, now lost, of the Old English translation of Gregory's *Regula Pastoralis* sent from King Ælfred to Bishop Swipulf, but otherwise the community must have accumulated only a few books before the arrival of the Norman bishops.[5]

---

[1] For a revised date, see Katherine M. Waller, *The Library, Scriptorium, and Community of Rochester Cathedral Priory C. 1080-1150* (Univ. of Liverpool doctoral thesis, 1980). An overview of the history of the library is provided by W. H. Mackean, *Rochester Cathedral Library* (Rochester, 1953), and a description of its surviving books by Rachael Stockdale in "Benedictine Libraries and Writers," *The Benedictines in Britain*, ed. D. H. Turner, et al. (New York, 1980), 62-69. See also James W. Thompson, *The Medieval Library*, rpt. with a supplement by Blanche B. Boyer (New York, 1957), 278-82, and E. Anne Read, *The Cathedral Libraries of England*, Oxford Bibliographical Society Occasional Publication no. 6 (Oxford, 1970), 40-42.

[2] See Smith, "The Early Community of St. Andrew at Rochester," 289-99, and Anne M. Oakley, "The Cathedral Priory of St. Andrew, Rochester," *Archaeologia Cantiana*, 91 (1976 for 1975): 47. Less accurate is the account by R. C. Fowler in *The Victoria History of the Counties of England, Kent* (London, 1926), 2:121-26. The economic condition of the priory has been studied in detail by Ann F. Brown in *The Lands and Tenants of the Bishopric and Cathedral Priory of St. Andrew, Rochester, 600-1540* (London Univ. doctoral thesis, 1974).

[3] Smith, "The Early Community of St. Andrew at Rochester," 294.

[4] Helmut Gneuss associates only four extant books with Rochester before 1100. See "A preliminary list of manuscripts written or owned in England up to 1100," *Anglo-Saxon England*, 9 (1980): 1-60. None of the texts described by F. A. Rella in "Continental Manuscripts Acquired for English Centers in the Tenth and Early Eleventh Centuries: A Preliminary Checklist," *Anglia*, 98 (1980): 107-16, is connected with Rochester.

[5] Neil R. Ker, *Catalogue of Manuscripts Containing Anglo-Saxon* (Oxford, 1957), 385. Ker, 257, quotes an inscription copied from the first leaf of BL MS. Cotton Tiberius B. XI before the fire of 1731: " + Plegmunde arcebisc. is agifen his boc. 7 Swipulfe bisc. 7 Werferpe bisc." See also Kenneth Sisam, "The Publication of Alfred's *Pastoral Care*," in his *Studies in the History of Old English Literature* (Oxford, 1953), 140-47, and Dorothy M. Horgan, "The Relationship between the O.E. MSS of King Alfred's Translation of Gregory's *Pastoral Care*," *Anglia*, 91 (1973): 164 and 169. The kinds of books owned by the canons would not have formed a library in the modern

As evidence of this state of affairs, just five pre-Conquest manuscripts surviving today have been assigned a Rochester provenance, and three of these may have originated elsewhere.[6] The oldest, a late tenth-century copy of Statius' *Thebaid* (BL MS. Royal 15 C.X) in a continental hand, seems to be a post-Conquest acquisition.[7] The work does not appear in the first inventory of the Rochester library recorded in the cartulary of the *Textus Roffensis* about 1124, yet it is listed in the second catalogue made in 1202.[8] Gneuss associates the volume tentatively with Canterbury, a center with continental connections in the late tenth century.[9] Thus, although the date of acquisition is uncertain, there is no evidence to suggest that the Statius belonged to Rochester before the middle of the twelfth century.

Another pre-Conquest classical work, an eleventh-century copy of Juvenal's *Satires* (Oxford MS. Bodleian Wood B.3), has a fourteenth-century Rochester *ex libris* yet is mentioned in neither medieval catalogue of the library. According to the *Summary Catalogue*, the text was copied in Italy, and Gneuss can find no evidence that it came to England before 1100.[10] A third pre-Conquest manuscript, "Goda's Gospels" (BL MS. Royal 1 D.III), can also be eliminated from the canons' ownership. This volume, an eleventh-century book once owned by Godgifu, half-sister to Edward the Confessor, did not reach Rochester until the reign of William I. (1087-1100).[11]

Aside from possible links to Ely and Norwich, only the fourth and fifth items, contemporary collections of vernacular homilies from the early eleventh century (Oxford MSS. Bodley 340 and 342 and Cambridge MS. Corpus Christi College 162), have a substantial claim to Rochester ownership prior to the refoundation of the see.[12] The Bodley set is mentioned in both catalogues of the library and it contains materials specifically designated for Rochester.[13] It is closely related to MS. 162, which also contains materials of local interest. From a southeastern textual tradition, these homiliaries contain the type of materials that might have been useful to the unlearned canons in their own services as well as in those for the laity.[14]

---

sense, as shown by David Dumville in "English Libraries Before 1066: Use and Abuse of the Manuscript Evidence," in *Insular Latin Studies*, ed. Michael Herren, Papers in Mediaeval Studies I (Toronto, 1981), 1:165.

[6] See Ker, *MLGB*, 160-64.

[7] See T. A. M. Bishop, *English Caroline Minuscule* (Oxford, 1971), xxii, xxv, 20, and no. 6. Description in *Catalogue of Western Manuscripts in the Old Royal and King's Collections*, ed. George F. Warner and Julius P. Gilson (London, 1921), 2:168. See also the entry, 542-43, in B. Munk Olsen, *L'Etude des auteurs classiques latins aux XIe et XIIe siècles*, 2 (Paris, 1985).

[8] See Table 1, item 199.

[9] Gneuss, "A preliminary list," 32, no. 497. See also *Texts and Transmission: A Survey of the Latin Classics*, ed. L. D. Reynolds (Oxford, 1983), xxxii and Helmut Gneuss, "Dunstan and Hrabanus Maurus zur HS. Bodleian Auctarium F.4.32," *Anglia*, 96 (1978): 146 and n. 36.

[10] See *A Summary Catalogue of Western Manuscripts in the Bodleian Library at Oxford* (1895-1953), 2:1193: no. 8574, reference provided by Professor Gneuss; Olsen 1: 580.

[11] *Catalogue of Western Manuscripts in the Old Royal and King's Collections*, 1:16.

[12] The evidence of Rochester provenance is described in detail in Chapter IV, 88-90.

[13] Ker, *Catalogue*, 361-67.

[14] Mary P. Richards, "Innovations in Ælfrician Homiletic Manuscripts at Rochester," *Annuale Mediaevale*, 19 (1979): 16-17.

In summary, unlike its neighbor Christ Church, Canterbury, the Anglo-Saxon foundation at Rochester lacked direct involvement in events associated with the Benedictine Revival and never became a comparable center of learning. On the positive side, however, Rochester seems to have participated actively in the transmission of Old English homiletic materials in the eleventh century, a reflection perhaps of its role as a secular cathedral serving also as the parish church. The canons would have been able to interact with the larger community to a much greater extent than monks, and could train others for parochial duties if they did not undertake such themselves.[15] But with the Conquest came a significant change. The monks installed in the refounded Benedictine cathedral priory undertook the development of a monastic scriptorium and library. For this purpose, as we will see, they drew most heavily on Christ Church, Canterbury, resources and augmented those with continental texts and materials borrowed from other English libraries. These new efforts, reflecting a closer relationship between the sees of Canterbury and Rochester, began a decade after the Conquest, soon after the last Anglo-Saxon bishop of Rochester, Siward, died in the fall of 1075.

The first Norman named to the Rochester episcopate was the monk Arnost, who held office for only one year before his death.[16] With the subsequent consecration of Bishop Gundulf in 1077, fortunes of the Rochester see began to improve.[17] Owing to a long, close friendship and working relationship with Lanfranc, first at Bec, then Caen, and afterwards at Canterbury, Gundulf was able to use his subordinate role to advantage.[18] He worked with Lanfranc to model the Rochester foundation upon that of Christ Church, Canterbury. He replaced the secular canons with a body of twenty-two Benedictine monks, some from Bec, adopted the monastic constitutions of Lanfranc, imitated the financial system of Canterbury, and began rebuilding the cathedral church, seemingly on the plan of Christ Church.[19]

In the course of these activities, Gundulf established a scriptorium, probably in temporary wooden buildings, and organized the effort that resulted fifty years later in a library with more than ninety books.[20] It appears that Gundulf formed his scriptorium on the pattern he had used in many other matters, that of Christ Church, Canterbury. The affinity in styles of script

---

[15] David Blake, "The Development of the Chapter of the Diocese of Exeter," *Journal of Medieval History,* 8 (1982): 1.

[16] John Le Neve, *Fasti Ecclesiae Anglicanae 1066-1300,* comp. Diana E. Greenway, II. *Monastic Cathedrals* (London, 1971), 75. Siward took part in Lanfranc's consecration ceremony of 29 August 1070 and remained in office under the new Norman archbishop. See Margaret Gibson, *Lanfranc of Bec* (Oxford, 1978), 115. For an account of the Norman takeover of the English church, see John Le Patourel, *The Norman Empire* (Oxford, 1976), 35-38; on p. 51, he gives the provenance of Rochester bishops, 1066-1144.

[17] Ibid.

[18] Gibson, 155-56.

[19] Reginald A. L. Smith, "The Place of Gundulf in the Anglo-Norman Church," in *Collected Papers,* 92-94.

[20] Ibid., 97, quoting W. H. St. John Hope.

and illumination, together with instances of joint Canterbury-Rochester productions of manuscripts and Rochester copies made from Canterbury originals, bespeaks a close relationship between the two scriptoria.[21] Similarly, the collections of books produced bear a resemblance to each other, though the Christ Church library was of course the larger and contained several volumes in Greek.[22] To a certain degree, the affinity of the collections derived from the scriptorium and library of the Norman abbey of Bec. Both Lanfranc and Gundulf professed vows and received early training there. When Lanfranc sought to augment the library at Christ Church, Canterbury, he began by acquiring books from Bec and having others copied by Bec scribes.[23] The Bec influence reached Rochester indirectly through its connections with Canterbury encouraged by Gundulf, himself a monk of Bec, as well as through newcomers from Bec who came to live at the refounded Rochester priory.[24]

Specific Bec influences on the copying of texts at Rochester will be explored in more detail in the course of this study, but it will be useful here to summarize them briefly. The distinctive script style developed at Christ Church and adapted at Rochester originated at Bec.[25] So did the emphasis on plain books, which demonstrated greater care taken in textual accuracy than in decoration.[26] The impetus to catalogue the growing Rochester library may have come partly from Bec monks, for the library of the Norman abbey was recorded in at least two medieval catalogues.[27] And, more generally, the shape of the new collection followed the Benedictine model that Lanfranc brought from the continent. His first acquisitions for the Canterbury library, some of which he solicited from Bec, included a set of canon laws and works of the fathers—Augustine, Ambrose, Jerome, and Gregory the Great.[28] When we compare these materials with a list of Rochester books copied in turn from Canterbury manuscripts, we find a similar group of selections—Augustine, Ambrose, Gregory, Eusebius, Jerome, John Chrysostom, and Solinus.[29] These volumes were basic to a medieval monastic library, but,

---

[21] On this topic, see particularly Charles R. Dodwell, *The Canterbury School of Illumination* (Cambridge, 1954), 119.

[22] Henry Eastry's catalogue of the Christ Church, Canterbury, library is printed in Montague R. James, *The Ancient Libraries of Canterbury and Dover* (Cambridge, 1903), 13-142. The extant books are listed in Ker, *MLGB*, 29-39.

[23] Gibson, 179-81.

[24] Oakley, 47-48.

[25] See Neil R. Ker, *English Manuscripts in the Century after the Norman Conquest* (Oxford, 1960), 25-26.

[26] Dodwell, 16-17.

[27] The Bec catalogues are printed by Gustav H. Becker in *Catalogi Bibliothecarum Antiqui* (Bonn, 1885), as no. 86, pp. 199-202, and no. 127, pp. 257-66. For an important discussion of terminology, see Albert Derolez, *Les Catalogues des Bibliothèques*, Typologie des Sources du Moyen Age Occidental, fasc. 3 (Turnhout, 1979).

[28] Gibson, 180.

[29] Ker, *English Manuscripts in the Century after the Norman Conquest*, 14-15. See also James S. Beddie, "Libraries in the Twelfth Century: Their Catalogues and Contents," in *Haskins Anniversary Studies in Medieval History*, ed. Charles H. Taylor and John L. La Monte (Boston, 1924), 1-23.

under the set of conditions outlined above, they can be traced to the specific, if indirect, influence of Bec.

The nature of Gundulf's role in the actual acquisition of books remains something of a mystery. The *Vita Gundulfi* by a contemporary monk at Rochester is silent on Gundulf's reputation as a scholar and founder of the scriptorium and library.[30] The author commemorates Gundulf's tears of compunction rather than devotion to learning.[31] In fact, the evidence remaining of Gundulf's contributions to the library dates from the thirteenth century, more than a hundred years after his death. First, he is memorialized in a list of donations recorded in BL MS. Cotton Vespasian A. XXII, fol. 88r, for having given two missals "sine epistolis et sine ewangeliis" and a benedictional, none of which has survived.[32] Additionally, an inscription on the flyleaf of each volume in a two-part Vulgate (Huntington Library MS. HM 62) attributes the donation to Gundulf,[33] but descriptions of this Vulgate in the medieval Rochester catalogues do not mention a donor. Thus there are no extant books that we can connect definitely with Gundulf. The bits of evidence we have suggest that his concern was to provide liturgical and devotional texts for his fledgling foundation of monks. The close relationship he established between Rochester and Christ Church, Canterbury, together with the interests and training of the new monks from Bec, must have led naturally, however, to a more ambitious program of collecting and copying texts.

Gundulf's successor, Ralph d'Escures, held office at Rochester for six years, 1108-14, before acceding to the archbishopric of Canterbury.[34] Credited with a bequest of a handsome volume containing the *vita* and history of St. Andrew, Ralph continued to develop the library and maintain the building program, probably by expanding the church begun by Gundulf.[35] Ralph's interest in learning is well documented, and his removal to Canterbury at this critical point in Rochester's development must have strengthened its ties to Canterbury.[36] As evidence of this, the Rochester library experienced its greatest period of growth, including the copying of numerous Canterbury books, during the episcopate of Ralph's successor, Ernulf (1114-24) who, coincidentally, had served earlier as prior of Christ Church. Dr. Katharine Waller, who has attempted to define the Rochester house style

---

[30] Printed in PL 159: 813-36, and newly edited by Rodney M. Thomson for Toronto Medieval Latin Texts, v. 7.

[31] Thomson, 10-11.

[32] Excerpts from the donation list are printed by W. B. Rye in *Archaeologia Cantiana*, 3 (1861): 62-63. See also the useful description of the MS. in Andrew G. Watson, *Catalogue of Dated and Datable Manuscripts c. 700-1600 in the Department of Manuscripts, The British Library* (London, 1979), 1:108.

[33] For the text of the inscriptions, see Chapter III, 69.

[34] Le Neve, 75.

[35] See Rye's edition of the thirteenth-century donation list, 62, and W. H. St. John Hope, "The Architectural History of the Cathedral Church and Monastery of St. Andrew at Rochester," *Archaeologia Cantiana*, 23 (1898): 216-17.

[36] Waller, 28-29.

of book production during this period and after, believes that as many as twelve scribes were at work preparing books in the years 1107-1122/23.[37]

In addition to fostering an expanded scriptorium and library, Ernulf consolidated the work of his predecessors and completed the monastic establishment at Rochester. Specifically, he had built a dorter, refectory, and chapter house, and he probably commissioned the *Textus Roffensis*, an ambitious undertaking designed to preserve records of Rochester's Anglo-Saxon heritage.[38] Although he clearly appreciated the resources available through a close relationship with Canterbury, Ernulf took the lead in establishing a separate identity for Rochester. The compilation of the *Textus Roffensis*, the development of a distinctive Rochester variant of the prickly script style originating at Christ Church, and the establishment of a new Rochester style of illumination together bespeak a tendency toward independent developments at least in manuscript production during Ernulf's episcopacy.

Another important area revealing Ernulf's initiative is the acquisition of exemplars. Waller has shown provisionally, and the present study will confirm, that the Rochester scriptorium looked to Norman and other English sources for texts that Christ Church, Canterbury, was unable to provide.[39] On occasion St. Augustine's, Canterbury, contributed to the Rochester library. Thus it comes as no surprise to learn that the post-Conquest Rochester Priory participated in what we today would call a network of textual traditions, some pre-Conquest in origin, available in southeastern England. Waller has suggested that Rochester may have acquired texts from as far north as Peterborough, owing to Ernulf's having served there just prior to his episcopacy. This may be the case, but there is no firm evidence to support it. Only the Old English version of the life of St. Neot, which occurs uniquely in a homiletic manuscript associated with Rochester, betrays an East Anglian connection. On the other hand, clear links to centers in London to the north, and Canterbury to the southeast, define a geographical area roughly equivalent to Kent, from which Rochester seems to have drawn the bulk of materials from English libraries.

The matter of sources will be addressed in greater detail in the chapters to follow. At this point it is important to stress that because of its history, Rochester Priory not only possessed Old English homiletic collections of the type extremely popular in the eleventh century, but it also acquired a monastic library in a matter of three decades in the early twelfth century. Both undertakings meant that neighboring resources had to be tapped extensively and, therefore, that texts produced at Rochester during this period represent a microcosm of locally available manuscript traditions.

Ernulf's pride in the library is evident in the catalogue of holdings entered into the cartulary of the *Textus Roffensis* about 1124. Any study of the

---

[37] Ibid., 134.
[38] Richard W. Southern, *Saint Anselm and His Biographer* (Cambridge, 1963), 269-70.
[39] Waller, 177-92.

Rochester library must begin with this remarkable full documentation of its contents just after the period of greatest growth. Three additional catalogues trace the further expansion of the library into the early thirteenth century. However, none of these catalogues has been studied as a text, to determine the cataloguer's method and what it reveals about the make-up of the library. Nor has a composite edition of the catalogues been attempted. Table 1, therefore, following this chapter, presents the medieval booklists in parallel columns, with the catalogue in the *Textus Roffensis* serving as the base text to which the others are compared, and cites the extant manuscripts where they are known.

The catalogue begun under Ernulf is organized similarly to the continental model used at Bec, as opposed to those from Christ Church, Canterbury, and its cell at Dover which are arranged alphabetically by author or title, and by donor. The Rochester catalogue opens with individual lists for works of the Fathers—Augustine, Jerome, Ambrose, Gregory, and Bede. Each list is rubricated by author. Augustine heads fol. 224r, Ambrose fol. 227r, Gregory fol. 227v, Bede fol. 229r, leaving only Jerome's rubric to fall in the middle of a page (fol. 225r, l. 16). The remaining volumes in the inventory are entered after Gregory's works on fol. 227v and after those of Bede on 229r, continuing on to 229v. An additional leaf, fol. 230, was added later in the twelfth century and eight more volumes are listed there.[40] Blank spaces were left at the bottom of fol. 226r, all of fol. 226v, the bottom of 228r, and all of 228v. These may have been intended to accommodate further additions to the catalogue such as have been made in part of the blank space on fol. 228r.[41]

Within the catalogue, volumes are assigned to author lists based on the first text in the codex, as illustrated by item 18 under Augustine's rubric. Augustine is the author only of the first of fifteen items in the volume, today Cambridge MS. Corpus Christi College 332.[42] This entry provides an illustration typical of the method of the cataloguer. Unlike many medieval cataloguers, he goes beyond the first item in a volume to give a sense of the entire contents. He does not, however, list every text, as we can discover from examining the extant manuscripts to which he refers. In the present entry, he has skipped a sermon by Jerome on the consecration of the Virgin, and a sermon by Ambrose on the assumption of the Virgin which follows the sermon on her nativity.[43] Further, he abbreviates descriptions, as in the

---

[40] See the facsimile edition of the *Textus Roffensis*, ed. P. Sawyer, v. 7, fols. 224r-30r.

[41] See T. A. Heslop, "'Dunstanus Archiepiscopus' and painting in Kent around 1120," *The Burlington Magazine*, 126 (1984): 195-203. The scribe must have intended originally to copy the author lists sequentially because Jerome's list begins in the middle of the page, directly after Augustine's. Cramped entries just preceding Jerome's rubric indicate that this scheme was inadequate to accommodate further volumes that came to hand and needed to be added to the author lists, and so the scheme was modified to allow for this contingency.

[42] Ker, *MLGB*, 160.

[43] Compare the description made by Montague R. James, *A Descriptive Catalogue of the Manuscripts in the Library of Corpus Christi College* (Cambridge, 1912), 2: 158-60.

reference to *sermones de assumptione sanctae mariae*, a group which in fact includes five sermons attributed to two authors, Rathramnus and Jerome. Nor does he specify two works connected with Anselm occurring in the volume, *De eterna beatitudine* (a sermon written down by Eadmer) and *De conversatione monachorum*. Despite these types of inaccuracies, the cataloguer manages to give a good picture of the range of works available at Rochester, and his detailed entries provide great help in identifying extant manuscripts with volumes listed in the catalogue.

Aside from the author rubrics, the catalogue in the *Textus Roffensis* contains no internal references to the arrangement of the books, nor does it indicate donors. The presentation of works clearly implies that the writings of the Fathers are fundamental, and the remaining volumes supplementary. Perhaps a sign of the haste with which the collection was assembled, works of amazing variety can be bound together within a single volume, as in item 43, where selections from Ambrose accompany Justin's abbreviation of Pompeius Trogus. Although the cataloguer aims to give a sense of the full contents of each volume, he says nothing of the physical condition of the books, i.e., bound or unbound, complete or incomplete. In short, the first catalogue of the Rochester library conveys an excellent sense of the works available there, but little additional information.

The analysis of the Rochester library to follow will be based on the two major medieval catalogues (compiled c. 1124 and 1202) and supplemented by information from two partial catalogues and from extant manuscripts identified with entries in the catalogues as presented in Table 1. Entry numbers are indicated in parentheses after the works mentioned in the course of the present chapter. Where the volumes have been lost and the catalogue descriptions are sketchy, there will be gaps in the account that can never be filled. There are some additional volumes, however, which have been associated with Rochester on evidence of provenance but are not recorded in the catalogues. As mentioned earlier, a fourteenth-century *ex libris* inscription beginning *Liber de claustro Roffensi* is entered at the foot of the flyleaf of many volumes attributed to the Rochester library.[44] When there are sound reasons of this kind to believe that certain codices were part of the medieval library, they too will be described after the catalogues have been analyzed. Since their dates of acquisition are uncertain in many cases, these uncatalogued volumes are better treated apart from the medieval book lists.

In 1124 the Rochester library consisted mainly of patristic and devotional texts, a fairly typical collection for a Benedictine foundation of its age and stature, yet one containing some individual items of interest for the light they shed on the development of the scriptorium and its relationship to other southeastern centers, especially Christ Church, Canterbury. Among the Fathers, the works of Augustine and Jerome predominate. Most of Augustine's works appear, including *De civitate dei* (2), *De doctrina christiana*

---

[44] Ker, *MLGB*, 160.

(10), the *Confessiones* (15), the *Retractationes* (16), and numerous commentaries, treatises, and sermons. Jerome is represented by his commentaries on Matthew (20), the twelve prophets (21), Daniel (21), the epistle to Titus (23), Isaiah (27), the Psalter (28), Ezekiel (31), Jeremiah (34), and Ecclesiastes (35), and many other works including the famous tract against Jovinian (22) and the *Interpretationes hebraicorum nominum* (29). Works by Ambrose include *De officiis* (36), the *Hexameron* (37), *De fide* (42), two tracts on virginity (38), his exposition of Luke (41), and the *De mysteriis* (44). The booklist wrongly attributes to him the *De conflictu vitiorum atque virtutem* of Ambrosius Autpertus (39). From Gregory appear the *Liber Regulae Pastoralis* (46) in Latin and Old English, the *Dialogi* (46), *Moralia in Job* (45), the *Registrum* (48) of his letters, a work entitled *Speculum* (49), and two volumes of his homilies on Ezekiel (50).[45] Bede is well represented with the *Historia Ecclesiastica* (65), *De temporibus* (66), *De aequinoctio* (i.e., his letter to Wicthed—66), *De arte metrica, De schematibus*, the metrical life of St. Cuthbert (all together in 67), *De tabernaculo Dei* (35), commentaries on Acts (35), Apocalypse (69), Mark (70), Nehemiah, Ezra, and Tobias (all in 68), and his *Martyrologium* (71).

Moving to other early Christian writers, we find six works mentioned for Isidore (in 16, 23, 67, 96, but not including the *Etymologiae*), two for Alcuin (*De dialectica*—67, *De trinitate*—59), two attributed to Ephraim the Syrian (*De compunctione cordis*—39 and a volume of homilies together with unspecified works—76), and one each for John Chrysostom (*De reparatione lapsi*—59), Prosper of Aquitaine/Julianus Pomerius (*De vita contemplativa et activa*—52), Julian of Toledo (*Prognosticon*—39), Paschasius Radbertus (*De corpore et sanguine Domini*—39), and Defensor (*Liber Scintillarum*—60). There are several anonymous biblical commentaries and collections of patristic excerpts in the list, along with a group of devotional texts and service-books, including at least three homiliaries, two lectionaries, a passional, two benedictionals (possibly the gift of Gundulf as mentioned in his donation list), a Psalter, and an Epistolary. No doubt the priory owned a larger supply of Bibles and service-books than is indicated in the catalogue, but these probably were stored apart from the main library.[46] Several volumes are devoted to monastic life: the rules of Augustine (11), John Cassian (72), and Benedict (71), Amalarius' *De officiis divinis* (63), the *Diadema Monachorum* of

---

[45] The work in question may be a copy of the *Speculum* often attributed to Augustine, a compendium of biblical extracts arranged in 144 chapters. This is printed, with an introduction, by Angelus Maius in *Novae Patrum Bibliothecae, tomus primus, continens Sancti Augustini novos ex codicibus Vaticanis Sermones* (Rome, 1852), 2:i-viii and 1-115. A *Speculum* attributed to Gregory occurs in a late tenth-century manuscript from Christ Church, Canterbury (Cambridge, Trinity College MS. B.4.27[141]); see Nicholas Brooks, *The Early History of the Church of Canterbury: Christ Church from 597-1066* (Leicester, 1984), 267, and the description in Montague R. James, *The Western Manuscripts in the Library of Trinity College, Cambridge, A Descriptive Catalogue* (Cambridge, 1900), 1:166-67.

[46] Beddie, 9-10. Particulary useful on this point is Michael Lapidge, "Surviving booklists from Anglo-Saxon England," in *Learning and Literature in Anglo-Saxon England*, ed. Michael Lapidge and Helmut Gneuss (Cambridge, 1985), 34-36.

Smaragdus (61), Lanfranc's *Constitutiones* (71), and Ralph of Battle's *Octo Puncta* (80).[47]

One suspects Ernulf's influence behind the collection of legal texts in the early Rochester library: these include at least four sets of decretals (16, 56, 57, 98) and a volume of laws of the English kings (now part of the *Textus Roffensis*—62). Histories, too, are numerous. Works by Josephus (89), Hegesippus (53), Orosius (58), Eusebius in the translation by Rufinus (55), Jordanes (58), Bede (65), Paul the Deacon (73), Nennius (90), and a *hystoria normannorum* (64)[48] appear in the first catalogue. Grammatical treatises include Cassiodorus' *Institutiones* (16) and *Collationes* (75), Bede's *De arte metrica* and *De schematibus*, and Alcuin's *De dialectica* (together in 67). Additionally, we find a volume containing Bede's *De temporibus* together with Alberic's treatise on the computus, and another containing the *De spera mundi* of Hyginus accompanied by an excerpt from the *Somnium Scipionis* of Macrobius (73). No Greek texts appear in the catalogue, but a handful of classical texts were available in Latin and Latin translation:[49] Justin's abbreviation of Pompeius Trogus (43), an abridgement of Julius Valerius' translation of the *Gesta Alexandri* (73), the so-called letter of Alexander the Great to Aristotle (73), Solinus' *De mirabilibus mundi*, Dares' *History of the Trojan Wars*, Priscian's rendering of the *Periegesis* of Dionysius, and the tenth sibyl's prophecy prefaced by Lactantius and followed by the acrostic (all four in 90). Also of interest are copies of Palladius' *Paradysus* attributed to Heraclitus (25), and the *Itineraria* of Peter (54).

Mention has been made of the early patristic texts identified by Ker as having been copied from Canterbury originals.[50] Numerous other volumes underline the close relationship between the Rochester and Canterbury scriptoria. Rochester owned works related to former archbishops of Canterbury, including Lanfranc's treatise against Berengar of Tours, Lanfranc's letters (79) and those of his pupil, Ivo of Chartres (44), the two works associated with Anselm mentioned previously and his *Cur Deus Homo* (6), the treatise *De ratione et peccatore* by Ralph d'Escures (80),[51] and the lives of SS. Dunstan and Elphege (77). Masses for Dunstan and Elphege representing formularies used at Christ Church, Canterbury, are found in a now

---

[47] The *Octo Puncta* is the second item in the volume described *Liber de ratione et peccatore cum pluribus opusculis in uno uolumine*. See Hugh Farmer, "Ralph's Octo Puncta of Monastic Life," *Studia Monastica*, 2 (1969): 19-29.

[48] Probably that of Dudo of St. Quentin, perhaps in the abridgement by William of Jumièges.

[49] Helpful on this subject are James S. Beddie, "The Ancient Classics in the Mediaeval Libraries," *Speculum*, 5 (1930): 3-20; *Texts and Transmissions*; M. David Knowles, "The Preservation of the Classics," and R. M. Wilson, "The Contents of the Mediaeval Library," in *The English Library before 1700*, ed. Francis Wormald and C. E. Wright (London, 1958), 136-47 and 85-111; R. A. B. Mynors, "The Latin Classics Known to Boston of Bury," in *Fritz Saxl*, ed. D. J. Gordon (London, 1957), 199-217.

[50] Waller gives evidence for several additional Christ Church exemplars of Rochester books, 155-66.

[51] Richard W. Southern, "St. Anselm and His English Pupils," *Medieval and Renaissance Studies*, 1 (1941-43): 27-29.

fragmentary Rochester manuscript at the Vatican, MSS. Reg. lat. 646 fols. 1-48; 458 fols. 1-36; 598 fol. 8r.[52] Of the three volumes in English so designated in the catalogue—*Pastoralis anglicus* (51), *Institutiones regum anglorum* (62), and *Sermonalia anglica* (83)—the latter two survive today as witnesses to vernacular traditions common to Christ Church, St. Augustine's, and Rochester, to be explored in Chapters II and IV. The Vulgates with a Rochester provenance are closely related to texts from Canterbury and Dover, as will be seen in Chapter III.

The catalogue in the *Textus Roffensis* was continued well into the twelfth century on fol. 230, a leaf added specifically for that purpose containing items 91-98. In its manuscript context, the catalogue was part of a larger effort to document the priory's holdings, responsibilities, and privileges, and, as with certain other records in the collection, it was kept up to date for decades after initial compilation. This circumstance may have been inspired unintentionally by Ernulf's successor John I, a former archdeacon of Canterbury. The first post-Conquest bishop at Rochester without monastic affiliation, John tried to separate the holdings of bishopric and priory to the disadvantage of the monks.[53] The question of ownership was not settled until 1145, when the Pope's legate, Imar of Tusculum, issued a report in favor of the monks.[54] In this unsettled atmosphere, a full record of the library might have been needed as a way to record ownership of books in threat of dispersal. Despite individual volumes of interest, and certain areas of strength, however, the early Rochester library clearly was not that of a great cathedral priory and center of learning in England. It lacked, for instance, scientific, mathematical, and musical texts. But as the library continued to grow through the twelfth century, the deficiencies in the collection diminished. A fragmentary catalogue compiled soon after 1124, and two catalogues from the early thirteenth century, document further expansion.

The second twelfth-century booklist of the monastic library appears on two butterfly-shaped fragments once intended to line seal bags, now part of the archive of the dean and chapter of Rochester Cathedral (DRc/Z18,1-2).[55] The remains of the word CHIROGR[APHUM] at the top of Z18/1 indicate that a duplicate copy of the list was made. When compared with the earlier list in the *Textus Roffensis*, the fragmentary catalogue is seen to have been copied directly from its predecessor, with new items added to the end of the earlier list. The fragments have been cut from a single sheet, which appears to have contained the entire inventory written full across the page, with horizontal spaces left to separate author groupings. Using the current numeration of the fragments, we can piece together the puzzle. Fragment 1r

---

[52] Daniel Sheerin, "Masses for Sts. Dunstan and Elphege from the Queen of Sweden's Collection at the Vatican," *Revue Bénédictine*, 85 (1975): 199-207.

[53] Oakley, 50.

[54] *TR*, fols. 203v-204.

[55] My thanks to the Assistant County Archivist of Kent, Miss Kathleen M. Topping, for providing photocopies of the catalogue fragments, and of the transcription and description made by Miss Anne Oakley.

contains the first portion of Augustine's list as copied on fol. 224r, ll. 2-21, of the *Textus Roffensis*. Ten volumes from those attributed to Augustine in the *Textus* can be identified, and two of these, *Contra faustum manicheum* and *De trinitate*, have been moved forward within the list. Fragment 2r preserves the latter portion of Jerome's list as found on fol. 225v, ll. 14-24, and 226r, ll. 1-12, of the *Textus*. This fragment, it seems, was cut from the bottom portion of the same sheet as 1r, and so its material once was positioned below 1r. *Expositio super psalterium* has been moved forward but otherwise the list follows the entries in the *Textus Roffensis* exactly.

The versos of the fragments bear out the conjecture that the list was copied on a single sheet. Fragment 1v contains most of Gregory's list from fol. 227v, ll. 2-4, of the *Textus* and a portion of Bede's list from 229r, ll. 2-11. The present cataloguer adheres more rigorously to the independence of the author lists, for he skips the miscellaneous volumes that fill out Gregory's page in the *Textus*, and moves at once to Bede. Fragment 2v, preserving the end of the list, describes miscellaneous works grouped roughly by topic. The first portion of this fragment is devoted to saints' lives and biographies, including those of an unknown abbot of Cluny, the Ely saints Etheldreda, Witburga, and Sexburga, a *Miracula sancti brandani*, a work dealing with St. Augustine of Canterbury, and another on the popes of Rome. Following these are portions of the Bible, the *Sententiae* of Peter Lombard, glossed volumes and a book of sermons. Several of the miscellaneous items appear again in the 1202 Rochester catalogue as indicated in Table 1. Further, within fragment 2v occurs an interesting phrase following an incomplete description of a volume: *que seorsum a ceteris libris in arca cantoris recondunt*. This phrase indicates that books were stored separately in the *arca cantoris*, decades before the location was to be mentioned by the 1202 cataloguer.

As Ker states, the hand of this fragmentary catalogue is roughly contemporary with that of the *Textus Roffensis*.[56] It has been annotated and updated by later twelfth-century hands. At least three volumes in the miscellaneous group have been lined through: the miracles of St. Brendan, one concerning St. Augustine of Canterbury, and a volume of sermons. Neither of these saints' legends appears in other catalogues of the Rochester library, and, unfortunately, the book of sermons is impossible to identify. An author's name, Alcuinus, has been entered in a later hand over the work *De arte metrica*, fol. 1v, just as it is in the *Textus Roffensis* inventory. In a similar hand, a notation *prima pars est perdita* appears over the entry for a two-volume set of Gregory's commentary on Ezekiel, also fol. 1v. Finally, in fragment 2v, at least two works have been added in a blank space among the miscellaneous volumes: the books of Ezekiel, Daniel and the twelve prophets in one volume, and the *Sententiae* of Peter Lombard.

Though fragmentary, the present catalogue reinforces the conclusion that cataloguing the library was an ongoing concern of the Rochester monks,

---

[56] *MLGB*, 160.

and that multiple copies were desirable. Normally, the word *Chirographum* is used for duplicate copies of charters, to verify a true copy in support of later claims. Without pressing too far the evidence in these fragments, the impression they give is one of the need to document ownership of possessions against external threats.

By the time the second major catalogue was compiled in 1202, the Rochester library had more than doubled in size. This new booklist differs from the first, which had been copied into the *Textus Roffensis* as part of a larger records-keeping effort. The 1202 catalogue, by contrast, has been added to a volume of Augustine's works recorded in the 1124 catalogue. The compilation of the new inventory may, however, have been motivated by similar circumstances. Again, real threats to the monks coincided with the production of new records of their possessions.

In this case, the uncertainty was caused by Bishop Gilbert Glanville (1185-1214), former archdeacon of Lisieux and clerk to Baldwin, archbishop of Canterbury.[57] With the support of Henry II and Archbishop Baldwin, Gilbert planned to set up a college of secular canons at Rochester, part of a widespread movement to lessen the power of the regular orders of England. The plan failed only because Henry died in 1189. It was the first in another series of attempts to encroach upon the influence and possessions of the monks. Without consulting them, Gilbert appropriated several of their properties to support a hospital in Strood. Further, he assumed the right to appoint incumbents to vacant livings inside and outside the diocese. These incidents, plus lesser disputes over the distribution of the bishop's *xenium* and the right to appoint servants in the priory, coincided with the initiation of a series of efforts by the monks to establish their possessions. They made a catalogue of the full library and a separate list of books copied and acquired by Alexander the precentor.[58] At approximately the same time, they compiled a chronicle and a list of donations to the priory now found in BL MS. Cotton Vespasian A. XXII.

The catalogue made in 1202 is a compact, but neat, list in double columns copied on two leaves added to a volume of Augustine's works.[59] Although the codex in which it is found dates from the first quarter of the twelfth century, the cataloguer in 1202 intended his list to accompany this particular book, as evidenced by entry 11:

De doctrina christiana et de vera religione et de penitencia in uno volumine id est iste liber

in the main hand under the works of Augustine. The relatively crowded format, however, meant that the descriptions of volumes had to be abbreviated more severely than those in the first catalogue. For example, the exten-

---

[57] Oakley, 50-53.
[58] Alexander's list is copied on fol. 111v of BL MS. Royal 10 A. XII, and printed in Warner and Gilson's catalogue of the Royal Library, I:308-309.
[59] Quire 1 begins on fol. 4.

sive description of item 18 from Augustine's list in the 1124 catalogue is rendered as follows in 1202:

De presencia Dei ad Dardanum, et alia plura, in uno volumine.

Were it not for the earlier full descriptions of Rochester books, the task of identifying volumes and describing the extent of the medieval library would be far more difficult than it is. Like the first catalogue, however, the 1202 inventory was a working document used over a period of time. Hence spaces were left for additional items, often donated volumes, recorded in different inks and later hands. A typical addition occurs, for instance, in item 23 at the end of Augustine's list:

Duo libri veteris et novi testamenti Willemi de heth'ame.[60]

Another noteworthy feature of the 1202 catalogue is the effort made to identify the condition of the works in question:

Duos quaternii de spera mundi [a work unbound];
Prisciani magni.iiii duo perfecti et duo imperfecti.

The 1202 catalogue divides into five author lists, two groups of miscellaneous volumes, and three donor lists. Each classification has its own organizing principle, but the overall structure may reflect the arrangement of volumes within the priory. To begin, this inventory does not seem to have been made with the first at hand. The author lists follow a new order, with Gregory and Jerome exchanging positions. The revised order is Augustine, Gregory, Ambrose, Jerome, and Bede. Within the author lists, the volumes are rearranged and a few additions are made to the items mentioned in the first catalogue. Augustine's list is expanded by five volumes, including commentaries on John (3), Romans (13), I-II Corinthians (14), and Genesis (20), along with a book of sermons. The only other obviously new volume in the author lists is a glossed portion of the Old Testament under volumes attributed to Jerome (49). On the other hand, several volumes disappear from the author lists in the first inventory. In a few cases, these may be listed elsewhere in the 1202 catalogue within a slightly different description, but otherwise they have simply vanished. Specifically, two volumes containing multiple works of Augustine, and at least one volume of Jerome, are omitted by the later cataloguer. Another Jerome volume containing the lives of the Desert Fathers disappears from his author list, but may be subsumed in the reference

Vita Sanctorum Patrum, in duobus voluminibus (58)

found in one of the miscellaneous groups in the second catalogue. Two items from Gregory's list disappear, a two-volume set of the *Moralia* and the English translation of *Liber regulae pastoralis*. A volume containing several of

---

[60] The identity of the donor is uncertain, but perhaps he came from Ightham, Kent. See J. K. Wallenberg, *The Place-Names of Kent* (Uppsala, 1934), 153, for similar versions of the name.

Bede's works, Alcuin's *De dialectica,* and items attributed to Peter Damian, Isidore, Augustine, and others no longer appears under Bede's list, but may be the referent of a miscellaneous entry

Alquinus, cum ceteris operibus, in 1 vol. (97).

The work of Ambrosius Autpertus (82), wrongly listed under Ambrose in the first catalogue, moves to a miscellaneous group of texts in the later catalogue.

Given the extensive changes in the organization and content of the author lists, the 1202 catalogue must have been made independently of its predecessor. Yet, before proceeding to the subsequent lists of miscellaneous items, we need to account for another important feature of the second catalogue. That is, despite the kind of reorganization described above, items repeated in the 1202 catalogue appear invariably in the first half of the list. Of the first 115, approximately 83 occur in the earlier catalogue. As far as can be determined, no items from the first catalogue appear after number 115, a one-volume New Testament.

The early books occur together in the 1202 booklist, it seems, because they were stored together. Following the author lists, the designations for groups of miscellaneous books, *Item commune librarium* and *aliud librarium in archa cantoris,* suggest that physical location was at least one classifying principle in the 1202 catalogue. This is confirmed by item 110 under the *commune librarium:*

Ysidorus Ethimologia Roberti de Hecham in i volumine. Item aliud in arca cantoris.

A similar set of entries referring to two copies of glossed Pauline Epistles (items 68 and 69) shows that *Item alius* means another copy of the previously described volume. In the example above, then, one copy of the *Etymologia,* donated by Robert de Hecham, is said to be in the *commune librarium,* while a second resides in the *arca cantoris.* The donation list in MS. Cotton Vespasian A. XXII is helpful on this point, for it contains the entry:

Robertus de Hecham librum Ysidori Ethimologiarum posuit in armarium claustri.[61]

It would seem, then, that the *commune librarium* was a group of books stored in cupboards within the cloister. The arrangement of items in the booklist supports this interpretation, for they are grouped together roughly by author and by topic, just as they might have been arranged for reference in cupboards. For example, the *commune librarium* list begins with devotional books, followed by decretals, Psalters, Epistolaries, histories, the works of Isidore, and so forth. The groups are neither rigid nor exclusive, but they do convey the impression of conscious organization consistent with the preceding arrangement by author lists. Some inconsistencies likely were occasioned by the size of the volumes and the size and location of the cupboards.

---

[61] Rye, donation list, 63.

The second group of miscellaneous volumes, said to be stored in the *archa* (or *arca*) *cantoris*, continues to be arranged roughly by topic—glossed portions of the Vulgate, saints' lives and miracles, classbooks, classical authors, and so on. The exact nature of the location is a mystery with some clues. Elsewhere in the 1202 catalogue, the term *cantor* is used to describe the precentor, Alexander. An *archa* can mean an arch or a chest, possibly in the present context an arched cupboard under the supervision of the precentor.[62] Near the time when the catalogue was compiled, Bishop Glanville is reported to have finished the cloister in stone. More recently, archaeologists have found a series of sunk recesses with trefoil heads in one wall that might have served as storage areas for books when fitted out with shelves.[63] Although the evidence does not allow us to locate the *archa cantoris* with certainty, we can state that the more recent acquisitions recorded in the catalogue formed an independent group of volumes, organized by topic, within the new location.

The two collections of miscellaneous volumes in the 1202 inventory are worth examining in more detail. As mentioned previously, the *commune librarium* list is comprised of items found in the first catalogue together with later acquisitions which strengthen the early holdings in particular areas. The number of Epistolaries, glossed and unglossed, is increased from two to six, and three Psalters are added. The collection of decretals has been increased by three volumes of Gratian (61). Several new histories appear: those by Pseudo-Turpin (122), William of Malmesbury (120), and Peter Comestor (104). The works of Isidore are increased by the additions of *Synonyma* (80), *De summo bono* (80), and the *Etymologia* (110). Along with assorted volumes of sermons, biblical commentaries, florilegia, and saints' lives are at least two volumes of apocrypha—the miracles of St. James the Apostle (122) and a Latin Infancy Gospel (123).

Here and in the following group of miscellaneous volumes stored in the *archa cantoris*, donors' names are supplied for certain items. The ascriptions probably are accurate, for they refer only to volumes acquired since the first catalogue was made, and those donors who can be identified date from the twelfth century. The following donors appear under the *commune librarium*:

Master Hamo, probably a teacher at Rochester c. 1150-1200—first volume of Gratian's *Decretals*; first volume of Peter Lombard's *Sententiae*; one part of a glossed two-volume Psalter attributed to Peter Comestor (*unum Magistri H. antiqui, et aluid Magistri Hamonis iunioris*); a glossed Epistolary attributed to Comestor; and a glossed Pentateuch.

Radulph de Frend', probably from Frindsbury, Kent—second volume of *Decretals*.[64]
Roger de Derteford, from Dartford, Kent—third volume of Gratian's *Decretals*.[65]

---

[62] Having the precentor in charge of the library was typical monastic practice. See Francis Wormald, "The Monastic Library," in *The English Library Before 1700*, 20-21.
[63] W. H. St. John Hope, "The Architectural History of the Cathedral Church and Monastery of St. Andrew at Rochester, 2—The Monastery," *Archaeologia Cantiana*, 24 (1900): 30-34.
[64] J. K. Wallenberg, *Kentish Place-Names* (Uppsala, 1931), 49.
[65] Wallenberg, *The Place-Names of Kent*, 31-32.

Willem de Bradest, probably from Bradsted, Kent—second volume of Peter Lombard's *Sententiae*.[66]
Ascelin, bishop of Rochester 1142-48—one volume from each of two sets of volumes with glosses attributed to Gilbert of Porrée, namely, a Psalter and an Epistolary; an anonymous commentary on Matthew.
Waleran, bishop of Rochester 1182-84—the second volume in each of the two sets attributed to Gilbert of Porrée, and a volume of sermons.
Robert de Hecham, mentioned in MS. Cotton Vespasian A. XXII, f. 127 as a "monachus, fuit custos de manerio de Suffliete" during the episcopate of Gilbert Glanville, 1185-1214—Isidore's *Etymologiae*.[67]

The second group of miscellaneous texts, stored in the *archa cantoris*, continues some of the special interests noted in the first catalogue—glossed books of the Vulgate, canon law (*Acta Pontificum*—136, the *Panormia* of Ivo of Chartres—127, *Exceptiones Gundulfi de libris canonicis*—138), histories (Gregory of Tours—137, Apollonius of Tyre—168, and a chronicle by Adam of Cobham—166), sermons in Latin and Old English, and monastic treatises. Many of the newer acquisitions also fill significant gaps in the Rochester collection. There is a marked increase in hagiographic materials: the *Miracula* of Paulinus, bishop of Rochester, 633-44 (148); two copies each of the *Vita* and *Miracula* of Ithamar, the first Anglo-Saxon bishop of Rochester, 644-60 (147, 148, 169); the *Miracula* of Thomas à Becket (146); a *Vita Malchi* by Reginald of Canterbury (145); and two *sanctoralia* (151, 152) containing, among other unspecified items, the lives of SS. Etheldritha (of Ely), Wulfram (of Sens), and Mildred (of Thanet, Kent). Numerous texts for teaching appear for the first time, including works of Priscian (175, 176, 177), Donatus (180), *Remigius super Donatus* (179), Cato (192), Arator (186), Adam of Balsham (grammar—164), William of Conches (*Philosophia*—197), Peter Helias (*Summa*—200), and untitled volumes of dialectic, rhetoric, orthography, arithmetic, and music. The new, modest group of classical authors includes Terence, Sallust, Virgil, Horace, Ovid, Persius, Lucan, Statius, Seneca, Macrobius, and Boethius. Additional volumes of poetry include verses by Ernulf (167), hymns of Prudentius (189), his *Psychomachia* (196), and the miracles of the Virgin in verse (201). Also of interest are the letters of Sidonius Apollinaris (157), a Mappa Mundi (161)—possibly the work of Gervase of Canterbury,[68] and a lapidary (195). Our knowledge of these volumes can only be sketchy, because in most cases the books have disappeared.

Donations are specified, as follows:

Master Hamo, the elder—the *Lamentations of Jeremiah*.
Alexander, presumably Alexander the cantor, responsible for a list of donations appearing further on in the catalogue—two volumes of sermons, the letters of Sidonius Apollinaris.

---

[66] Ibid., 70.
[67] A. F. Brown, 175.
[68] Authorship proposed by Rye, 59, no. 160.

Wib', possibly Wibert, subprior and then prior of Christ Church, Canterbury, 1152-67—*Cantica Canticorum* and other unnamed works.
Master Robert, a fifth copy of Priscian.

Immediately following the list of books preserved in the *archa cantoris* are three lists of donated books that may have been stored in the same place, since no further designation of location is given and there is some repetition from the miscellaneous lists. Two of the three donors, Master Hamo and Alexander the cantor, are mentioned earlier in the catalogue, and a few of the books attributed to them appear again in these separate lists. The third name, one prior Robert of Walton, in Suffolk, site of Rochester's cell at Felixstowe, could be the donor called "Master Robert" mentioned above; the volumes on his list actually may have comprised a branch library at Felixstowe.[69] The first list of donations (items 202-17), attributed to Master Hamo, contains sixteen books, including two volumes of canon law, glossed portions of the Bible, the *Sententiae* of Peter Lombard, the *Summa* of John of Cornwall, a computistical and mathematical treatise, two sets of grammatical and rhetorical treatises, a grammar by Ralph of Beauvais and, finally, some classical texts in Latin—Aristotle's *Organon*, *Rhetorica ad herennium*, Cicero's *De officiis*, Ovid, Suetonius, and a volume of Claudian's poetry. In the second donation list (items 218-40), Alexander "quondam cantor" is credited with twenty books, mainly medical texts, including a copy of the *Viaticus* in the version by Constantine of Monte Cassino, the *Practica* of Bartholomeus, and the works of Odo of Meung, Quintus Serenus, Dynamides, Dioscorides, Oribasius, and Razi, the Arab. At least nine composite volumes are mentioned, along with one in English—*Medicinale anglicum*—probably the Old English version of Pseudo-Apuleius.

Lastly, in a slightly later hand, occurs a third list of six donations (items 241-46) by Robert of Walton, four of which have survived. These six include an abridgement of Gratian's *Decretals* made by Omnibonus; a commentary on the Psalter by Letbert, abbot of Ruf, that may once have belonged to the nunnery at Malling (*Spalterium Magalonensis*); a compendium of the Old and New Testaments; John of Salisbury's *Policraticus*; Gilbert Foliot's commentary on the Song of Solomon; and the *In unum ex quatuor* of Zacharias Chrysopolitanus, a commentary on Victor of Capua's Latin version of the *Diatessaron* of Tatian.

Additionally, there are some works copied and/or bound together with texts identified by catalogue entries and *ex libris* inscriptions as having been part of the Rochester library that deserve to be mentioned in this survey of the medieval holdings. Only those works that can be confidently associated with Rochester will be noted here. Among works of the Fathers, we find Jerome's commentaries on Paul's epistles to Titus and Philemon (BL MS. Royal 3 B. I), and numerous sermons of Augustine. From other early Chris-

---

[69] See the *Catalogue of Western Manuscripts in the Old Royal and King's Collections*, 2:63, and Stockdale, 69.

tian writers appear the *Expositio Hymnorum* by Hilary of Poitiers (Oxford MS. Bodley Laud misc. 40), and a *Vita beati Fursei* ascribed to Bede (A.A.S.S. 16 January) in MS. Royal 5 A. VII, which appears to have circulated separately as an unbound manuscript packet judging from the worn appearance of its outer leaves.

A few works have survived in two copies: Solinus' *De mirabilibus mundi*, Dares' history of the Trojan Wars, and the tenth sibyl's prophecy, copied together in volumes that also contained originally Nennius' *Historia Brittonum* and *De miraculis Britanniae*;[70] and the *Flores Psalterii* by Letbert, Abbot of Ruf.[71] Doubtless there were other duplicates or renewals that have since disappeared. For example, the existence of two copies of Gregory's *Dialogi* can be inferred from the fact that the extant copy with a Rochester *ex libris* (BL MS. Royal 6 B. II) was made in the thirteenth century, but the work is recorded as early as the catalogue of 1124.

A few extant Rochester books do not appear in either catalogue, but can be assigned to the medieval library on other evidence. First, BL MS. Royal 10 A. XII, containing legal treatises and miscellaneous theological materials, was part of the medieval library by the early thirteenth century when a list of Rochester books, said to have been copied or acquired by Alexander, was made on fol. 111b in the bottom of the left column. Alexander's list is cramped and rubbed, and hence illegible in several places, but still it adds a few bits of information about the library in the early thirteenth century. The list is contemporary, or almost so, with the 1202 catalogue, a date confirmed by marginal notations in the latter. In the 1202 list, Alexander's name is entered by two volumes, *De arca Noe et al.* and the third volume of a multivolume Vulgate set, books which are attributed to him again in BL MS. Royal 10 A. XII. Whether the Alexander credited with nineteen scientific and medical texts at the end of the 1202 catalogue is the Alexander of the separate short list is less certain. Not one of the technical volumes appears in the separate list. On the other hand, a few additional texts do occur there, most notably the letters of Sidonius, works of Ailred of Rievaulx, and a supply of service-books. Further, Alexander's catalogue mentions an *armarium* where the new Bible, of which he has copied a portion, is stored.[72]

Other volumes not mentioned in any catalogue, but which probably formed part of the medieval library at Rochester, include a twelfth-century volume with a Rochester *ex libris* containing Ernulf's *De incestis conjugibus*, excerpts from Augustine and Gregory, and Gilbert Crispin's treatise against the Jews (Brussels, Bibliothèque Royale de Belgique MS. 1403);[73] and a portion of the Old Testament (BL MS. Royal 1 C. VII) (see Chapter III).

---

[70] BL MSS. Royal 15 A. XXII (twelfth century) and 15 B. XI (early thirteenth century).
[71] BL MSS. Royal 2 D. VI and 4 B. VII, both from the thirteenth century, with a Rochester *ex libris*.
[72] "Scripsit tertiam partem novi bibli armarii Roffensis..."
[73] Mary P. Richards, "On the Date and Provenance of MS. Cotton Vespasian, D. XIV, fols. 4-169," *Manuscripta*, 17 (1972): 163-67.

Another twelfth-century volume with a Rochester *ex libris*, Cambridge MS. Corpus Christi College 318, contains saints' lives and histories, including Eadmer's life of Anselm and the life of Herlewin of Bec. Additional noteworthy works attributed by Ker to Rochester include a copy of the compilation of proverbs by Publilius Syrus and Pseudo-Seneca and *De corpore et sanguine Domini* by Guitmund of Aversa, a student of Lanfranc at Bec (BL MS. Royal 12 C. 1). Two vernacular homiliaries (Cambridge MS. Corpus Christi College 303 and BL MS. Cotton Vespasian D. XIV, fols. 4-169) and three Latin collections (BL MS. Royal 2 C. III, Edinburgh N.L. Adv. 18.2.4, and Vatican Lat. 4951) from the late eleventh and early twelfth centuries also are associated with Rochester on the basis of script and internal evidence (see Chapter IV), but they may have been kept in locations apart from the main library and hence were omitted from the catalogues.

There are at least twenty-seven items with the characteristic Rochester *ex libris* copied too late for inclusion in the medieval catalogues. Thirteenth-century volumes include a bestiary and lapidary (BL MS. Royal 12 F. XIII); several theological collections containing the works of authors such as Honorius of Autun, and the *Summa de vitiis et virtutibus* of Guillaume Perault (BL MSS. Royal 10 B. II); Anselm, Peter Damian, the *Historia scholastica* of Peter Comestor (BL MS. Royal 2 C. I); the *Distinctiones* of Peter Cantor (BL MS. Royal 10 A. XIV); and the *Pantheologus* of Peter of Cornwall (BL MS. Royal 7 E. VIII, 7 C. XIII, and 7 C. XIV). Later acquisitions from the thirteenth and fourteenth centuries include four volumes of Aristotle in Latin (BL MS. Royal 12 D. XIV, 12 G. II, 12 G. III, 12 F. 1); a volume of canon law (BL MS. Royal 11 B. XV); Peter Lombard's *Sententiae* (BL MS. Royal 11. C. I); a copy of the *Volumen Parvum* of the *Corpus Iuris Civilis* (BL MSS. Royal 11 D. I); a volume of works of St. Bonaventure (BL MS. Royal 10 C. XII); the metrical bible of Peter Riga (BL MS. Royal 15 A. XIX);[74] a concordance to the Bible (BL MS. Royal 4 E. V); Book III of the *Summa* of Alexander of Hales (BL MS. Royal 9 E. XI); St. Thomas Aquinas' commentary on book IV of Peter Lombard's *Sententiae* (BL MS. Royal 9 C. IV); and John Bromyard's *Summa predicantium* (BL MS. Royal 7 E. IV).

Some sixteen medieval Rochester books remaining today have shelf-marks on the flyleaves, but the shelf-marks do not correlate with the catalogue entries.[75] Bold Roman numerals are used most frequently, and these may have been assigned to cupboards or shelves, rather than volumes, because the same number can be found in two or more unrelated volumes. Other marks are in Arabic numerals and in a more complicated form (E. Vi. m). Since the shelf-marks are found latest in thirteenth-century volumes, they could be related to the cataloguing and construction activities described above.

From the foregoing account of the catalogues and of the volumes remaining from the medieval Rochester library, it should be clear that the collection

---

[74] Ker, *MLGB*, 163, n. 7.
[75] Ibid., 160-64.

was modest both in the scope of works represented and in the availability of multiple copies of key works. By contrast, Eastry's catalogue of the Christ Church, Canterbury, library, made early in the fourteenth century, lists 1831 volumes, often in multiple copies.[76] Late in the fifteenth century, a catalogue was made of the St. Augustine's, Canterbury, library, listing 1837 volumes. Even the library at Dover Priory had some 450 books in 1389. We can surmise from the number of extant volumes copied or acquired too late for inclusion in the second Rochester catalogue that the library increased gradually up to the fourteenth century. It is doubtful, however, that the Rochester collection ever surpassed the one at Dover. For the purposes of the present study the surviving books make all the difference, and here the Rochester collection has the advantage. From it we can document the growth, the strengths, and the idiosyncrasies of a medieval library relatively undistinguished in its time, but invaluable because of its preservation.

The chapters to follow present the most significant features of the Rochester collection as it has survived. Some of these features, especially paleographic characteristics, have been studied individually, but never has there been assembled an analysis of the library based on an intensive examination of texts and textual traditions and their relationship to the history of the priory. Yet even the library catalogues themselves seem to relate to events in Rochester's history. Thus it is possible, in the case of Rochester, to examine links between the library and external forces and hence to gain a clearer perspective on the development of a post-Conquest Benedictine foundation.

Equally important is the fact that key texts for documenting the history of the scriptorium have survived, in many cases where their Canterbury exemplars have not, with the result that Rochester materials are crucial to an understanding of the English and continental manuscript traditions flourishing in southeastern England from the eleventh through the thirteenth centuries. As the present study will demonstrate, most of these textual traditions are distinct to the area and derive in great part from the influence of Christ Church, Canterbury. They can only be defined, however, through examination of the Rochester books which preserve them. Those books selected for analysis here contribute to our knowledge of textual traditions while at the same time giving new insights into the liturgical practices (as evidenced by Vulgates, Gospel books, and homiliaries) and documentary history of Rochester Cathedral Priory. By fortunate coincidence, the kinds of books that relate most closely to the life of the foundation, namely, its records, Bibles, and homiliaries are also the most interesting from a textual point of view. To give a monk's-eye view of the Rochester scriptorium and library, then, is the purpose of our enterprise.

---

[76] For the Christ Church, St. Augustine's, and Dover catalogues, see James, *The Ancient Libraries of Canterbury and Dover*. Also helpful is C. R. Haines, "The Library of Dover Priory," *London Bibliographical Society Transactions*, N.S. v. 7 (1927): 73-118.

Prefatory Note to Table 1

In the Table to follow, all four of the medieval catalogues of the Rochester library have been reedited in parallel columns to demonstrate, as far as possible, continuity and change in the collection. Rye's earlier numeration of items in the 1202 catalogue is inaccurate. Since Ker cites Rye's numbers in *MLGB* wherever he connects an extant MS. to a catalogue reference, the reader will have difficulty matching all of Ker's citations to the present edition. To overcome this problem, Table 1 includes a list of extant MSS. that can be associated with the various catalogue entries. The list is heavily dependent on the second edition of *MLGB*, and includes Ker's symbols indicating evidence of provenance. Additional information gathered from entries in the shorter catalogues and from study of individual MSS. has led to firmer identifications in a few instances, and new identifications in others. By means of question marks, where the evidence is inconclusive, and footnotes pointing the way to relevant discussion within the text of the present study, the basis for such judgments is indicated.

Subsequent to the completion of this table, a *Supplement to the Second Edition of MLGB* has appeared (London, 1987), edited by Andrew G. Watson. Watson adds several identifications of extant manuscripts with catalogue entries from Rochester (pp. 58-59), and includes identifications from a list, dated 1390, of thirteen books lent by the prior and convent. All of the identifications, with the exception of those from the 1390 list, have been anticipated in Table 1.

TABLE 1

THE MEDIEVAL CATALOGUES OF ROCHESTER CATHEDRAL LIBRARY

TR	Royal 5 B XII	Other	MS. Extant
1. Expositionem eiusdem super psalterium in iii vol.	6. Super psalterium in tribus magnis vol.		e Royal 5 D. I e Royal 5 D. II e Royal 5 D. III
2. Librum ipsius de civitate dei in i vol.	1. De civitate dei in uno vol.		e Royal 5 D. IX
3. Expositionem eiusdem super epistolam sancti iohannis apostoli in i vol. in quo et sermo ipsius inter pressuras et apocalipsis et cantica canticorum.	12. Super epistolam Johannis in i vol.	DRc/Z18:Expositionem super epistolam sancti iohannis a...	e Royal 5 B. VI
4. Item augustinum contra faustum in uno vol.	8. Contra faustum manicheum in uno vol.	DRc/Z18:anicheum in i vol.	e Royal 5 B. X
5. Enkiridion eiusdem et librum beati ambrosii de bono mortis, librum quoque domini lanfranci archiepiscopi contra beringerium in i vol.	9. Encheridion et alia opuscula in i vol.	DRc/Z18:dions eiusdem, et librum beati ambrosii de bono mortis, librum quoque domini lanfranci arch...	e Royal 5 A. XV
6. Item librum eiusdem contra felicianum et librum domini anselmi archiepiscopi Cur deus homo, et librum de asseneth cum quibusdam aliis opusculis in i vol.	10. Contra felicianum et alia opuscula in i vol.	DRc/Z18:ntra felicianum, et librum domini anselmi archiepiscopi Cur deus homo, et libellum de asseneth cum...	
7. Item librum ipsius de trinitate in i vol.	2. De trinitate in uno vol.	DRc/Z18:Librum de trinitate in i vol.	e Royal 5 B. IV
8. Item librum ipsius contra v. hereses, et sermonem eiusdem de muliere forti, et librum didimi de spiritu sancto, expositio quoque baede super xxx. quaestiones in librum reges, item expositio eiusdem de templo solomonis et expositionem super canticum abbacuc, epistolam quoque mansueti episcopi ad constantinum in uno vol.	15. Contra v hereses et alia diversa opuscula in uno vol.	DRc/Z18:rti, et librum didimi de spiritu sancto, ex... de super xxx quaestionibus in libris regum ...stantinum in i vol.	e Royal 5 B. VII

TABLE 1 *(Continued)*

TR	Royal 5 B XII	Other	MS. Extant
9. Item librum ipsius de concordia evangelistarum, et ipsius expositionem de sermone domini in monte et librum ipsius de blasphemia in spiritum sanctum, et sermonem ipsius de decem plagis in i vol.	4. De consensu evangelistarum in uno vol.	DRc/Z18:positio eiusdem de sermone domini ...	e Rochester Cathedral
10. Item de doctrina christiana, et de vera religione et de poenitentia in uno vol.	11. De doctrina christiana et de vera religione et de penitencia in uno vol. Id est iste liber.		e Royal 5 B. XII
11. Item contra caelestianos et pelagianos et de natura boni et dialogus eiusdem ad ieronimum, et de cura pro mortuis gerenda, et regula eius ad monachos in i vol.			
12. Item exceptiones de augustino super iohannem, et aliae plures exceptiones de libris ipsius in i vol.	19. Sentencie excerpte de diversis libris augustini in uno vol.		e Royal 5 B. XIII
13. Item librum eiusdem de agone christiano cum aliis pluribus minutis opusculis in i vol.	17. De agone christiano et alia plura in parvo.		
14. Sermo eiusdem de pastoribus, et sermo de ovibus, liber quoque adversus donatistas de baptismo, liber eiusdem etiam de baptismo parvulorum, et epistola ad marcellinum et liber de unico baptismo, et liber eiusdem de spiritu et littera in i vol.	7. De ovibus et pastoribus et alia plura in uno vol.		s Camb. U. L. Ff.4.32
15. Liber confessionum eiusdem et liber eiusdem de diversis heresibus in i vol.	21. Libri confessionum eius et diversis heresibus in i vol.		e Royal 5 B. XVI
16. Item liber retractationum eiusdem et liber de ortu vita vel obitu sanctorum patrum, qui in scripturarum laudibus efferuntur, liber etiam sancti ysidori quidam catalogus quoque beati	22. Liber retractationum et alia plura in i vol.		e Lambeth Palace 76, fols. 1-147.

TABLE 1 *(Continued)*

TR	Royal 5 B XII	Other	MS. Extant
ieronimi de catholicis scriptoribus, et catalogus gennadii episcopi post ieronimum, et catalogus ysidori de illustribus viris, et decretalis epistola gelasii papae de recipiendis et non recipiendis libris, liber quoque catholici senatoris de institutionibus divinarum litterarum et liber prohemiorum sancti ysidori episcopi in i vol.			
17. Item liber eiusdem de nuptiis et concupiscentia et responsio eiusdem sancti augustini contra cartulam missam valerio comiti, a quodam reprehendente eundem librum, et libros vi contra iulianum episcopum pelagianae heresis defensorem in i vol.	16. De nupciis et concupiscencia et contra iulianum hereticum et alia plura in i vol.		s Bodley 134
18. Item de praesentia dei ad dardanum et epistole senice ad paulum et pauli ad senicam, et liber rathramni de eo quod christus ex virgine natus est, et liber eiusdem de anima, et sermones de assumptione sanctae mariae, et sermo pascasii diaconi in genealogia christi et sermo sancti ambrosii de nativitate sanctae mariae, et quoddam scriptum anselmi archiepiscopi in i vol.	18. De presencia dei ad dardanum et alia plura in uno vol.		s Camb., Corpus Christi College 332
Libri beati ieronimi sunt isti.			
19. Epistolae ipsius in i vol.	37. Epistole in i vol.		e Royal 6 D. II
20. Commentarium eiusdem super matheum in i vol.	41. Super matheum in i vol.		
21. Item libri eiusdem super xii prophetarum et super danihelem in duobus vol.	42. Super xii prophetas et Danielem in ii vol.		

TABLE 1 *(Continued)*

TR	Royal 5 B XII	Other	MS. Extant
22. Item liber eiusdem contra iovinianum hereticum in uno vol.	47. Contra Jovinianum in i vol.		s Eton College 80
23. Item expositio eiusdem super epistolam ad titum, et isidorus super genesim in i vol.	79. Ysidorus super Genesim cum aliis in i vol.		e Royal 3 B. I
24. Item liber eiusdem de essentia et ineffabilitate dei cum aliis pluribus minutis opusculis in i vol.			
25. Item liber eiusdem in vitam sancti pauli heremitae et sancti hilarionis et aliorum plurimorum sanctorum patrum, etiam actus monachi captivi, cum vita sancti antonii, et liber heraclidis qui paradysus appellatur in i vol.	58? Vita sanctorum patrum in ii vol.	DRc/Z18:radysus appellatur in i vol.	i
26. Vetus et novum testamentum, quam [sic] transtulit de hebreo in latinum in ii vol., Quorum primum continet hos libros. Quinque libros moysi. Iesum nave Iudicum. Ruth. Psalterium. Proverbiorum. Ecclesiastes. Sapientiae. Ecclesiasticum. Hezram et neemiam. Paralipomenon duos libros. et iiii evangelia. In alio vero volumine continentur iiii libri regum. Iob. Liber tobie. Iudith. Hester. Libri machabeorum ii. Libri prophetarum omnes. Actus apostolorum. Epistolae pauli. Aliorumque apostolorum. Apocalypsis.	48. Vetus et novum testamentum secundum translationem ieronimi in ii vol. veteribus.	DRc/Z18:Vetus et novum te . . . inque libros moysi, Iesum nave, Iudicum . . . Psalterium, Proverbiorum, Ecclesiastes, S . . . lia. In alio vero volumine continentur quatuor libri regum, Iob, liber tobie, Iudith . . .	e Huntington Library MS. HM 62
27. Item expositio eiusdem super ysaiam prophetam in i vol.	38. Super ysaiam in i vol.		
28. Expositio quoque eiusdem super psalterium in i vol.	39. Psalterium eius in i vol.	DRc/Z18:Expo . . . alterium in i vol.	
29. De hebraicis quaestionibus in genesi, et de mansionibus filiorum israhel, et de distantiis locorum, et inter-	46. De hebraicis questionibus cum aliis in i vol.	DRc/Z18:estionibus in genesi, et de mansionibus filiorum israelis et	e Camb., Trinity College 1238

TABLE 1 (Continued)

TR	Royal 5 B XII	Other	MS. Extant
pretationes hebraicorum nominum, et quaestiones in librum regum, et de decem temptationibus, et canticum debborae, et lamentationes ieremiae in i vol.		de distantiis locorum, et inter . . . et de decim temptationibus, et canticum debborae, et lamentationes, ieremiae in i vol.	
30. Item tratatus [sic] eiusdem in libro iesu nave, libri quoque duo beati augustini doctoris de adulterinis coniugiis, et liber unus de mendacio et aliis contra mendacium, et liber eiusdem ad renatum de natura et origine animae, et alius liber de eadem re ad petrum presbyterium, ad vincentium victorem quoque duo libri de eadem re, et sermo arrianorum, et liber sancti augustini respondentis contra arrianorum perfidiam, et libri duo eiusdem contra adversarium legis et prophetarum in i vol.	45. Super iesu nave et pluribus operibus Beati augustini in i vol.	DRc/Z18:adulterinis coniugiis, et liber unus de mendacio et alius contra mendacium et liber ei . . . vincentium victorem quoque duo libri d . . . re, et sermo arrianorum, et liber sancti aug . . . legis et prophetarum in i vol.	es Bodley 387
31. Expositio super ezechielem prophetam in i vol.	40. Super ezechielem in i vol.	DRc/Z18:Ex . . . prophetam in i vol.	
32. Item quinque libros moysi in uno vol. novo.	112. Pentateuchi moysi in vol. Novo.	Royal 10 A. XII: tertiam partem novi bibli armarii Roffensi quarum i pars est Genesis.	
33. Iesum nave. Iudicum. et Ruth. in uno vol. novo.	113? Item Iosue, Iudicum, Regum iiii in alio Novo.	Royal 10 A. XII: ii Iosue Iudicium Regem.	s Royal I C. VII?[1]
34. Item explanatio eiusdem in ieremiam prophetam in i vol.	43. Super ieremiam in i vol.		
35. Item super aecclesiastem, et Bedam de tabernaculo et vasis eius, et super actus apostolorum, et improperium ad monachos et responsiones cuiusdam in i vol.	44. Super ecclesiasten et aliis pluribus operibus in i vol.		

[1] See Chapter III.

TABLE 1 *(Continued)*

TR	Royal 5 B XII	Other	MS. Extant
Libri beati ambrosii sunt isti			
36. De officiis in uno vol.	35. De officiis in i vol.		e Royal 6 A. IV
37. Exameron eiusdem in uno vol.	34. Exameron in i vol.		e Royal 6 A. I Royal 7 A. XI, fols. 19-24.
38. Item liber eiusdem de virginitate et de viduis et de lapsu virginis in i vol.	33. De virginitate et viduis in i vol.		
39. Item liber eiusdem de conflictu vitiorum et virtutum, et oratio sancti effrem de compunctione, libri etiam iuliani episcopi de prognosticis, et plures sermones sancti augustini, et liber paschasii de corpore et sanguine domini in i vol.	82. De conflictu vitiorum atque virtutum cum aliis in i vol.		e Royal 5 A. VII
40. Epistolae ipsius in i vol.			
41. Item expositio in evangelium lucae evangelistae in i vol.	32. Super lucam in i vol.		
42. De fide ad gratianum imperatorem in i vol.	31. De fide ad gratianum in i vol.		e Royal 6 C. IV
43. Item de poenitentia contra novatianos, et liber sancti augustini de utilitate credendi, et liber eiusdem de fide ac simbolo, et liber illius ad inquisitiones ianuarii, et epistola ad armentarium et paulinam, et sermo de periurio, et sermo de excidio urbis romae, et sermo de faciendis elemosinis, et sermones de fide, de caritate, de timore domini, et liber iustini in libris trogi pompeii in i vol.	36. De penitentia cum trogo pompeio et aliis in i vol.		
44. Item liber de mysteriis sive initiandis, et sermo de sacramentis neophitorum habitus in synodo, et epistolarium ivonis carnotensis episcopi in i vol.	30. De sacramentis cum epistolis yvonis et aliis in i vol.		e Royal 6 B. VI

THE ROCHESTER CATHEDRAL LIBRARY

TABLE 1 (Continued)

TR	Royal 5 B XII	Other	MS. Extant
Libri sancti Gregorii papae sunt hi			
45. Moralia eiusdem in duobus vol.	24. Super iob in duobus vol.		e Royal 3 C. IV e Royal 6 C. VI
46. Pastoralis et dialogus in ii vol.	26. Pastoralem et Gregorium Nanzanzenum in uno vol.	DRc/Z18:ogus in i vol.	e Royal 5 E. II?
	27. Dialogus in i vol.		e Royal 6 B. II (later copy?)
47. Liber ipsius super ezechielem in i vol.		DRc/Z18:Liber ipsius super ezechielem in duobus vol.	
48. Registrum in i vol.	29. Registrum eius in i vol.	DRc/Z18:Registrum in i vol.	e Royal 6 C. X
49. Speculum in i vol.	25. Speculum in uno vol.	DRc/Z18:Sp . . .	
50. Gregorius super ezechielem in duobus vol.	28. Super partem primam ezechielis et super secundam in duobus vol.		e Royal 4 B. I
51. Pastoralis anglicus in i vol.			
52. Prosper in i vol.	92. Prosper in i vol.		e Royal 5 E. X
53. Egesippus in i vol.	73. Egesippus in i vol.		is Edinburgh N.L. Adv. 18.3.9
54. Itinerarium Petri in ii vol.	94. Itinerarium petri in i vol.		
55. Rufinus in aecclesiasticam hystoriam in uno vol.	95. Ecclesiastica historia Ruffini in i vol.		m Camb., Corpus Christi College 184?
56. Canones et decreta pontificum in 1 vol.	96. Canones et concilia in i vol.		
57. Exceptiones de eiusdem in i vol.	89. Exceptiones ex decretis pontificum et registro Gregorii in i vol.		
58. Orosius cum gothorum hystoria in i vol.	72. Orosius cum historia gothorum in i vol.		
59. Iohannes crisostomus de reparatione lapsi, libri quoque eiusdem de compunctione, liber etiam ipsius de psalmo quinquagesimo, et liber ipsius de eo quod nemo leditur nisi a se[met] ipso, et de expulsione sua, sermonesque beati augustini de simbolo et oratione dominica, quoddam quoque miraculum	75. Iohannes crisostomus cum aliis in i vol.		e Royal 6 A. XII

TABLE 1 *(Continued)*

TR	Royal 5 B XII	Other	MS. Extant
sancti martini. et scriptum fulberti de eo quod [sic] tria maxime sunt necessaria christianae religioni, item scriptum fulberti de sacerdote et hostia quam accipit cum ordinatur, libri quoque alcuini ad karolum de trinitate in i vol.			
60. Liber scintillarum in i vol.			
61. Diadema monachorum in i vol.			
62. Institutiones regum anglorum in i vol.			e Textus Roffensis
63. Librum amalarii abbatis de officiis divinis in i vol.	62. Amalarius in i vol.		
64. Descriptio locorum que vidit bernardus sapiens quando ivit ierusalem vel rediit, et vita karoli magni regis, et itinerarium christianorum in ierusalem contra paganos, et hystoria normannorum in i vol.	85? Hystoria ierusalem cum pluribus aliis in i vol.		
Libri venerabilis baedae presbyteri sunt isti:			
65. Hystoria anglorum in ii vol.	50? Hystoria anglorum in i vol.		e Harley 3680?
66. Eiusdem de temporibus, et de aequinoctio, cum Alberico de compoto in i vol.	52. De temporibus in i vol.	DRc/Z18:ribus, et de aequinoctio cum alberico de c . . . poto in i vol.	
67. (Alcuinum) De arte metrica, et de scematibus et de miraculis sancti cuthberti versificae compositus, cum libro karoli et alcuini de dialectica, libellus quoque petri damiani cuius nomen dominus vobiscum, et sexaginta sex quaestiones orosii ad augustinum, et sermo beati isidori de corpore et sanguine domini et liber sancti augustini de agone christiano in i vol.	97? Alquinus cum ceteris operibus in i vol.	DRc/Z18: (Alcuinus) De arte metrica, et de sc . . . de dialectica libellus quoque . . . cuius nomen dominus vobiscum, et lx . . . domini, et liber sancti augustini de . . .	e Camb., Trinity College 1128

TABLE 1 *(Continued)*

TR	Royal 5 B XII	Other	MS. Extant
68. Super tobiam et ezram, et liber eiusdem in verbis neemiae in i vol.	53. Super tobiam in i vol.	DRc/Z18:Super tobiam et ezram, et liber ...	
69. Item expositio eius super apocalipsin cum alia expositione sine titulo in i vol.	51. Super apocalipsim in i vol.		
70. Commentarius eiusdem super marcum evangelistam in i vol.			
71. Item martyrologium de nataliciis sanctorum, et regula sancti benedicti, consuetudinesque lanfranci archiepiscopi in i vol.	54. Martirologium cum aliis in i vol.		
72. Regula sancti Johannis cassiani in i vol.	90. Regula Johannis cassiani in i vol.		e Royal 8 D. XVI
73. Iginus de spera mundi, et hystoria longobardorum et gesta alexandri regis macedonum in i vol.	91. Yginus de spera cum historia longobardorum et aliis in i vol.		e Royal 12 C. IV (later copy?)
74. Expositio super apocalipsin sine titulo in i vol.			
75. Collationes de dictis vel factis patrum in i vol.	59? Collationes patrum cum multis aliis in i vol.		
76. Collationes abbatis moysi et libri sancti effrem, cum pluribus omeliis et multis aliis opusculis in i vol.			
77. Vita sancti dunstani, et passio sancti Ælphægi cum sermonibus de dedicatione aecclesiae in i vol.	81. Vita S. Dunstani et sancti Ælfegi martyris in i vol.		s Vatican MSS. Reg. Lat. 646, fols. 1-48; 458 fols. 1-36; 598 fol. 8r
78. Epistolae sancti pauli glosatae in i vol.	68? Item epistole pauli glosate in alio vol. parvo.		
79. Epistolae domini Lanfranci archiepiscopi, cum aliis minutis opusculis in i vol.	83. Epistole lanfranci et anselm[i] cum aliis in i vol.		
80. Liber de ratione et peccatore cum pluribus opusculis in i vol.	98. De ratione et peccatore et aliis in i vol.		e Royal 12 C. I
81. Liber prognosticorum in i parvo vol.			

TABLE 1 *(Continued)*

TR	Royal 5 B XII	Other	MS. Extant
82. Passionalia in iiii vol.	56. Passyonaria iiii.		
83. Sermonalia anglica in ii vol.	111. Omeliaria anglica ii.		c Bodley 340, 342[2]
84. Sermones diversarum solennitatum [sic] diversorumque auctorum in i vol.	102? Leo ad flavianum et sermones annui diversorum auctorum in i vol.		e Vat. Lat. 4951?[2]
85. Omeliaria duo in duobus vol. Unum de dominicis, aliud de sanctis.	57. Omeliaria ii.		
86. Lectionarii duo ad matutinas in duobus vol. Unus de dominicis, aliud de sanctis.	55? Lectionaria v.		
87. Benedictionalia in duobus vol.			
88. Tripartitum psalterium in i vol.			
89. Iosephus in ii vol.	74. Iosephus in ii vol.		
90. Solinus et dares, et liber pergesis i. de situ terrae prisciani grammatici urbis romae, et vaticinium sybillae, et historiam britannorum in i vol.	99. Solini duo cum ceteris operibus in ii vol.		e Royal 15 A. XXII s Cotton Vespasian D. XXI, fols. 1-17 e Royal 15 B. XI e Cotton Vitellius A. XIII
91. Epistolas beati pauli in uno vol.	70? Item epistole pauli sine glosa.		
92. Collationes diversorum auctorum in uno vol.			
93. Lectionaria in tribus vol.	55? Lectionaria v.		
94. Novum testamentum in uno vol.	115. Item Novum testamentum in vol. Novo.		c Baltimore, Walters Art Gallery 57[3]
95. Haimonem in uno vol.	101. Haymo in i vol.		
96. Ysidorum de ordine creaturae et miracula sanctae mariae in uno vol.	78. Ysidorus de ordine creature cum miraculis sancte Marie et aliis in i vol.		
97. Quinque libri moysi, et iosue et iudicum in uno vol.			
98. Collectiones ecclesiasticarum regularum domini ivonis carnotensis.	60? Decreta yvonis in i vol.		

[2] See Chapter IV.
[3] See Chapter III.

TABLE 1 *(Continued)*

	Royal 5 B XII	Other	MS. Extant
	3. [Aug.] Super iohannem in uno vol.		e Royal 3 C. X
	5. [Aug.] De verbo domini et de verbo apostoli in uno vol.		e Royal 5 C. VIII
	13. [Aug.] Super epistolam ad Romanos ex compilacionibus bede in uno vol.		gs Royal 4 C. IV?
	14. [Aug.] Super duas epistolas ad corinthios in altero vol.		
	20. [Aug.] Super genesim ad litteram in i vol.		e Royal 5 C. I
	23. Duo libri veteris et novi testamenti Willelmi de heth[enhame].		
	49. Leviticus et de liber numeri et liber deuteronomii in uno vol. glosatus—Walter de Maidestane.		e Royal 3 C. IX
	61. Decreta gratiani in iii vol., unum magistri hamonis et aliud Radulphi de frend[sbury], tercium magistri Rogeri de derteford.		
	63. Sententie magistri petri in ii vol. unum magistri h[amonis] et aliud Willelmi de Bradest'.	DRc/Z18:ntentiarum magistri petri.	
	64. Psalteria secundum petrum comestorem ii, unum magistri h[amonis] antiqui, et aliud magistri hamonis junioris.		
	65. Alia duo secundum magistrum Gilebertum porratanum, unum fuit ascelini episcopi, aliud Galaranni.		
	66. Item secundum eundem Gilebertum. Epistole Pauli Glosate, unum vol.		

TABLE 1 *(Continued)*

	Royal 5 B XII	Other	MS. Extant
	fuit ascelini, aliud Galaranni.		
67.	Epistole pauli secundum comestorem, que fuerunt magistri hamonis.		
69.	Item alie epistole Glosate que fuerunt apud Waleton.		
71.	Item sermones diversi qui fuerunt Galaranni.		
76.	Arma contra iudeos cum pluribus operibus in i vol.		
77.	Prophetarum xiiii liber in uno vol.		
80.	Sinonima ysidori et de summo bono in i vol.		e Royal 5 E. I
84.	De arca noe et pluribus aliis in i vol.	Royal 10 A. XII: Item de arca noe et cum pluribus operibus.	
86.	Liber florum cum aliis in i vol.		e Royal 2 D. VI (a later copy?)
87.	Super matheum liber unus qui fuit ascelini episcopi in i vol.		
88.	Liber magistri hugonis de sacramentis in i vol.		e Royal 8 D. V*
93.	Item prosper et liber odonis et scintillarum in i vol.		e Royal 6 D. V
100.	Sermones habiti in synodis in parvo vol.		
103.	Vita sancti Bernardi cum aliis in i vol.	Royal 10 A. XII: Item vitam S. Bernardi et Malachie in i vol. et alia in eodem.	e Camb., Corpus Christi College 62, fols. 49-208
104.	Hystoria magistri Petri in i vol.		
105.	Hystoria britonum in i vol.		
106.	Martirologium novum.		

TABLE 1 (Continued)

	Royal 5 B XII	Other	MS. Extant
	107. Textus evangeliorum annuorum in ii vol. novis.		
	108. Aurea gema ecclesie in i vol.		
	109. Radulfus super leviticum in i vol.		
	110. Ysidorus ethimologia Roberti de Hecham in i vol. Item aliud in arca cantoris.		
	114. Tercia pars incipiens a salomone cum multis aliis, in alio vol. novo.	Royal 10 A. XII: iii predictus liber continens libros salomone. Iob. Iudith. Hester. Esdras. Machabeorum.	
	115. Deest adhuc quarta pars veteris testamentum, hoc est xvi prophete et paralipomena.	Royal 10 A. XII: iiii pars est xvi prophete et paralipomena.	
	117. Item pentatheuchus glosatus qui liber fuit Magistri Hamonis.		e Royal 4 C. X?
	118. Ysaias glosatus.		
	119. De claustro anime.		
	120. Hystoria Willelmi Malmesburiensis.		e Harley 261 Harley 23
	121. Magister andrea contra Judeos.		
	122. Miracula sancti Jacobi apostoli cum ystoria de runcievallo.		
	123. De infancia salvatoris.		
	124. Vita sancte Marie egiptiace.		
	125. Versus Magistri Geoffrey vinisalvi.		
	Item aliud librarium in archa cantoris		
	126. De divinis.		e Royal 6 A. XI?
	127. Panormia in i vol.		
	128. Glose super epistolas pauli in duobus vol.		

TABLE 1 (Continued)

Royal 5 B XII	Other	MS. Extant
129. Matheus glosatus in i vol.		e Royal 4 A. XVI
130. Item matheus cum epistolis canonicis in i vol.		e Royal 4 A. XII
131. Item aliud cum apocalypsi.		
132. Lamentationes ieremie in i vol. Magistri Hamonis antiqui.		
133. Parabole salamonis glosate in i vol.		e Royal 1 B. IV?
134. Sententie excerpte de epistolario ieronomi in i vol.		
135. De monacho et abbate i vol.		
136. Acta beatorum pontificum i vol.	DRc/Z18: ta romanorum pontificum.	e Cotton Otho A.XV?[4]
137. Cronica francorum i vol.		
138. Exceptiones Gundulfi de libris canonicis i vol.		
139. Liber de predestinatione et li[bero] ar[bitrio], et arator, et alia in i vol.		
140. Magister anselmus super psalterium et bina cantica in i vol.		
141. Item glose super psalterium in predicto libro.		
142. Excerpta de Registro in parvo vol.	DRc/Z18: Exceptiones de registr . . .	
143. De novitiis et liber Bernardi de Diligendo deo in i vol.		
144. Exceptiones questionum Regum et paralipomenon in i vol. parvo.		
145. Malchus in i vol.		
146. Miracula Sancti Thome i vol.		

[4] See *MLGB*, 161, n. 1.

THE ROCHESTER CATHEDRAL LIBRARY 37

TABLE 1 *(Continued)*

	Royal 5 B XII	Other	MS. Extant
	147. Miracula Sancti ythamari i vol.		
	148. Item miracula sancti paulini et sancti ythamari i vol.		
	149. Beda super vii epistolas canonicas i vol.	DRc/Z18: Expositio bede super epistolas canoni...	e Camb., Corpus Christi College 62, fols. 209-74
	150. Liber translationis Sancti Augustini cum ceteris operibus in i vol.		
	151. Vita sancte etheldrithe et aliorum sanctorum in i vol.		
	152. Vita sancti Wulfranni et mildride virgine cum aliis in i vol.		
	153. Glose super epistolas pauli in i vol.		
	154. Sermones æilmeri prioris in glosis in i vol.		
	155. Liber sermonum cum multis aliis in i vol., qui fuit alexandri.	Royal 10 A. XII: Item vol. aliud sermonum diversorum et alia plura.	
	156. Item alius liber sermonum eiusdem alexandri.	Royal 10 A. XII: Item sermonum volumen aliud quod perditum est.	
	157. Epistole Sydonii eiusdem i vol.	Royal 10 A. XII: Item epistolas Sidonii in i vol.	
	158. Super iohannem glosatum in i vol.		
	159. Cantica canticorum Wib[erti] et alius libellus eius.		
	160. Iudaismus i.		
	161. Mappa mundi i.		
	162. Item laur[entius] in parvo vol.		

TABLE 1 (Continued)

Royal 5 B XII	Other	MS. Extant
163. Alfricus i.		
164. Grammaticam magistri Ade de parvo ponte.		
165. Duos quaternos de spera mundi.		
166. Cronica ade de cobeham.		
167. Versus magistri ernulfi prioris de conflictu vitiorum et virtutum in duobus locis.		
168. Istoriam apollonii tyrii.		
169. Vitam sancti hytamari in duobus locis.		
170. Item Dialectica i.		
171. Rethorica i.		
172. Arithmetice ii.		
173. Musica Boetii et Wido simul i vol.		
174. Item alius liber de musica		
175. Prisciani magni iiii duo perfecti et duo imperfecti.		
176. Quintus Priscianus Magistri Roberti.		
177. Prisciani de constructione iii.		
178. Ortographia i vol.		
179. Remigius super Donatum cum pluribus auctoribus in i vol.		
180. Liber antonii in quo due editiones donatati cum ceteris pluribus regulis.		
181. Oratii ii.		
182. Boetii iiii.		
183. Virgilii ii.		
184. Sallustii iiii.		
185. Terentii iii.		
186. Arator unus glosatus per se.		
187. Persius glosatus i.		

TABLE 1 *(Continued)*

	Royal 5 B XII	Other	MS. Extant
	188. Lucani iii.		sc Camb., Trinity College 610?
	189. Prudentii ymnorum ii.		
	190. Macrobius i.		
	191. Saturnalia macrobii in alio vol.		
	192. Cato vel seneca de causis i.		
	193. Ovidius fastorum i.		
	194. Bucolica et georgica in i vol.		
	195. Lapidarius i.		
	196. Prudentius sicomachia.		
	197. Philosophia magistri Willelmi.		
	198. Glose diverse tum de divinitate, tum de artibus, vel auctoribus in xvi locis in vol. et in quaternis.		
	199. Statius unus.		e Royal 15 C. X
	200. Summa magistri p. helie.		
	201. Miracula sancte marie virginis metrice.		
	Librarium magistri hamonis		
	202. Pentateuchus glosatus in i vol.		e Royal 4 C. X?
	203. Decreta gratiani i vol.		
	204. Epistole pauli glosate in i vol.		
	205. Psalterium glosatum in i vol.		
	206. Sententie magistri Petri in i vol.		
	207. Bine summe super decretalia, una secundum Johannem, alia secundum magistrum Gerardum.		
	208. Suetonius i.		

TABLE 1 (Continued)

	Royal 5 B XII	Other	MS. Extant
	209. Liber unus de compoto et algorismo.		
	210. Topica aristotelis et analitica et elenchi in i vol.		
	211. Rethoria [sic] cum Tullio de officiis in i vol.		
	212. Philosophica iiii in i vol.		
	213. Bina vol. de glosis diversis, unum de Rethorica, aliud de dialectica et Grammatica, cum pluribus summis.		
	214. Grammatica magistri R. Belvacensis in i vol.		
	215. Ovidius magnus i.		
	216. Claudianus minor et maior in i vol.		
	217. Summa magistri Johannis corn[ubiensis] de homine assumpto.		
	Sic ordinavit libros et sic scripsit. *Alexander huius ecclesie quondam cantor.*		
	218. Liber de phisica.		
	219. Liber aureus i.		
	220. Viaticus i.		
	221. Experimenta.		
	223. Afforismi i cum aliis pluribus.		
	224. Liber stomachi cum phisica magistri W[alteri] i.		
	225. Liber odonis i.		
	226. Quintus serenus et nomina herbarum i.		
	227. Diete [sic] dinamedes.		
	228. Aurelius et liber febrium et antidotarium in parvo vol.		

THE ROCHESTER CATHEDRAL LIBRARY 41

TABLE 1 *(Continued)*

	Royal 5 B XII	Other	MS. Extant
	229. Graduum et experimenta i.		
	230. Alexander i.		
	231. Diascorides et oribasius in i vol.		
	232. Antidotarius i.		
	233. Phisica fulconis i.		
	234. Super Johanicium novum vol.		
	235. Practica bartholomei, cum breviario Johannis de S[ancto] P[aulo].		
	236. De simplici medicina i.		
	237. Medicinale vetus.		
	238. Medicinale anglicum.		
	239. Liber graduum in i vol.		
	240. Razi qui fuit magistri alexandri.		
	Hii sunt libri Prioris Rodberti de Waletune		
	241. Decreta abbreviata		e Royal 10 C. IV
	242. Spalterium magalonensis.		e Royal 2 F. XI
	243. Compendium novi et veteris testamenti.	? Royal 10 A. XII: Biblium gestatorium vetus et novo in i vol.	
	244. Policraticus.		e Royal 12 F. VIII
	245. Cantica Gileberti londoniensis episcopi.		e Royal 2 E. VII
	246. Unum ex quatuor.		e Royal 3 C. VII (a later copy?)

Additional items listed in DRc/Z18:

... abbatum cluniacensium.

Vita ... virginis, et Witburge,
et sexburge

miracula sancti brandani abbatis
in i vol.

... sancti augustini et de adventu eius in ...

Libri Ezechielis et danielis et xii
prophetarum in i vol.

... chorum et auctorum cum glosis, que seorsum a ceteris libris in arca cantoris recondunt ...

... canticorum glosata libri tres, et glose ... liber i.

Questiones in paralipomenon.

... continue super epistolas pauli gemine ...

Additional items listed in Royal 10 A. XII:

Item Decreta gratiani plenaria cum
decretalibus et summam quandam
pauperum vel si placet compila-
tionem in i vol.

Item primam partem Ezechielis in i vol.

Item volumen presens in quo plura continentur.

Item summam verborum usus et
regulas in i opus.

Item apocrifa exce[rpta] et magistri
petri de tropis loquendi, et liber
gregorii [cura] pastorum et plura
alia in i vol.

Item senecam, platonem, Boetium
in i vol.

Item opuscula ailredi de oneribus
Ysaie, Speculum karitatis et
cantica canticorum et alia in
ii vol. Qui liber dicitur ailredi
abbatis Ryevall.

Item missalia ii vol. quorum unum penes
sancti martinum.[1]

Item psalteria v.

Sinodolia ii, quorum unum penes
Wal[etunam].[2]

Item apud Waletu[nam] excerptum
epistolarum An[selmi] var[iorum].[2]

Item v libros de eccl. hist.
magistri petri.

---

[1] One volume (or copy) may have been sent to St. Martin's, Dover.

[2] One synodal book and a volume of excerpts from Anselm's letters, both copied by Alexander, apparently were sent to the library at Walton.

II. THE *TEXTUS ROFFENSIS*

From the time of Bishop Gundulf, who endowed the monks at Rochester with properties and privileges intended to support them in perpetuity, the community attempted to guard its possessions against encroachments from his successors. They had little to fear from the monk-bishops Ralph d'Escures and Ernulf, but their concerns proved valid in subsequent years when bishops who were not in monastic orders came to occupy the episcopal seat. As had Gundulf before him, Ernulf may have foreseen potential threats to the economic security of the monks when he commissioned the *Textus Roffensis*, a compendium of laws and charters in Latin and Old English—the most distinctive book remaining from the medieval library of Rochester.[1] Although there is no absolute proof of Ernulf's involvement in this undertaking, the fact that it is contemporary with his term in office supports such a conclusion. Moreover, the connection with Ernulf was traditional at Rochester, as exemplified by the fourteenth-century inscription "Textus de ecclesia Roffensis per Ernulfum episcopum" entered on the flyleaf of the codex.

But concerns about the endowments of the Rochester community were not all that motivated the book known today as the *Textus Roffensis*. In order to establish a full account of Rochester's glorious past, the monks at Rochester also compiled the most comprehensive collection of Old English laws surviving today. As R. W. Southern has observed, an extraordinary effort lies behind such a compilation, a sign of the post-Conquest monastic commitment to preserve the Anglo-Saxon heritage in the face of Norman advances into every sphere of English civilization.[2] In fact, the Rochester

---

[1] An excellent facsimile of the manuscript has been edited by Peter Sawyer as Early English Manuscripts in Facsimile vols. 7 (Laws) and 11 (Cartulary) (Copenhagen, 1957 and 1962 respectively). Its history is outlined in 7:20-21, from the detailed accounts by Samuel Pegge, "An Historical Account of that venerable monument of Antiquity The Textus Roffensis; including Memoirs of the Learned Saxonists Mr. William Elstob and his sister," *Bibliotheca Topographica Britannica*, 1:25 (1784), 1-47, and by Felix Liebermann, "Notes on the Textus Roffensis," *Archaeologia Cantiana*, 23 (1898): 101-12. Thomas Hearne published the first edition of the *Textus* (Oxford, 1720), which is incomplete. Working from a transcript made by Sir Edward Dering, Hearne lacked a number of texts omitted by Dering on the grounds that they were already printed, or in the process of being printed. Most of the omitted legal texts had been published in William Lambarde's *Archaionomia* (London, 1568).

[2] "Aspects of the European Tradition of Historical Writing: 4. The Sense of the Past," *Transactions of the Royal Historical Society*, 5:23 (1973), 243-63, esp. 253. See also Southern's essay, "The Place of England in the Twelfth Century Renaissance," in *Medieval Humanism and Other Studies*, ed. Richard W. Southern (Oxford, 1970), 174-75. Simon Keynes observes that the compiler of the *Textus* went so far as to incorporate relevant information from the Domesday survey into the Anglo-Saxon documents, in *The Diplomas of King Aethelred "The Unready" 978-1016* (Cambridge, 1980), 6, n. 5.

collection bears a close relationship to post-Conquest materials from London and Christ Church, Canterbury, where extensive legal compendia already were available. Our question is, therefore, why did the monks at Rochester determine to make their own legal compendium at the same time they were assembling a cartulary?

We know that the *Textus Roffensis* originally was compiled in two separate volumes. Their independence from one another can be demonstrated by the separate sequences of quire signatures within the codex, and the fact that the law book is listed as a self-contained volume in the first catalogue of the library entered into the cartulary.[3] On the other hand, both parts are written by the same Rochester scribe, one of several who worked there c. 1124; the parts share certain Kentish dialect features, and the similarities in organization and layout are such that the volumes appear to have been planned as a composite book.[4] For example, each collection is arranged historically and includes materials attributed to the earliest kings of Kent. Further, the parts have similar formats, viz., continuous sequences of texts with titles in red entered by the main scribe. The original leaves are ruled in hard-point, usually twenty-four lines to the page. Two vertical lines delimit the written space, which measures 170 x 95 mm. throughout.[5] Paleographically, the cartulary is distinct from the law book in two minor respects only: it has numerous additions in later hands, the result of efforts to keep the records up to date throughout the twelfth century; and it has an illumination on the recto of fol. 1, the sole decoration in the joint codex.

The cartulary and the law book, then, seem to have been contemporary productions meant to accompany one another. Furthermore, each collection harkens back to the first Christian kings of Kent, to a time when kings and bishops associated with Rochester played a leading role in establishing Christianity in England. It is this conscious historical focus, I would argue, that makes the law book and the cartulary unique, and helps to explain the motivation behind the paired collections. As will be shown in more detail in the course of this chapter, chronological arrangement of these types of records is extremely unusual, despite the fact that they are obviously historical materials.[6] But at Rochester the laws could help to verify the claims of the charters. Just as the Canterbury monks tried to preserve, and even revive, the legends of important local saints in the post-Conquest years, and other monasteries turned to Bede's *Historia* to increase their prestige, so the Rochester monks may have hoped to preserve the Anglo-Saxon laws in such a way as to glorify the heritage of their own episcopal foundation.[7]

---

[3] Item 62: "Institutiones regum anglorum in i volumine."

[4] Ker, *Catalogue*, 447. The legal codes and charters of Kentish origin preserve the dialect features summarized by Campbell in *The Charters of Rochester*, xxix-xxx. These features occur sporadically in the other texts throughout both parts of the *Textus Roffensis*.

[5] Sawyer, *TR*, 7:12-13, 11:12-13.

[6] Mary P. Richards, "The Manuscript Contexts of the Old English Laws: Tradition and Innovation," in *Studies in Earlier Old English Prose*, ed. Paul E. Szarmach (Albany, NY, 1986), 171-92.

[7] See Eadmer's account of Anselm's defense of St. Elphege as a true Canterbury saint in his *Life of Anselm*, ed. and trans. R. W. Southern (London, 1962), 51. Antonia Gransden shows how Bede was used in the Anglo-Norman period in "Bede's Reputation as an Historian in Medieval England," *Journal of Ecclesiastical History*, 32 (1981): 404-12.

Tradition supported the monks in this undertaking. Bede describes Æthelberht's founding of St. Andrew's at Rochester, and eulogizes him for the many benefits he brought to his kingdom, including the code of laws established with the advice of his counsellors.[8] The preface to the laws of Ælfred and Ine, often attributed to Ælfred himself, links Æthelberht's laws with the establishment of Christianity in England, and ultimately to Mosaic law, hence the pride a Rochester compiler might have taken in showing the posterity of his founder.[9] More importantly, a comprehensive legal collection could balance the scope and arrangement of the monastic cartulary and give authority, as it were, to claims of possessions dating from the establishment of the see and those same early Christian kings of Kent.

The significance of the parallel collections to Rochester becomes clear when we examine the appellation *textus*. Normally this word was used for Gospel books in the Middle Ages, but it seems to have carried a wider meaning at Rochester, namely, a valuable book often stored apart from the monastic library in the cathedral church.[10] The list of donations to St. Andrew's recorded in BL MS. Cotton Vespasian A. XXII, fols. 88r-v (early thirteenth century) uses *textus* to describe four books given to the library by Gundulf and others.[11] Three of these are indicated to be extremely valuable, and these same three are excluded from inventories of the monastic library. Goda's Gospels, now BL MS. Royal 1 D. III, is mentioned as one of these precious books ("Textus aureum Gode comitisse") because it had been redeemed from mortgage by Prior Helyas about 1200. The others are a life and history of St. Andrew and a second Gospel book.[12] Unfortunately, Goda's Gospels is the only book among those called *textus* to survive. But, interestingly enough, it has an inscription on the flyleaf almost identical to that in the *Textus Roffensis*.[13] Both inscriptions read "Textus de ecclesiae . . .," rather than "de claustro" as is usual in Rochester books, leading to the conclusion that the two were not, in fact, part of the monastic library, but were stored in the cathedral church because of their value. This conclusion is supported by the omission of both volumes from the 1202 inventory of the library where, it will be recalled, books are listed according to location within the priory.

The *Textus Roffensis*, then, merited esteem equivalent to that awarded precious Gospel books and the life of Rochester's patron saint. Exactly when the two parts were combined under one title is impossible to know, but the donation list cited above shows that Goda's Gospels were designated *textus* at least a century before the appellation was entered in the book itself. The

---

[8] *Bede's Ecclesiastical History of the English People*, ed. and trans. Bertram Colgrave and R. A. B. Mynors (Oxford, 1969), 142-43 and 150-51.
[9] Liebermann, *Die Gesetze*, 1:46-47.
[10] Sawyer, *TR*, 7:19.
[11] Printed by Rye, 62-63.
[12] "Textus pulchrum de auratum, in quo vita et historia Sancti Andree; textum evangeliorum aureum." The fourth *textus*, a gift from Ernulf described as "textum cum evangeliis et lectionibus in principalibus diebus," may appear in the 1202 inventory as "Textus evangeliorum annuorum, in ii voluminibus novis," item #107.
[13] "Textus de ecclesia Roffensi per Godam comitissam," so noted also by Sawyer in *TR*, 7:19.

same could be true for the *Textus Roffensis*, especially as the cartulary contains a manumission.[14] This type of document normally was entered in Gospel books or Bibles, the two exceptions being ritual books, the Leofric Missal at Exeter and the *Liber Vitae* of Durham, both of which apparently were kept on the altar.[15] In light of the circumstantial evidence, it seems probable that the two parts of the *Textus Roffensis* were combined late in the twelfth century after the cartulary was completed, and moved at that time to a place of honor and security in the cathedral church at Rochester.

Because its two parts are superficially so distinct—legal materials of great scope bound up with internal documents relating mainly to Rochester Priory—the *Textus Roffensis* has been little studied as a single book. As is obvious by now, however, there is much to link the two parts. Our curiosity ought to be excited by an unusual volume so highly valued in its time, one that served as a kind of *liber vitae* for the foundation. Following this theme, we will examine each of the parts in detail and then consider the aims and achievements of the book as a unit.

Despite the fact that the law book in the *Textus Roffensis* preserves the codes of the earliest Christian kings of Kent, it is a Norman document. As such it embodies a subtle argument for the continuity of Anglo-Saxon legal authority in a vastly changed society. In this feature lies its purpose to accompany the cartulary, where benefactions from the Anglo-Saxon period are renewed periodically by Norman kings, but with the financial fabric and even the founding of St. Andrew's dependent ultimately on the earliest records entered there. The law book is extraordinary, for it brings together up-to-date legal treatises in Latin with the lengthy Old English tradition from which they were drawn. As Sawyer has shown, the original order of the gatherings gave first place in the law book to the Norman codes. His reconstruction of the original state of the legal collection is taken as the basis of this study.[16]

The conceptual framework of the collection is typically Norman. Our compiler resembles most closely the Norman author of the *Quadripartitus*, who a decade earlier compiled and translated into Latin an extensive group of codes, including all of the Old English laws found in the Rochester

---

[14] David Pelteret, *Late Anglo-Saxon Slavery: An Interdisciplinary Approach to the Various Forms of Evidence* (Univ. of Toronto doctoral thesis, 1976), 215. Also see Pierre Chaplais, "The Origin and Authenticity of the Royal Anglo-Saxon Diploma," *Journal of the Society of Archivists*, 3:2 (1965): 53, and his "The Anglo-Saxon Chancery: From the Diploma to the Writ," 3:4 (1966), 174-75.

[15] Dorothy Whitelock, *English Historical Documents*, 2nd ed., 1:384, and Elaine M. Drage, *Bishop Leofric and the Exeter Cathedral Chapter* (Oxford Univ. doctoral thesis, 1978), 142-43, 254. The text of the manumission is printed as no. 975 in John Kemble, *Codex Diplomaticus Aevi Saxonici* (London, 1846; rpt. 1964), 4:305. Max Förster lists the extant Anglo-Saxon manumission documents in *The Exeter Book of Old English Poetry*, with introductory chapters by R. W. Chambers, Max Förster, and Robin Flower (Bradford, 1933), 45, with additional manuscripts listed in his *Der Flussname Themse und seine Sippe*, Sitzungsberichte der Bayerischen Akademie der Wissenschaften, phil.-hist. Abt., Jahrgang 1941, Band 1: 794, n. 3 (reference provided by Dr. Pelteret).

[16] Sawyer, *TR*, 7:11-12.

collection excepting the Kentish codes and the short text *Becwæp*.[17] The Rochester man was, however, deliberately producing a work for his own foundation. Not only did he locate and include the Kentish laws, but he modified historical lists accompanying the laws with references of special interest to his house. For many of these items, our compiler probably turned to sources from Christ Church, Canterbury, but the evidence is problematic. At present, signs of Canterbury origin appear mainly in the accompanying historical lists rather than within the laws themselves. For example, the genealogies of English kings and the episcopal lists copied at the end of the Rochester law book have been assigned independently by their most recent editors to a lost Canterbury source.[18] To these lists the Rochester scribe added local references such as the names of three early bishops of the see unknown from any other source.[19]

The general type of collection used by our compiler can be seen today in two other post-Conquest manuscripts whose materials are closely related to those in the *Textus Roffensis:* Oxford MS. Bodley Rawlinson C. 641 (twelfth century, provenance unknown) and Cambridge MS. Corpus Christi College 383 (late eleventh/early twelfth century, associated with St. Paul's, London).[20] MS. Rawlinson C. 641 contains most of the Latin texts found in the *Textus*, while MS. 383 has fifteen Old English texts in common with the Rochester law book. These two collections differ significantly from each other as well as from the Rochester collection, and cast into relief the aims of our compiler. The former is a scrappy collection of a few Norman texts in Latin, while the latter is a handbook exclusively of vernacular codes providing a concise guide to English custom, with special emphasis on laws meant to govern hostile peoples forced to live together.[21]

By contrast, the organization of the law book in the *Textus Roffensis* resembles that of Book I of the Latin *Quadripartitus*, which begins with the codes of Cnut and then returns to those of *Ælfred-Ine*, the earliest in its collection. From there Book I proceeds forward in rough chronological order through two codes of William I. Similarly, the *Textus Roffensis* opened originally with Cnut's codes, as translated and edited by a Norman author in the *Instituta*

---

[17] Felix Liebermann, *Quadripartitus, Ein Englisches Rechtsbuch von 1144* (Halle, 1892), vii; Sawyer, *TR,* 7:20. See also Edgar B. Graves, *A Bibliography of English History to 1485* (Oxford, 1975), 300-303.

[18] David M. Dumville, "The Anglian Collection of Royal Genealogies and Regnal Lists," *Anglo-Saxon England,* 5 (1976): 27-28, 46; Raymond I. Page, "Anglo-Saxon Episcopal Lists, Part I," *Nottingham Medieval Studies,* 9 (1965): 81-83.

[19] Page, 73.

[20] Sawyer, *TR,* 7: 19-20. For descriptions see Liebermann, *Die Gesetze,* 1:xix and xxxviii. The scope of Liebermann's work is reviewed by H. W. C. Davis in "The Anglo-Saxon Laws," *English Historical Review,* 28 (1913): 417-30. A fuller description of Cambridge MS. Corpus Christi College 383 is in Ker, *Catalogue,* 110-13. Sawyer, 7:20, offers the conjecture that the Kentish laws may have been included on the missing leaves that originally opened MS. 383.

[21] A related point about MS. Corpus Christi College 383 is made by Patrick Wormald in "Æthelred the Lawmaker," *Ethelred the Unready,* ed. David Hill, British Archaeological Reports British Series, 59 (1978): 60-61. More detailed analysis of the MS. can be found in Richards, "The Manuscript Context of the Old English Laws," 181-84.

Cnuti,[22] and two further Norman texts in Latin, before returning to the Kentish laws and moving forward through the Anglo-Saxon period. A closer examination of our compiler's selections reveals much about the milieu in which he worked and the aims of his own project.

To begin, our compiler used the curious rendition of Cnut's codes known as the *Instituta Cnuti*, in which the laws of Cnut are translated into Latin and supplemented with extracts from the codes of *Ælfred-Ine*, *II Eadgar*, and anonymous legal prescriptions to provide a range of statements, anachronistic and even contradictory, on a given topic. The author addresses Peter's Pence, for instance, with the strict provisions of *II Eadgar* 4.1 and more lenient statements drawn from *I Cnut* 9.[23] The Rochester copy of the *Instituta Cnuti* is the earliest and most accurate remaining today. Textually it is closest to the version copied c. 1175 into Oxford MS. Bodley Digby 13, which Ker has linked tentatively to Christ Church, Canterbury, or its cell at Dover.[24] The two texts share a unique title and a number of individual readings against other extant versions of the *Instituta*. It is possible, therefore, that the Rochester version was copied from a Canterbury original now lost, of which a later copy remains in MS. Digby 13. From the compiler's point of view, this text must have seemed a handy recasting of lengthy materials that coincided with the overall theme of his project, namely, the continuing authority and viability of the Old English laws.

As if to strengthen this theme, our compiler follows the *Instituta Cnuti* with the *Ten Articles* of William I, the stated purpose of which is to preserve the peace between the English and Normans living together in England.[25] This author draws on the *Instituta* for the purpose of combining Anglo-Saxon legal custom with Norman practice. To this end, he resolves conflicts between the two by offering alternatives. Englishmen, for instance, are given the choice of defending themselves from criminal accusations either by ordeal of iron, the traditional means, or by combat, the French method. The Rochester version of the *Ten Articles* is again the earliest and most accurate remaining, but this text is closest to one found in Oxford MS. Bodley Rawlinson C. 641, mentioned above, which may have had a common ancestor with portions of the *Textus Roffensis*.[26]

The third and final Norman composition in the series that originally opened the law book is an excerpt from the Decretals of Pseudo-Isidore, entitled *De accusatoribus* by Liebermann.[27] The decretal collection had been

---

[22] See Felix Liebermann, "On the Instituta Cnuti Aliorumque Regum Anglorum," *Transactions of the Royal Historical Society*, N.S. 7 (1893): 77-107. Printed in Jan L. A. Kolderup-Rosenvige, ed., *Legum Regis Canuti Magni* (Havn, 1826), 4-118.

[23] Liebermann, *Die Gesetze*, 1:612-16.

[24] Ker, *MLGB*, 59.

[25] Liebermann, *Die Gesetze*, 1:486-88; translated in A. J. Robertson, *The Laws of the Kings of England from Edmund to Henry I* (Cambridge, 1925; rpt. 1974), 225-26. See also David C. Douglas and George W. Greenaway, eds., *English Historical Documents*, 2nd ed. (London, 1981), 2:431.

[26] Sawyer, *TR*, 7:20; Liebermann, "Instituta," 102.

[27] "De accusatoribus aus Pseudo-Isidor," *Deutsche Zeitschrift für Kirchenrecht*, 1 (1901): 1-5.

brought to Canterbury from the Norman abbey of Bec by Lanfranc, archbishop of Canterbury under William I, and from there had circulated throughout England during the post-Conquest period. Apparently Norman ecclesiastics excerpted certain portions from the larger collections to address specific topics within a wider legal context, for the present text seems to have been known to the author of the *Quadripartitus*.[28] *De accusatoribus* addresses the question of accusations against ecclesiastics, and its inclusion at this point in the Rochester law book is most interesting: following the *Ten Articles* of William I as it does, the text provides authority from canon law to accompany the new civil code, and thus provides a sign of the growing separation of civil from ecclesiastical law during William's reign.[29]

Having assembled three important Norman legal documents, our compiler fortunately turned to the earliest laws in Old English to continue his collection. The fact that he chose to preserve these materials in their original language sets him apart from his contemporaries, and may indicate that he, unlike they, concerned himself with the matter of authenticity. This is especially probable because many of the early Rochester charters contain Old English, and the existence of parallel legal documents could only strengthen their statements. Certainly our compiler had schooled himself in Anglo-Saxon language and history to the extent that he was able to organize the vernacular codes by dynasty, from Æthelberht through Æthelred II, and then to supplement these with anonymous codes related by topic.

His method is clear in the first group of English laws—the Kentish codes of Æthelberht, Hlothhære and Eadric, and Wihtræd.[30] He sets these forth in historical order and follows with the anonymous short code, *Hadbot*, now attributed to Archbishop Wulfstan (d. 1023).[31] Despite the disparity in date of composition, *Hadbot* relates topically to Wihtræd's code, which addresses the clergy and offenses against the church, since *Hadbot* lists penalties for offenses to the seven ranks of clergy. The compiler then follows these materials with the West Saxon regnal table through Æthelred II (978-1016), which leads into the West Saxon codes. The table probably descended from a Canterbury text, but it is closely related to one copied into MS. Corpus Christi College, Cambridge 383.[32]

Because the arrangement of codes is key to understanding the method and motives of our compiler, it is worthwhile to examine more of his work in detail. From the West Saxon dynasty he includes the codes of Ælfred/Ine, Æthelstan, Eadward, Eadmund, and Æthelred. The particular version of

---

[28] Suggested by a comparison between the passages from Pseudo-Isidore cited by Liebermann as sources for Henry's laws in Book II of the *Quadripartitus* (*Die Gesetze*, 1:548 ff.), and the contents of *De accusatoribus* listed by Liebermann in the article cited above, n. 22.

[29] This was a gradual process, as shown by Colin Morris in "William I and the Church Courts," *English Historical Review*, 82 (1967): 449-63.

[30] Liebermann, *Die Gesetze*, 1:3-14.

[31] Ibid., 464-68. On the question of authorship, see Dorothy Bethurum, "Six Anonymous Old English Codes," *Journal of English and Germanic Philology*, 49 (1950): 459-60.

[32] Sawyer, *TR*, 7:15.

Ælfred/Ine in the *Textus Roffensis* has a chapter on incendiaries and murderers following Ine's code that appears elsewhere only in MS. 383.[33] But in the *Textus*, two further short, anonymous codes follow *Ælfred/Ine* and give a Norman flavor to the compilation of English materials. The first of these, *Ordal*, lists procedures for the ordeal used to determine the guilt or innocence of the accused.[34] The second, *Walreaf*, is a statement which prohibits robbing the dead.[35] Liebermann believed that the latter is Scandinavian in origin because of its terminology.[36] Both pieces occur here uniquely in Old English, but they also appear in *Quadripartitus*, where the Norman author translated them into Latin. Our compiler, then, follows in detail the methods of his contemporaries as he makes selections from the Danelaw to include alongside English practices. Although he preserves the materials in their original language, he nevertheless produces a collection appealing to Norman interests.

Just how closely he follows his contemporaries can be seen in the next selections in the Rochester law book, three codes of Æthelstan. These are out of chronological order because they precede Eadward's codes, but this same arrangement occurs in the *Quadripartitus*, which also aims to set forth royal codes in historical order. Since the West Saxon regnal table was close at hand, but clearly not consulted, it seems probable that the anachronism stems from a common source used by the two compilers. The treatment of Æthelstan's codes in the *Textus* is interesting in itself. Under the rubric *Æthelstanes gerænesse* [sic] occur II *Æthelstan*, V *Æthelstan* with a unique addition from IV *Æthelstan*, and the short code *Pax*. II *Æthelstan*, the most accurate version remaining today, addresses the issues of thieves, lordless men, landless men, exchange and purchase, ordeals, and refusal of justice. V addresses fugitives from the law and corruption among reeves, with the addition of a statement from IV on sanctuary for outlaws. *Pax*, on the extent of the king's peace, completes the group.[37] It is yet another text found elsewhere only in *Quadripartitus*. As a group, these materials address criminal activity and prosecution in Æthelstan's time.

Thus far in our analysis, a number of parallels regarding selection and arrangement of texts have emerged between the *Textus Roffensis* and the Norman compilation *Quadripartitus*. But within the historical scheme of the Rochester collection, some groups of texts are arranged topically, more in the manner of the other great Norman compendium, the *Instituta Cnuti*. Such is the case with a group of anonymous codes following Æthelstan's laws.

---

[33] The chapter is actually numbered CXXI. in the *Textus*, but not so in MS. 383, where no chapters in the laws of Ine are numbered. The *B* of the title, *Be Morþslihtum*, is in red in the latter MS., however, leading Liebermann to conclude that the scribe thought it was a separate text. See *Die Gesetze*, 1:388.

[34] Liebermann, *Die Gesetze*, 1:386-87.

[35] Ibid., 1:392.

[36] Ibid., 3:230.

[37] Ibid., 1:309; 3:230. Although clearly following the theme of the preceding codes, *Pax* is thought by Liebermann to be a slightly later composition.

Under the rubric *Hu se man sceal swerie* are gathered *Swerian*, directions for swearing oaths;[38] *Ap*, in a unique version having the two parts reversed from normal order, ranking men by the value of their oaths;[39] and *Mircna laga*, stating the wergild for different ranks in Mercia.[40] The two latter texts, written by Wulfstan, are translated together in the *Instituta Cnuti* along with *Hadbot*, which, it will be recalled, cited penalties for offenses to the seven ranks of clergy. Next in the *Textus Roffensis* occurs the unique Old English version of *VI Æthelstan*, showing early guild organization in the City of London, a text known also in the *Quadripartitus*.[41] Two further laws attributed to Wulfstan, *Geþyncþo* and *Norþleod*, return to the theme of defining social status and wergilds found in the previous group of codes.[42] The final group of anonymous pieces is practical—sets of directions for marriage, retrieving stolen cattle, and making wills, all found as well in the post-Conquest compilation, MS. Corpus Christi College, Cambridge 383.[43] Clearly the Rochester compiler was well acquainted with the range of legal materials produced in his time and attempted to develop an up-to-date collection for his priory. He himself must have had a strong interest in legal materials to have undertaken such an effort—and the same could be said of a group of collaborators, since we do not know who actually made the compilation. But the motivation to produce an exemplary, even state-of-the-art collection to accompany the Rochester cartulary could only have originated in the belief that such work was valuable for the priory.

Our compiler concludes the lawbook in the *Textus Roffensis* with a series of royal codes in historical order: the laws of Eadward and Guthrum governing relations between English and Danes, including *Wer*, a statement of the wergild owing for different ranks of men;[44] *I-II Eadmund*;[45] and *I and III Æthelred*,[46] separated by William's decree settling disputes between the English and French.[47] In the latter series, the pieces address the English, the English and French, and the Danes, respectively, on topics such as surety, witness, and keeping the peace, and thus illustrate again the eclectic approach to legal materials we have come to associate with the Normans. Both William's decree and *III Æthelred* exist only in the *Textus Roffensis* and the *Quadripartitus*.

---

[38] Ibid., 1:396-98.
[39] Ibid., 1:464.
[40] Ibid., 1:462.
[41] Ibid., 1:173-83.
[42] Ibid., 1:456-58, 458-60.
[43] Ibid., 1:442-44 (*Wif*), 400 (*Becwæp*). The charm is printed in Godfrid Storms, *Anglo-Saxon Magic* (The Hague, 1948), 11B, p. 204. Its motifs are discussed by Thomas D. Hill, in "The Theme of the Cosmological Cross in Two Old English Cattle Theft Charms," *Notes and Queries*, 25 (1978): 488-90, and Raymond J. S. Grant, *Cambridge, Corpus Christi College 41: The Loricas and the Missal*, Costerus, N.S. v. 17 (1978): 7-9 and 114.
[44] Liebermann, *Die Gesetze*, 1:128-34, 392.
[45] Ibid., 1:184-90.
[46] Ibid., 1:216-20, 228-32.
[47] Ibid., 1:483-84.

Following the royal codes, the compiler adds certain ceremonial pieces necessary to the church's role in the judicial process and a series of historical lists, as follows: three forms of exorcism in Latin (*Iudicia Dei I-III*)—for water, iron, and bread;[48] the coronation charter of Henry I in its earliest version;[49] two forms of excommunication in Latin;[50] and four sets of lists— the West Saxon genealogy, genealogies of Anglo-Saxon kings, lists of popes, emperors, and patriarchs, and lists of English archbishops and bishops. The episcopal lists, at least, were copied from a Canterbury manuscript, for the archbishops of Canterbury continue in the main hand through the obit of Ralph D'Escures in 1122, while the Rochester list ends with Godwin II (d. c. 1050). Curiously, there has been no effort to bring the Rochester list up to date, although three early bishops of the see known only from their inclusion here have been added to the Canterbury source. This reinforces the impression that our compiler was interested primarily in documenting the Anglo-Saxon history of Rochester, probably to balance and strengthen the claims of the cartulary.

Coming as it does among texts preserving church rituals, Henry's coronation charter seems almost to have been included as an afterthought—at least as a text found apart from the major sources of legal material in the collection. Its separation from the main body of laws, however, has a parallel in the arrangement of the *Quadripartitus*, where Henry's charter begins Book II, an incomplete collection of documents from his reign recording legislation and the investiture controversy.[51] With Henry, as opposed to William, Norman authors and compilers seemingly recognized that a new era of legislation had begun, for Henry declared himself free of many practices of his predecessors in the coronation charter and all of his codes were issued in Latin. Thus, although Henry's charter is properly included among the Norman texts which comprise MS. Bodley Rawlinson C. 641, it is separated from the English and English-influenced Norman texts in the *Textus Roffensis* as it is in the *Quadripartitus*.

Henry's charter leads back to fundamental questions about the law book in the *Textus Roffensis*. As mentioned previously, the text is preserved here in its earliest copy. Its separate existence as a charter is recorded only in inventories of the treasury of the archbishop of Canterbury made c. 1277 and 1330.[52] Possibly, then, our compiler found it among other sources he used at Canterbury. The question remains why so many legal texts are preserved in their most accurate and complete versions in the Rochester lawbook. The answer, though it cannot be complete, draws on the many individual features of the collection we have observed. The first is its aim for comprehensiveness within a Norman framework, which led to the inclusion of a wide

---

[48] Ibid., 1:401-409.
[49] Ibid., 1:521-23, and in Whitelock, et. al., *Councils and Synods*, 1, 2:652-55.
[50] Liebermann, *Die Gesetze*, 1:439-40.
[51] Liebermann, *Quadripartitus*, 150-51.
[52] Whitelock, et al., *Councils and Synods*, 1, 2:653.

range of texts. Secondly, the appellation *textus* suggests that it was regarded as part of a precious book meriting special treatment not normally accorded legal materials, possibly including storage in the cathedral church. Thus the *Textus Roffensis* probably was not subject to borrowing or even frequent consultation, and was not as exposed to the elements as books stored in the cloister might be. Most importantly, our compiler seems to have regarded the law book, including its historical materials, as a means to give authority to the cartulary; hence he sought out the most authoritative sources he could locate. He shared an interest in the English laws with his contemporaries, but he also had specific motives for developing a collection for Rochester priory. We have seen how those motives shaped the law book; the cartulary bears similar signs of conscious organization toward preserving the history and security of St. Andrew's.

On first examination, the cartulary differs from the lawbook in several fundamental respects: it is composed primarily of materials originating at Rochester; it was augmented throughout the twelfth century; it even was "corrected" by erasures and replacements of leaves.[53] Nevertheless, it closely resembles its companion volume in appearance and organization. Unlike most medieval cartularies, it is arranged chronologically, from the spurious foundation charter of Æthelberht through donations and confirmations made during the reign of Henry I.[54] Most of the texts have titles in red, written by the main scribe, which refer to the properties mentioned within the piece: *De Bromleage, De Hallinges,* and so on. These rubrics may well be unique to the copies in the *Textus Roffensis*, for they occur neither in the originals of the charters where they still exist, nor in the fourteenth-century *Liber Temporalium*, still the property of the dean and chapter, which contains copies of most texts in the present collection.[55] The advantage to the system in the *Textus* is that the reader can locate quickly documents referring to particular holdings, while the collection as a whole demonstrates an ancient and valuable history of royal patronage parallel to the materials set forth in the law book.

To appreciate fully the achievement represented in the *Textus* cartulary, we need only compare it with the other surviving medieval cartularies from Rochester.[56] Ours is the earliest in the group of four, all of which stress the holdings of the priory over those of the bishop. Indeed, certain post-Conquest items preserved in these cartularies record disputes over properties between monks and bishops which were resolved in favor of the priory. Each cartulary, however, has its own distinct features. Only the *Liber Tem-*

---

[53] Sawyer, *TR*, 11:12, 15.
[54] G. R. C. Davis, *Medieval Cartularies of Great Britain* (London, 1958), xii. See also David Walker, "The Organization of Material in Medieval Cartularies," in *The Study of Medieval Records (Essays in honour of Kathleen Major)*, ed. Donald A. Bullough and R. L. Story (Oxford, 1971), esp. pp. 134-36.
[55] Campbell, xv, argues that certain texts in the *Liber Temporalium* were copied directly from the *Textus Roffensis*.
[56] Davis, 92-93.

poralium mentioned above contains Anglo-Saxon materials, and most of its documents are arranged topographically. On the other hand, the two thirteenth-century collections differ from the *Textus* in that they contain post-Conquest records exclusively. The larger of these collections, now fols. 90-208 in BL MS. Cotton Domitian A. X, covers a century and a half of episcopal and royal charters, beginning with the work of Gundulf and Lanfranc. The struggles of the monks to retain their properties are recorded here, along with deeds and confirmations of holdings arranged by location. The second set of records from the late thirteenth century appears in a quire in BL MS. Royal 5 A. IV among a hodgepodge of unrelated texts.[57] The charters copied here cover roughly fifty years, from 1177 to c. 1227-38. They are so messy that they may have been drafts for a proper set of records. In addition to these collections of charters, a register, mainly in the form of lists, was compiled in the thirteenth century in BL MS. Cotton Vespasian A. XXII, together with two sets of annals, one universal and the other ecclesiastical. The *Textus* cartulary stands apart from these collections because of its emphasis on the Anglo-Saxon heritage of the see and priory. At the same time, the later cartularies continue to reflect the concerns we have attributed to the compiler of the *Textus*, namely, to insure the financial independence of Rochester Priory. Hence, records of the same properties, confirmations, disputes, and agreements can be found from collection to collection, at times in slightly different versions. As a whole, the cartularies parallel the various library catalogues compiled well into the thirteenth century with the aim of protection through documentation.

The historical focus of the *Textus* cartulary is clear from the start, as it opens with the spurious foundation charter of Æthelberht I.[58] Whether or not it reflects an actual transaction, this text is essential to the compiler's efforts to link Rochester to the earliest Christian kings of Kent and, at the same time, to demonstrate its independence from Canterbury. Subsequent Anglo-Saxon charters, recorded in the present collection as having been issued by the kings of Kent and Mercia to the bishop and "monasteria" of St. Andrew's, have been judged authentic.[59] These materials trace through the early ninth century Rochester's growing endowment in properties, pasture-rights, and privileges such as the free access of a ship into the port of London. They document grants of land from Sigered of Kent and Offa of Mercia made specifically for the purpose of enlarging the monastery.[60] After A.D. 811, however, the charters recorded are almost exclusively from the kings of Wessex: Ecgberht, Æthelwulf, Æthelberht, Æthelred I, Eadmund I,

---

[57] *Catalogue of Western Manuscripts in the Old Royal and King's Collections*, 1:95.
[58] Campbell, no. 1. See also Peter H. Sawyer, *Anglo-Saxon Charters* (London, 1968), 69, no. 1; Vivian H. Galbraith, "Monastic Foundation Charters of the Eleventh and Twelfth Centuries," *Cambridge Historical Journal*, 4 (1934): 221-22; and Margaret Deanesly, "English and Gallic Minsters, Appendix: The Charters of King Æthelberht," *Transactions of the Royal Historical Society*, 4th ser., 23 (1941): 66-69.
[59] But see Keynes, *The Diplomas of King Æthelred "The Unready," 978-1016*, 10.
[60] Campbell, no. 5 and no. 13.

Eadgar, and Æthelred II. In all, thirty-one charters arranged historically record the possessions of St. Andrew's prior to the Conquest.

The shaping spirit behind the *Textus* becomes clear when we compare the texts included by our compiler with materials he omitted: separate charters still extant and documents recorded only in the *Liber Temporalium*. These materials are published together with the pre-Conquest documents from the *Textus Roffensis* in Campbell's edition of the Anglo-Saxon charters from Rochester.[61] Campbell no. 16 and no. 23 provide examples of royal grants of land and other rights to two individuals termed *minister* (probably in its most general meaning of *thane*), which our compiler selected for inclusion in the *Textus* cartulary. Campbell no. 16, a grant from Coenwulf of Mercia and Cuthred of Kent to one Swithhun, is followed by a brief note recording the latter's bequest of the property to St. Andrew's. In Campbell no. 23, Æthelwulf of Wessex makes a grant to Dunn in Latin, to which is added Dunn's will in Old English deeding the lands to Rochester at his death.[62] By contrast, two Anglo-Saxon documents known only in the *Liber Temporalium*, Campbell no. 21 and no. 22, record royal grants of land to important individuals but lack any clauses deeding the properties to Rochester. The same is true of Campbell no. 25 and no. 30, two further charters from the tenth century where the original parchments remain, yet are not recorded in the *Textus Roffensis*. These four items may have been kept for safety by the chapter, possibly in hopes of a bequest, but since they did not record actual gifts or possessions, our compiler excluded them from his cartulary.

Our compiler did not ignore struggles over properties rightfully belonging to the monks, for he includes short histories of certain disputed estates within the larger compilation of documentary materials. The first of these, Campbell no. 34, relates Rochester's attempts to regain possession of Wouldham, Kent, which had been granted by charter to St. Andrew's.[63] The report ends with a judgment against one Leofsunu, who had usurped the property. The question may not have been settled by the early twelfth century, for this text alone among the three mini-histories in the *Textus Roffensis* has been translated into Latin following the Old English version. In Campbell no. 36, Bishop Ælfstan of Rochester has a stronger case against those who had alienated the estates of Snodland, Kent, in the time of King Eadgar, for he bases his claims on the actual deeds which had been stolen from him by certain priests and then sold. According to the present account, the bishop appealed to the king, who in turn forced the widow of the man who bought them to return the deeds and to forfeit her other property to the crown. Subsequently, the bishop persuaded the king to let him buy the

---

[61] Reviewed by Bernard Wigan in *Archaeologia Cantiana*, 88 (1973): 229-30. Additional reviews are listed in *Anglo-Saxon England*, 5 (1976): 274, and 6 (1977): 308. For a discussion of the volume and the series it inaugurates, see Nicholas Brooks, "Anglo-Saxon Charters: the work of the last twenty years," in *Anglo-Saxon England*, 3 (1974): 211-31.

[62] Translated in Whitelock, *English Historical Documents*, 1: 525-26.

[63] For a history of the Wouldham estate, see David A. E. Pelteret, "Two Old English Lists of Serfs," *Mediaeval Studies*, 48 (1986): 492-503.

forfeited estates of Bromley and Fawkham, Kent.[64] After the king died, however, a kinsman of the widow seized the estates, and a group of influential churchmen and nobility was assembled to witness that the previous transaction of ownership to Rochester had taken place. The sequel to the history of Snodland occurs in Campbell no. 37, which relates Bishop Godwine's successful efforts to take possession of that estate on behalf of the priory after having produced the deeds that had been returned to his predecessor.

As these cases demonstrate, written evidence in support of claims to property was most helpful in resolving disputes. But materials collected together into a cartulary obviously were in handier, and even safer, form than were loose sheets which could be stolen and sold. A cartulary did not preserve the original documents and, hence, its materials could be open to the charge of forgery, but these considerations were secondary to the need to preserve historical documentation of ownership. With reference to the *Textus Roffensis*, it is striking that the monks of Rochester wanted to record not only grants and privileges, but also the history of disputed properties, perhaps as protection against claims made after the principals to the settlement had died.[65]

Similar considerations must have motivated our compiler to include Latin translations of additional documents in Old English having continued importance to the foundation, as illustrated by Campbell no. 35, the will of Byrhtric and his wife Ælfswith, and a text concerning Rochester Bridge. The complicated provisions of the will are mainly in favor of St. Andrew's, but the transaction must have taken decades to complete.[66] The couple leaves certain properties and gold outright to Rochester, to Christ Church, Canterbury, and to St. Augustine's, Canterbury. The remaining properties are divided among eleven kinsmen, to revert to Rochester upon each of their deaths. From the evidence of the historical accounts described above, the probability of disputes with the families of the eleven was great. Hence, it was only practical to have a Latin version of the will on hand to consult as needed. The same is true of the final Anglo-Saxon text in the cartulary, a list of estates liable for work on Rochester Bridge.[67] Both the Old English and Latin versions of the document have been altered, perhaps to reflect a change in responsibilities regarding different portions of the bridge. In any event, a Latin translation was needed for an obligation that had ongoing importance for the priory.

---

[64] Patrick Wormald examines these charters for evidence of negotiated settlements in "Charters, law and the settlement of disputes in Anglo-Saxon England," in *The Settlement of Disputes in Early Medieval Europe*, ed. Wendy Davies and Paul Fouracre (Cambridge, 1986), 158-61. On the tenurial history of Bromley, see E. E. Barker, "The Bromley Charters," *Archaeologia Cantiana*, 93 (1978): 181-83.

[65] See Brown, 5.

[66] Edited and translated by Dorothy Whitelock, *Anglo-Saxon Wills* (Cambridge, 1930; rpt. 1973), no. XI: 26-29 and 128-32.

[67] Edited and translated by A. J. Robertson, *Anglo-Saxon Charters*, 2nd ed. (Cambridge, 1956), 106-09.

Clearly, our compiler had a purpose for his collection of Anglo-Saxon materials: to provide an historical account of the priory's holdings that could be used, as necessary, in the future. He was a pragmatic archivist, and an extremely effective one. Through his selection and arrangement of materials, he was able to demonstrate the continuing validity of past agreements essential to the independence of Rochester Priory, both from the bishop and from Christ Church, Canterbury.

This theme is reinforced strongly by the post-Conquest documents, which begin with an account of the celebrated trial at Penenden Heath, where Lanfranc forced Odo of Bayeux to return properties in Kent that he had usurped from Canterbury and Rochester.[68] The decision was of great value to Rochester, and it possessed another, fuller version of the settlement in MS. Cotton Vespasian A. XXII, fols. 120-121.[69] As do the Anglo-Saxon materials in the *Textus* cartulary, the post-Conquest charters follow in rough chronology yet continue to be titled by the property addressed within the text of each document. There are pieces devoted to the donation and subsequent confirmation of estates, but on the whole they are less colorful than the mini-histories in the Anglo-Saxon group. Occasionally one can extract bits of history from the post-Conquest documents. The text on Hedenham (fol. 173v), for instance, which records William I's donation of land there in return for Gundulf's services, contains the information that Gundulf built Rochester Castle.

The mass of post-Conquest material to be presented puts new demands on our compiler, who is determined to maintain the historical focus of his cartulary. In the process of recording all royal and episcopal donations from the time of refoundation and all properties given by individuals—on behalf of family members who joined the brotherhood of monks, for prayers and masses to be said for themselves and their families, and in thanks for the hospitality of the monks—our compiler provides summaries of these bequests in tables and lists near the end of the collection. Thus, on fols. 183-84 and fols. 185-91, the gifts of individuals are grouped together and recorded in formulaic style. Fols. 209-10 preserve a version of the Domesday account of the Rochester fief.[70] On fols. 215-16 occurs a list of royal donations from A.D. 738 through the reign of William II. Apparently these lists proved to be useful, for later in the twelfth century another such list of royal donations from Æthelberht of Kent through Henry I was added on a bifolium, fols. 177-78.

Our compiler must have been an admirer of Bishop Gundulf, whose role in the acquisition and retention of lands belonging to the see and priory

---

[68] On Lanfranc's role in helping Rochester recover its lands, restore its cathedral, and build a castle, see Gibson, *Lanfranc of Bec*, 214-15.

[69] John Le Patourel, "The Reports of the Trial on Penenden Heath," *Studies in Medieval History Presented to F. M. Powicke*, ed. Richard W. Hunt, et al. (Oxford, 1969), 15-19.

[70] Sawyer, *TR*, 11:16. See also David C. Douglas, ed., *The Domesday Monachorum of Christ Church, Canterbury* (London, 1944), 80-81, 95-98.

emerges in great detail from the documents within the cartulary. Gundulf was present at the trial on Penenden Heath and received the deeds for properties restored to Rochester. He also received confirmations from William I of properties and rights mentioned in the Anglo-Saxon charters. He was party to certain agreements benefiting the priory, and established a fund for clothing the monks. In fact, his close relationship to Lanfranc seems to have been instrumental in successful efforts to gain new properties as well as confirmations of older claims from the king. A case in point is the piece in Latin and Old English, fol. 170v, entitled *De frachenham* (Freckenham in Suffolk), where William affirms his grant to Lanfranc and the latter's donations of the property to St. Andrew's. Further on, fols. 211-12 record a series of royal donations of land and churches to Rochester, subsequently confirmed on fol. 213r by Lanfranc. In fact, the detailed accounts of Gundulf's activities in the *Textus* amount to a substantial biography of the bishop, echoed in many respects by the contemporary *Vita Gundulfi* written by a monk of Rochester. As evidence of this, the charter entitled *De subiectione et fidelitate abbatisse de mellingis* (fol. 198r) preserves an agreement made at the time Gundulf founded the nunnery, in which the abbess swears obedience to Gundulf and his successors in the Rochester episcopate. This event forms a major episode in the account of Gundulf's life.[71]

Several royal confirmations merit specific attention because they relate to matters associated with the Rochester library. On fol. 181r, William II confirms a gift of Countess Goda, half-sister of Edward the Confessor, involving the manor of Estuna, to Gundulf and St. Andrew's. This same Goda owned a *textus* described above, hence she must have been an important donor for Rochester. She is the only woman mentioned in the cartulary who makes a gift herself rather than as part of her husband's bequest.[72] In a text entitled *De waletuna* (fol. 182r-v), William II confirms Roger Bigot's gift of a church at St. Felicity, Walton, Suffolk, which later became a cell of Rochester and may have housed a small collection of books.

Henry I seems to have been quite friendly to Rochester. He visited there in 1101 and issued a series of charters at that time, which are now recorded on fols. 186v-87v.[73] These include grants of churches, protection of fishing rights in the Thames, and even a commemoration of the feast of St. Paulinus. His party, too, was generous, as the list of donations on fol. 188 proves. On another occasion, recorded on fols. 218-19, Henry confirmed the division of lands and privileges between the monks and bishop proposed by Gundulf with the consent of Anselm, then archbishop of Canterbury.

Gundulf's successor, Ernulf, is credited with extensive donations in two lists copied on fols. 196v-97v, the second made in honor of Gundulf. These demonstrate, above all else, the interest Ernulf had in the welfare of the priory during his relatively short tenure as bishop and the fact that his

---

[71] Thomson, *Life of Gundulf*, 65.
[72] Brown, 174, relates a later version of Goda's bequest as cited in the *Registrum Roffensis*, 119.
[73] Waller, 16-17, describes these in detail.

efforts were viewed as a continuation of Gundulf's. Ernulf's aggressiveness on the monks' behalf is evident in a document on fols. 198v-99r, where one Radulfus *clericus* concedes land adjoining the monks' cemetery and money to settle a feud over the property with Ernulf. He, further, is the last bishop to be mentioned as a donor in the cartulary, despite later additions through the twelfth century. When we reflect on the troubles the monks had with subsequent bishops who were not in monastic orders, it is clear why they are omitted from a compilation of grants and privileges to the priory. For example, on fols. 203v-204r is a judgment in favor of the monks at Rochester issued in 1144 by Imar of Tusculum, who happened to be traveling through England and was called upon to settle a long-standing property dispute dating from the episcopacy of John II.[74]

Later texts continue to confirm the priory's holdings. The Norman kings and archbishops of Canterbury regularly issued such confirmations as the cartulary shows. Fols. 206-208r contain a copy of a bull of Eugenius III, issued in 1146, addressed to the monks at Rochester. The funds owed the bishop of Rochester for performing episcopal duties in the absence of the archbishop of Canterbury are noted in an agreement on fol. 220r in a thirteenth-century hand. Another agreement between Gundulf and one Eadmer *anhaende* over property in London has been erased and recopied on fol. 210v. On fols. 220v-22r is a list of churches in the Rochester diocese with notations of payments due for chrism.[75] On fol. 222r are offices and masses to be said for members of houses in confraternity with Rochester.

Whether purposeful or not, the fact that Gundulf is mentioned in some of the latest documents in the cartulary reminds us of the role he played in reestablishing the see and priory at Rochester to something of its former glory. Our compiler seems to recognize Gundulf and Ernulf as fellow Normans who appreciated the Anglo-Saxon heritage of Rochester and who persuaded royal and ecclesiastical authorities to do likewise. Similar to the Norman authors of the *Quadripartitus* and *Instituta Cnuti*, these bishops renewed the Anglo-Saxon legacy rather than disregarding it. The compiler of the *Textus Roffensis* took inspiration from their work.

Following the extensive documentation of post-Conquest gifts, privileges, and other sources of income in the cartulary, comes the earliest catalogue of the Rochester library, a monument to the first Norman bishops of Rochester. In this way the priory concludes with obvious pride and tenacity the account of its holdings c. 1124, and some later additions. The Anglo-Saxon charters establish the ancient heritage of St. Andrew's, and the post-Conquest texts show it coming to life as a Benedictine priory and monastic see operating within the influence of Christ Church, Canterbury. This relationship nourished Rochester in many respects, not the least of which was providing the basis for its monastic library and, most likely, the legal portion of the present

---

[74] Whitelock, et al., *Councils and Synods*, 1, 2: 810-13.
[75] Gordon Ward attempts to identify the churches in "The List of Saxon Churches in the *Textus Roffensis*," *Archaeologia Cantiana*, 44 (1932): 44-53.

volume. But the proximity of Canterbury limited the growth of Rochester's see and priory in other ways, particularly in the acquisition of endowments. Waller has observed that all but one of the properties granted to Rochester in the *Textus Roffensis* are in western Kent, as opposed to the eastern portion of the kingdom dominated by Canterbury.[76] As the documents show, the monks had to struggle even to protect the endowments they already claimed, let alone attract new donations. In the law book and cartulary, however, they were able to show the authority of their claims and to bestow upon themselves a certain status through the accumulated evidence of an Anglo-Saxon heritage.

Perhaps it will not be analyzing too far the motives for a set of volumes like the *Textus Roffensis* to say that these books gave a certain weight and importance to a see that in fact was neither powerful nor independent. Being neither, it was concerned to guard those possessions and such other evidence of influence as it could lay claim to. For obvious reasons the lawbook and cartulary are characteristically Anglo-Norman products. But they also have a consciousness of Anglo-Saxon history and tradition that distinguishes them from contemporary collections of laws and charters. Because of its relative insignificance, Rochester, it seems, felt called upon to defend its existence through extensive documentation. Whoever first called these volumes *textus* understood how crucial they were to the priory's sense of identity.

---

[76] Waller, 21.

III. THE MEDIEVAL VULGATE TRADITION AT ROCHESTER

The picture of Rochester Cathedral Priory and its library now emerging is distorted to a degree, owing to the subjective nature of the materials we have examined thus far. In the booklists, related donation lists, and the *Textus Roffensis* we have traced a sense of defensiveness on the part of the monks towards encroachments by the bishops of Rochester, and of the need to establish an identity for Rochester separate from its relationship to Christ Church, Canterbury. These were parallel concerns in a sense, because the priory was at once indebted to Canterbury for extensive help with its collection of books and, indeed, for the very structure of its being, yet at the same time it was a competitor for donations and disputed properties, particularly in Kent. The texts which display these concerns obviously are those which record the ongoing life and the Anglo-Saxon heritage of St. Andrew's.

Aside from the more practical interests of the priory, however, lay its reason for being: a spiritual community united in the *opus dei*. Hence most of the books produced and acquired by Rochester in the post-Conquest era reflect the need to educate the monks and provide pious texts for reading and study. In Chapter I our survey of the booklists demonstrated that Rochester acquired the basic texts needed for a Benedictine foundation by the early twelfth century. Chapter II provided further evidence that the monks owned at least a few precious books, including Gospels, the *Textus Roffensis*, and a *vita* of St. Andrew. But what has not yet emerged is the fact that certain texts vital to the spiritual life of the priory, namely, its Gospel and Vulgate books and its homiliaries, have a history equally as telling as those works related directly to St. Andrew's and its possessions.

By a quirk of fate, key texts copied from Christ Church, Canterbury, or obtained through copying from other foundations in southeastern England, have survived at Rochester when their exemplars have often disappeared. Apparently Rochester was one of the first libraries encountered by Henry VIII's emissary as he began to gather books for what is now the Royal and King's Collection in the British Library, and possibly for that reason, a great proportion of rather ordinary—by Henry's standards—items was preserved. In practical terms this state of affairs provides an unusual opportunity to analyze groups of important texts that balance, by virtue of their place in the canon, the types of collections examined in Chapters I and II. The present texts relate to the spiritual, as opposed to the material, life of the foundation.

Our subject now is the Vulgate texts surviving from Rochester, their links to each other and to surviving books from pre-Conquest Canterbury and from Dover Priory, a dependency of Christ Church. The close relationships among these Vulgates are remarkable, and they raise several important questions: do the books possibly represent a distinctive textual tradition, perhaps a "use," and, if so, what are its genesis and distinguishing features? Why would the monks of Rochester trouble to adopt and maintain a Vulgate text from Canterbury? These questions are worth raising because similar trends have been documented in Vulgates associated with Winchester Cathedral Priory in the twelfth century, but the extent to which other English monastic chapters developed their own Vulgate text, or shared textual traditions with related foundations, has not been explored fully.[1] The case of the Rochester Vulgates is particularly interesting because, as we will see, the text found there has pre-Conquest origins, and seems to have been imported by Christ Church, Canterbury, during the Benedictine Revival of the tenth century. Although the Anglo-Saxon foundation at Rochester probably did not benefit directly from renewed emphasis on Latin learning, the new Benedictine monastery did receive certain continental texts and textual traditions imported during that period through copies made a century and a half later.

Given the close ties among Benedictine foundations in Kent, it must have been convenient for Canterbury to share basic ecclesiastical texts. Whether deliberate or not, however, this process resulted in common textual traditions, possibly amounting to a "use" in certain instances. To answer the questions raised earlier about a distinctive Vulgate text found at Rochester, its origin and defining characteristics, we must begin with a review of certain related Gospel and Vulgate manuscripts from the late Anglo-Saxon period associated with Christ Church, Canterbury. These books provide the essential context for interpreting the Rochester Vulgates and appreciating the enterprise of those who acquired texts for the cathedral priory of St. Andrew.

As will be demonstrated in the course of this chapter, the Rochester Vulgates, namely, the two-volume great Bible known as the Gundulf Bible (San Marino, CA, Huntington Library MS. HM 62) and two portions of a multi-volume Vulgate set (Baltimore, Walters Art Gallery MS. W. 18 and BL MS. Royal 1 C. VII), share a common textual type.[2] This text is Franco-Saxon in origin, containing variations transmitted in manuscripts from Northern France emended at St.-Germain-des-Prés. Copies of this type of text must have made their way to Kent as early as the tenth-century reforms of SS. Dunstan, Æthelwold, and Oswald, who imported books from France and Flanders to give renewed impetus to learning and scribal activity in En-

---

[1] Evidence defining and supporting a "use" at Winchester in the twelfth century is cited by Sandy Heslop in "Books for Use and Beauty," *Art History*, 5 (1982): 124-25. The term "use" refers here to the practice of conforming to an established Vulgate text.

[2] For descriptions of the MSS. respectively, see Seymour De Ricci, *Census of Medieval and Renaissance Manuscripts in the United States and Canada* (New York, 1937), 1:48; *Catalogue of Western Manuscripts in the Old Royal and King's Collections*, 1:16; De Ricci, 1:766; and *Catalogue of Western Manuscripts in the Old Royal and King's Collections*, 1:14-15. Further descriptive materials will be cited in the course of this chapter.

gland.³ Apparently from the late tenth century on, the Northern French textual tradition was established in Gospel books and great Bibles at Christ Church, Canterbury, from which it was transmitted to Rochester.

The term Franco-Saxon applies both to a particular style of illumination and to a distinctive type of Gospel and Vulgate text, and refers to the region of Flanders and lower Saxony where characteristic materials were produced beginning in the reign of Charles the Bald (second half of the ninth century).⁴ The most telling witness to this Vulgate tradition in England is a late tenth-century Bible, ascribed tentatively to Christ Church, Canterbury, by Ker, but attributed definitely to that library by Brooks. This manuscript, BL MSS. Royal 1 E. VII-VIII, is in two large volumes written in double columns with reduced script for the prefatory materials.⁵ It is the earliest example of the Northern French Vulgate in England and, at the same time, it is more closely akin to the Rochester Bibles than any other text known. Physically, the format and extensive corrections convey an overall impression very much like that of the Gundulf Bible, copied almost a century later for Rochester. The Canterbury Bible is considerably larger, however, and preserves evidence of its earlier date. The leaves now measure 562 x 335 mm., written space 453 x 241 mm. The MS. is ruled by stylus and gathered in quires of eight leaves numbered on the first recto. Rubrics and large initials are now a purplish color. It has only a single illumination, a colored drawing of the Creation on fol. 1v.

The similarity between the Canterbury and Rochester Bibles extends to a wide variety of textual matters, including: the same type of text, characteristic of Northern French Bibles influenced by St.-Germain-des-Prés;⁶ an

---

³ Knowles, *The Monastic Order in England*, 2nd ed. (Cambridge, 1963), 36-42. Gibson, 178-81, points out that this practice was continued by Archbishop Lanfranc a century later. A good overview is provided by Philip Grierson in "The Relations between England and Flanders before the Norman Conquest," *Transactions of the Royal Historical Society*, 4th ser. (1941), 23: 71-112.

⁴ See Rosamond McKitterick, *The Frankish Kingdoms under the Carolingians, 751-987* (London, 1983), 223.

⁵ *Catalogue of Western Manuscripts in the Old Royal and King's Collections*, 1: 20-21. Possibly item 321 in Eastry's catalogue, as printed by James in *Ancient Libraries of Canterbury and Dover*, 51. James, lxiv, excludes the possibility that MSS. Royal 1 E. VII-VIII are the so-called Bible of St. Gregory from St. Augustine's. Ker assigns the Bible to Christ Church, Canterbury, with a question mark indicating uncertainty, in *MLGB*, 36. See Brooks, *The Early History of the Church at Canterbury*, 268, and Terence A. M. Bishop, "Notes on Cambridge Manuscripts Part V: MSS connected with St. Augustine's Canterbury, Continued," *Transactions of the Cambridge Bibliographical Society*, 3 (1959-63): 94.

⁶ Northern French readings from BL MSS. Royal 1 E. VII-VIII:
Genesis 30:32 *rufum*
Exodus 2:25 *respexit filios israhel dominus et liberavit eos*
Deuteronomy 2:19 *in vicinia*
I Kings 21:7 *Hic pascebat mulas Saul*
    25:44 *alio viro*
II Kings 12:7 *qui fecisti hanc rem*
    15:34 *patere me vivere*
III Kings 1:8 *semei et cerethi*
Matthew 10:14 *de civitate*
    18:19 *quaecumque*
    21:31 *in regno*
    23:25 *pleni sunt*

extremely rare incipit to the chapters of Numbers (*Numerantur ex praecepto*);[7] the omission of canon tables; the peculiar order of prefaces to the Gospels, with identical chapters; a unique series of prefatory materials to Romans: argument, *Epistolae Pauli ad Romanos causa haec est*; list of fourteen Epistles (with Laodiceans as the fifteenth); *Omnis textus vel numerus*; preface by Rabanus Maurus, *Primum queriter* [sic]; preface to Romans, *Romani qui ex iudeis*; argument, *Romani sunt in partibus Italiae*; "Versus Damasi episcopi urbis Romae," *Iamdudum Saulus procerum precepta secutus*; capitula, *De nativitate Christi secundum carnum*; list of Pauline epistles omitting Laodiceans;[8] a long prologue to I Corinthians (*Corinthus metropolis civitas Achaiae*);[9] Laodiceans following Hebrews. More detailed analysis of these elements will follow in our consideration of the Gundulf Bible.

Although the affinity of the Canterbury and Rochester Vulgate texts is clear, the Gundulf Bible seems not to have been copied directly from MSS. Royal 1 E. VII-VIII. The order of the books differs considerably as do the chapters to Joshua-Judges and I-II Kings, and readings of particular verses.[10] Equally significant, however, is the evidence that the two were corrected to agree with a common tradition, at times by similar hands. A selection of readings that characterize the Northern French Vulgate text as corrected at St.-Germain-des-Prés illustrates the relationship between the two Bibles. In Acts, both of our Vulgates have the reading *Paulus vocans rogavit me* at 23:16.[11] At 18:10, both have the St.-Germain reading, but in slightly different

        26:47 *adhuc illo loquente*
        27:32 *venientum obviam sibi*
Luke 6:7 *unde accusarent illum*
    7:39 *mulier esset*
    11:3 *cotidie*
John 13:10 *nisi ut lavet pedes*
Acts 5:36 *Theodas dicens esse se aliquem magnum*
    18:2 *et salutavit eos*
II Peter 2:7 *iniuria inpudica*
    3:10 *terra autem et quae in ipsa sunt opera exurentur.*

[7] Berger, 344.
[8] Chapters in Wordsworth and White, *Novum Testamentum Latine*, pt. 2, Epistles, 44-60. The prefatory pieces are numbered by Friedrich Stegmüller as follows, in order of their occurrence here: 651, 670, 674, 677, 654; *Repertorium Biblicum Medii Aevi*, 1 (Madrid, 1940).
[9] Stegmüller, 684, 689.
[10] Gundulf Bible: Stegmüller 311, 307, 323, Chaps. I-II Kings: *Ubi orat Anna corde* (PL 28:603-8), Chaps. III Kings: *Senectus David et Adonia filius* (PL 28:721-24); MS. Royal 1 E. VII: 311; Berger, 346, Josue et Juges 1. Readings found only in MS. Royal 1 E. VII-VIII include:
II Kings 17:14 *et ut videretur esse consilium chusai bonum coram absolon*
Matthew 16:10 *et quattuor milia*
    24:26 *penetrabilibus*
    27:46 *lemasabathani*
Luke 6:26 *vae cum bene vobis dixerint*
    10:30 *suspiciens*
    19:37 *descendentium*
I Peter 2:21 *pro nobis relinquens vobis*
Apocalypse 1:3 *audiunt . . . servant*
    1:13 *zona auream*
    1:15 *oricalco*
[11] For this and the following readings from Bibles at St.-Germain-des-Prés, see Berger, 65-72.

forms; the Royal MS. reading is identical to the one found in Paris MS. B.N. Lat. 93, part of a Northern French Bible emended at St.-Germain-des-Prés:

Royal I. E. VIII: *et nullus nocere te poterit et nemo apponetur tibi ut noceat te*
Gundulf Bible: *et nullus tibi nocere poterit et nemo apponetur tibi ut noceat te.*

At Acts 2:7, however, the St.-Germain reading *ad invicem dicentes*, found in the Gundulf Bible, has been added to the Royal text. Other types of readings reveal a similar pattern. At Genesis 31:8, the reading in the Royal text, *pro mercede*, has been added by a corrector's hand to the Gundulf Bible. Elsewhere, differences in wording are not corrected:

Royal 1 E. VIII	Gundulf Bible
Mark 11:32 *timebant*	*timemus*
Acts 13:2 *segregate*	*separate*
James 5:12 *iuramentum*	*iuramentum vestrum*
I Peter 3:18 *mortificatus . . . vivificatus*	*mortificatos . . . vivificatos.*

Thus, much as it would be convenient to identify the Royal text as the exemplar of the Gundulf Bible, it cannot be done. What can be said, however, is that the two Bibles are representatives of a larger tradition shared by Canterbury and Rochester.

Such a tradition, however, remains to be established more fully. The Canterbury Gospel and Vulgate manuscripts have previously been studied individually, but the Rochester materials have received little attention and neither group has been considered as a whole. For example, Berger's *Histoire de la Vulgate* includes only Goda's Gospels, donated in the early twelfth century, which is the single Gospel book remaining from Rochester Priory.[12] The text is classified Anglo-Irish by Berger, and bears no relationship to the Franco-Saxon Gospel manuscripts linked to Canterbury.[13] Although the

---

[12] 386 and *passim*.
[13] Readings from BL MS. Royal 1 D. III (Goda's Gospels) are as follows:
Matthew 15:7 *esaias*
        16:18 *imferni*
        16:27 *opus*
        17:3 *apparvit*
        24:3 *discipuli secreto*
Mark 16:14 *crediderant*
      16:15 *illis*
      16:18 *eos nocebit*
Luke 6:26 *prophetis*
     6:38 omits *eadem vero mensura*
     6:42 *et quomo potest*
     7:39 *no esset*
     11:3 *hodie*
     19:37 *descentium*
John 5:4 *teneretur infirmitate*
Samuel Berger classes MS. Royal 1 D. III (*Catalogue of Western Manuscripts in the Old Royal and King's Collections*, 1:16) as an Irish text, 45. It may be, but the fourth preface, *Sciendam etiam*, was not a part of the Irish tradition in England; see, for example, the description of MS. Royal 1 B. VII in the *Catalogue of Western Manuscripts in the Old Royal and King's Collections*, 1:10-11. On the features of Irish MSS. see A. Cordoliani, "Le Texte de la Bible en Irlande du Ve au IXe siècle," *Revue Biblique*, 57 (1950): 5-39.

Canterbury Gospel books merit a separate, thorough study, they can be considered briefly here for their role in helping to define the tradition that ultimately reached Rochester. In the second quarter of the tenth century, King Æthelstan donated an important Gospel book to Christ Church, Canterbury.[14] This book, now BL MS. Cotton Tiberius A. II (ninth century, possibly from Lobbes in Flanders) has prologues, chapters and many readings of the Franco-Saxon type. Possibly influenced by this gift or other imported texts are two early eleventh-century decorated English Gospel books of the Franco-Saxon type associated with Canterbury: New York, Pierpont Morgan Library MS. 709 (second quarter of the eleventh century) and BL MS. Royal 1 D. IX (c. 1020).[15] These two MSS., from among at least a dozen surviving pre-Conquest Gospel books associated with Canterbury, are cited here because they are consistently termed Franco-Saxon by Vulgate scholars, and hence they have the greatest potential for establishing Canterbury's interest in that particular tradition.

MS. Morgan 709 was part of Judith of Flanders' legacy to Weingarten Abbey and formerly was attributed to New Minster, Winchester, on the basis of decorative style.[16] It is one of a group of four Gospel books produced, Bishop theorizes, by scribes and artists under lay patronage, perhaps in Judith's employ.[17] (This could explain why the textual type of Morgan 709 appears to be unrelated to that in Morgan 708, the Gospel book most closely linked to it on the basis of decorative style. The scribes may have found exemplars in several locations since they were not working within the limitations of a monastic context.) Morgan 709 appears to have lost seven leaves of the first quire, which would have contained, presumably, the prologues to the Gospels and the preface to Matthew. The prefaces to Mark, Luke, and John, however, are Franco-Saxon. No chapters to the Gospels appear.

By comparison, MS. Royal 1 D. IX, now incomplete after John 21:18 (*cum esses iunior . . .*), has the full set of Franco-Saxon prologues and prefaces to individual books that continue to appear in later Vulgate texts from Canterbury and Rochester. The two Gospel books share a number of characteristic Northern French readings found in these later manuscripts.[18] In fact, they

---

[14] Brooks, *The Early History of the Church of Canterbury,* 219-20; Watson, #548, 1:105; Temple, #12, 41. For the inscription and its context, see Simon Keynes, "King Athelstan's books," in *Learning and Literature in Anglo-Saxon England,* ed. Michael Lapidge and Helmut Gneuss (Cambridge, 1985), 147-53.

[15] For Morgan MS. 709, see De Ricci, 2:1485-86. The Canterbury attribution is made in The Pierpont Morgan Library, *Medieval and Renaissance Manuscripts: major acquisitions of the Pierpont Morgan Library, 1924-74* (New York, 1974), description facing pl. 8. For a summary of opinion, see Elzbieta Temple, *Anglo-Saxon Manuscripts, 900-1066, A Survey of Manuscripts Illuminated in the British Isles* V.2 (London, 1976), #93, 108-111. For BL MS. Royal 1 D. IX, see *Catalogue of Western Manuscripts in the Old Royal and King's Collections,* 1:17-18; Ker, *MLGB,* 36; and Temple, #70, 88-90.

[16] See Grierson, 111, and Meta Harrsen, "The Countess Judith of Flanders and the Library of Weingarten Abbey," *Proceedings of the Bibliographic Society of America,* 24 (1930): 1-13.

[17] Terence A. M. Bishop, *English Caroline Minuscule* (Oxford, 1971), xvi-ii.

[18] These include, for example, all of the Gospel readings shared by Paris, MS. B.N. Lat. 261 and the Gundulf Bible cited below in n. 47.

could have been copied from the same exemplar. The few differences in readings suggest that MS. Royal 1 D. IX was written by a less careful scribe.[19] This textual relationship helps to associate the two manuscripts more firmly with Canterbury and with each other.

These Gospel books contain a core of readings in common with the Vulgates produced at Canterbury and Rochester, but they also share a number of readings against the Vulgates, which suggests that the Gospel text was related to, but independent of that found in the great Bibles.[20] Unfortunately, there is no manuscript evidence to show whether this separate Gospel tradition was transmitted to Rochester. The Canterbury Gospel books thus provide important early evidence of the presence of a Northern French text in Kent, but they are of limited help in tracing the transmission of a Vulgate text to Rochester.

The surviving Vulgates from Rochester, however, show definite links to the Canterbury tradition. Glunz mentions the Gundulf Bible in his *History of the Vulgate in England*, but states incorrectly that it embodies a biblical revision made by Lanfranc.[21] There is no evidence for the attribution, as Gibson's recent study of Lanfranc has shown.[22] But as we will see, the Gundulf Bible does provide yet another example of a highly individual book created by Rochester from materials largely available at Christ Church, Canterbury. Further, the early twelfth-century Vulgates produced for Rochester and Dover Priory seem to demonstrate a continuing effort to maintain a common Vulgate text among the Benedictine foundations in Kent associated with Christ Church. For these reasons, and the fact that all three Vulgate books seem to descend from a pre-Conquest text, the tradition

---

[19] Of 111 readings checked, 23 differed: three involved a spelling variation (*e* for *ae*), two a disagreement in word order, and the others resulted from careless copying, as illustrated by the following:

Morgan 709	Royal 1 D. IX
Matthew 5:15 *ponunt eam*	*onunt ea*
5:18 *iota*	*lota*
Mark 2:16 *cum publicanis*	*cum plicanis*
Luke 1:26 *gabrihel*	*grabrihel*
11:28 *quin immo*	*quimimmo*

Linda L. Brownrigg, in "Manuscripts containing English decoration 871-1066, catalogued and illustrated: a review," *Anglo-Saxon England*, 7 (1978), discusses the ambiguous paleographical evidence for the origin of MS. Royal I D. IX on 264-66.

[20] The following is a sample of the distinctive readings found in the Gospel books compared with the Vulgate text as transmitted to Rochester:

Royal 1 D. IX and Morgan 709	Gundulf Bible
Matthew 10:14 *vel civitate*	*de civitate*
Mark 1:24 *qui sis*	*quis sis*
9:2 *fullo*	*solos*
Luke 6:38 *eadem quippe mensura*	*eadem vero mensura*
11:3 *hodie*	*cotidie*
John 5:4 *tenebatur infirmitate*	*detinebatur infirmitate*

[21] Hans Glunz, *History of the Vulgate in England from Alcuin to Roger Bacon* (Cambridge, 1933), 182.

[22] Gibson, *Lanfranc of Bec*, 241, rejects Lanfranc's connection to any textual revision of the Vulgate.

they embody is worth developing in detail. It reveals still more about the curious relationship between Canterbury and Rochester in the post-Conquest era.

As mentioned earlier, the Gundulf Bible dates from about 1075, contemporary with the refoundation of Rochester as a Benedictine cathedral priory. The question of its origin, however, is difficult to resolve. Paleographic data are inconclusive, so much so that a recent study has suggested that the Bible was copied in Normandy in an unidentified scriptorium.[23] The likelihood of a Norman scribe is very great considering the date of production and the state of the Rochester foundation in the years immediately following the Conquest. Analysis of the text narrows the possible geographic origin considerably. Given its close relationship to BL MSS. Royal I E. VII-VIII, the two-volume Vulgate ascribed tentatively to Christ Church, Canterbury, the Gundulf Bible probably originated in Kent.

Although long assumed to have been the gift of Gundulf, the second Norman bishop of Rochester (1077-1108), the Bible is linked to him only by a thirteenth-century entry on the flyleaf of each volume. A long description without reference to Gundulf appears in the first catalogue of the Rochester library (Table 1, #26). The Bible is recorded, again without attribution, in the second Rochester catalogue of 1202, and probably remained in the cathedral library until the Dissolution, though this cannot be proven definitely.[24] Around 1611 it was listed in the catalogue of Lord Lumley's collection as

Biblia vetusta quondam Gundolphi episcopi Roffensis.[25]

One searches in vain for other evidence of Gundulf's donorship. The early thirteenth-century list of donations to Rochester in BL MS. Cotton Vespasian A. XXII, for instance, omits the Bible while attributing other volumes to Gundulf.[26] The *Vita Gundulfi*, by a contemporary monk at Rochester, again does not mention the gift of a Bible.[27] By contrast, the gift of the Carilef Bible to the library at Durham by Gundulf's contemporary, Bishop William of St. Carilef (1081-1096), is recorded twice: first, in a late eleventh-century list of some fifty volumes bequeathed by him to the Durham library, which occurs on the flyleaf of the second volume of his Bible; second, in an account of his benefactions to the cathedral which includes the earlier list of books.[28]

---

[23] Waller, 80-83.

[24] See Rye's appendix, "Gundulph's Latin Bible," 61.

[25] Printed in the Concordance with Lord Lumley's Catalogue, *Catalogue of Western Manuscripts in the Old Royal and King's Collections*, 1:xl. See also item 111, p. 48, in Sears Jayne and Francis R. Johnson, eds., *The Lumley Library, The Catalogue of 1609* (London, 1956). In succeeding centuries the Gundulf Bible was in private hands, first in the Netherlands and later in England. In 1827 it was sold to Thomas Phillipps in London, in whose collection it remained until his death. Since 1924 it has been owned by the Huntington Library, San Marino, California.

[26] Fol. 88r, excerpts printed by Rye in *Archaeologia Cantiana*, 3 (1861): 62-63.

[27] *PL*, 159:812-35, and Thomson, ed., *The Life of Gundulf, Bishop of Rochester*. S. Harrison Thompson uses the evidence of the *Vita* to show that Gundulf made no revision of the Bible in "Bishop Gundulf of Rochester and the Vulgate," *Speculum*, 6 (1931): 468-70.

[28] R. A. B. Mynors, *Durham Cathedral Manuscripts to the End of the Twelfth Century* (Oxford, 1939), 32.

Nevertheless, the inscriptions on the flyleaves of the Gundulf Bible are of interest:

I. Prima pars biblie; per bone memorie Gundulfum Roffensum Episcopum. Liber de claustro Roffensis. quem qui inde alienaverit alienatum celaverit vel hunc titulum in fraudem deleverit excomunicatus est. ferentibus sentenciam sancto Episcopo. Priore et singulis presbiteris capituli Roffensis.

II. Secunda pars biblie. Per felicis recordacionis Gudulfum Roffensum episcopum. Liber de claustro Roffensis. quem qui inde alienaverit. alienatum celaverit. vel hunc titulum in fraudem deleverit. excomunicatus est. ferentibus sentenciam dicto sancto episcopo. Priore et singulis presbiteris capituli Roffensis.

These entries are significant for their thirteenth-century date and their placement at the head of each flyleaf. The usual Rochester *ex libris* and *ex dono* are from the fourteenth century and occur in that order at the foot of the flyleaf.[29] Thus, whatever the motive, the connection with Gundulf was recorded quite apart from the more general effort of the fourteenth century that has helped to identify former Rochester books. This could indicate that oral tradition lay behind the entry, to be written down at least a century after the donor's death. The anathemas on thieves are characteristic of Rochester inscriptions.[30]

Fresh analysis of the paleographic features of the Bible is crucial to the question of origin. First, the size and layout of the Gundulf Bible are typical of great Bibles from Norman England.[31] Though the margins have been trimmed, the pages still measure 400 x 265 mm. with a written space of approximately 340 x 200 mm. ruled in double columns. Possibly in keeping with Gundulf's background as a monk from Bec, where plain texts were the rule, the Bible has neither illuminations nor decorated initials, nor has space been left for them.[32] The volumes are nearly equal in length.[33] There are no scribal quire-signatures visible in volume I. Beginning with the eighth quire in volume II, there are signatures in Roman numerals remaining at the center of the foot of the first recto of nine quires.[34] According to Ker, the placement of these signatures in an Insular manuscript would indicate a date of copying before, or just after, the Conquest.[35]

---

[29] Ker, *MLGB*, xvii and 160.

[30] For instance, BL MS. Cotton Vespasian A. XXII, early thirteenth century, has a brief threat following the fourteenth century *ex libris* and *ex dono*:
Liber de consuetudine ecclesie Roffense. per benedictum monachum quem qui alienaverit anathema sit. amen.

[31] The great Bibles are contrasted to earlier English manuscripts, as described by Bishop, *English Caroline Minuscule*, xii.

[32] The plainness could mean that the Bible was intended for individual study rather than ceremonial use; see Walter F. Oakeshott, *The Artists of the Winchester Bible* (London, 1945), 1.

[33] Vol. 1: 240 leaves, 1-8^8, 9^9, 10-14^8, 15^{10}, 16-29^8, 30^5; Vol. 2: 262 leaves, 1-6^8, 7^9, 8-31^8, 32^9, 33^4. The foliation in Vol. 1 is incorrect after f. 170; 171 has been skipped. Mme. Jeanine Fohlen of the Institut de Recherche et d'Histoire des Textes in Paris assisted with the collation of the Bible.

[34] Quires 8, fol. 58r (I, partially visible); 9, fol. 66r (II, partially visible); 10, fol. 74r (III); 12, fol. 90r (V, partially visible); 14, fol. 106r (VII); 17, fol. 30r (X, partially visible); 20, fol. 154r (XIII); 24, fol. 186r (XVII); 31, fol. 242r (XXIV, partially visible).

[35] Ker, *English Manuscripts in the Century after the Norman Conquest*, 49-50. Waller, however, finds that this feature is uncharacteristic of manuscripts produced at Rochester before c. 1108, p. 84.

The main text of the Gundulf Bible has been written throughout by a Norman scribe, probably during the late eleventh century. The Norman characteristics are pronounced: sharply angled finishing strokes, short split ascenders, minuscule *g* with an elongated tail.[36] In addition, the scribe uses a horned *e*, often thought to be an early English feature (cf. Oxford MS. Bodley Auct. D. Inf. 2.9, part i from St. Augustine's, Canterbury, second half of the tenth century),[37] but persisting beyond the Conquest into the late eleventh century (cf. Cambridge MS. Corpus Christi College 191 from Exeter, third quarter of the eleventh century).[38] The latter date is confirmed by Oxford MS. Bodley 535 from Winchester, end of the eleventh century, where a Norman scribe has used a similar horned *e*;[39] this hand shares a number of features with that of the main scribe of the Gundulf Bible. In the latter, ascenders and descenders are double the height of the minims, but the letters do not fill the space between lines. The *ct* ligature and suprascript abbreviations are common, and a distinctive ligature for the genitive plural *-orum, -arum* occurs:p. A hooked sign is used for *-bus*. The hand of the principal emender is some forty years later, in the Rochester variant of the Christ Church, Canterbury, "prickly" style.

The vellum has been ruled in dry point on the hair side, usually 46 lines to a page spaced about 7.4 mm. apart.[40] Punctuation is mainly by mid and low point, with less frequent use of punctus elevatus, punctus versus, and punctus circumflexus. The ink shades from almost-black to light brown. The space between lines is sufficient to accommodate omissions in many cases, but, in others, a *signe-de-renvoi*, often .·., is used for entries in the margins. Occasionally, as on f. 89v, v. 1, a box is drawn around an "Al" reading placed in the margin in a later hand. As mentioned earlier, certain of these readings indicate that the Rochester and Canterbury Bibles may have been corrected to agree with one another. Trimming, however, has damaged many marginal notations. There are a few modestly decorated and colored initials, in red, purple, yellow, and blue. The Book of Baruch, added later, has fancier capitals in red, green, and white. Red display script is used in the Psalter, whereas elsewhere in the text red alternates with lines of square and rustic capitals in brown ink on a plain background.[41]

The weight of paleographic evidence suggests a Norman scribe working at Canterbury or Rochester, more probably Canterbury. The only features

---

[36] Ker, *English Manuscripts in the Century after the Norman Conquest*, 22-23.

[37] On this feature, see Ker, *Catalogue of Manuscripts Containing Anglo-Saxon*, xxix. A plate of fol. 67r is in Bishop, *English Caroline Minuscule*, pl. V.

[38] P. 100 is reproduced in Bishop, *English Caroline Minuscule*, pl. XXIV.

[39] Ker, *English Manuscripts in the Century after the Norman Conquest*, pl. 1b.

[40] The two top and bottom lines are extended to the edges of the page; less frequently the three top and bottom lines, or the first and third, are so extended. Two vertical bounding lines separate the written space from the margins. The vertical ruling between columns varies, with three or four lines dividing a space about 14 cm. in width. Information provided by C. W. Dutschke, Assistant Curator of Medieval Manuscripts, the Huntington Library.

[41] Waller, 82, mistakenly claims that the display script and initials are written on a yellow ground.

described above that may be uncharacteristic of Canterbury manuscripts from the decades immediately following the Conquest are the *ct* ligature and the frequency of suprascript abbreviations, whereas the variation in ink color, the punctuation, the *-bus* sign, and the quire signatures all differ from the early Rochester practices documented by Waller.[42] Our scribe is not, however, writing in the distinctive Christ Church, Canterbury, style of the late eleventh century. Rather, his work precedes that development as confirmed by the date of the quire signatures and ruling in dry point, the latter practice having given way to plummet by the late eleventh century. In summary, the Gundulf Bible presents relatively sophisticated script, punctuation, and abbreviation styles in a physical setting reflecting earlier English practices. Since Canterbury had one of the very few active scriptoria in England at the time of the Conquest, it was certainly a possible setting for a production like the Gundulf Bible. Textual, rather than paleographic, data, however, are the most telling in the case for Canterbury.

Two Carolingian traditions are apparent in the Gundulf Bible. The format and text are basically those of the revision attributed to Alcuin, first produced at Tours early in the ninth century.[43] The large size and Gallican Psalter are two obvious Alcuinian features. The use of a reduced script for prefatory pieces, chapters, and the Psalter, and the inclusion of Psalm 151 (*Pusillus eram*), however, are characteristic of the Theodulf Bible, revised by the Spanish prelate and contemporary of Alcuin who worked at Orléans.[44] Vulgates produced in England during the late tenth, eleventh, and twelfth centuries share many of these Carolingian features, but not the particular textual tradition reflected in the Gundulf Bible. Its text is of the so-called later form of the Alcuin Bible, identified by Rand, Köhler, and others, meaning that it has undergone two sets of revisions in its history.[45] The first set represents the incorporation of Theodulf's corrections; the second shows a Franco-Saxon influence. In a list of sixteen variant readings from the Gos-

---

[42] Waller, 149-54.

[43] "On Alcuin's revision of the Bible, see Berger, 185-242; Edward K. Rand, "A Preliminary Study of Alcuin's Bible," *Harvard Theological Review*, 24 (1931): 323-96; Donatien De Bruyne, "Notes sur la Bible de Tours au IXe siècle," *Göttingische gelehrte Anzeigen*, 193 (1931): 352-59; Bonifatius Fischer, *Die Alkuin-Bibel* (Freiburg im Breisgau, 1957); Bonifatius Fischer, "Bibelausgaben des Frühen Mittelalters," *Settimane di Studio del centro Italiano Sull'Alto Medioevo*, 10 (Spoleto, 1963): 586-93; Bonifatius Fischer, "Bibeltext und Bibelreform unter Karl dem Grossen," in *Karl der Grosse*, v. II, *Das Geistige Leben*, ed. Bernhard Bischoff and Wolfgang Braunfels (Düsseldorf, 1965), 169-77.

[44] For a description of the Theodulf Bible, see Rand's article above; M. Léopold Delisle, "Les Bibles de Théodulfe," *Annales de la Société d'Agriculture du Puy*, 33 (1876-77): 73-137; Berger, 145-64; Fischer, *Die Alkuin-Bibel*, 8-9; Fischer, "Bibelausgaben," 593-97; Fischer, "Bibeltext und Bibelreform," 177-83; Elisabeth Dahlhaus-Berg, *Nova Antiquitas et Antiqua Novitas* (Köln, 1975), 39-61.

[45] Rand, 383, following Wilhelm Köhler, *Die Karolingischen Miniaturen*, v. I, *Die Schule von Tours*, pt. 1 *Die Ornamentik* (Berlin, 1930; rpt. 1963), 340ff.

pels cited by Rand to distinguish among these three versions, five of each type occur in the Gundulf Bible, along with one Northumbrian reading.[46] This proportion obtains as well in the much longer list of Köhler, where the Bible shares at least seventeen unusual readings from the Gospels with Paris MS. Bibliothèque Nationale Lat. 261, one of the major texts in the Franco-Saxon group.[47]

The suggestion of a Franco-Saxon heritage is reinforced by other evidence. The Gundulf Bible reveals a heavy Spanish textual influence quite apart from readings adopted from Theodulf, but characteristic of Bibles from Northern France.[48] This influence is evident in a number of exclusively Spanish readings in both the Old and New Testaments, as well as the chapters to Matthew and Luke, indebted ultimately to those in the Codex

---

[46] Rand, 384. The readings from the Gundulf Bible, and their sources, are as follows:
Matthew 15:2 *traditionem* (Theodulf)
       15:7 *isaias* (Alcuin)
       15:38 *hominum* (Theodulf)
       16:18 *inferi* (Northumbrian)
       16:27 *opera* (Theodulf)
       17:3 *apparverunt* (Alcuin)
       21:31 *in regno* (Theodulf)
       23:15 *circuitis* (Alcuin)
       23:21 *quicumque* (2nd revision)
       23:23 *vae autem* (2nd revision)
       24:44 *quia qua nescitis hora* (Theodulf)
Mark 16:18 *eis nocebit* (Alcuin)
Luke 6:8 *in medium* (Alcuin)
       6:26 *pseudoprophetis* (2nd revision)
       6:38 *eadem vero* (2nd revision)
       6:42 *autem quomodo* (2nd revision)
Note that few manuscripts are of the later type having the second set of revisions. For example, BL MS. Royal 1 B. XI, twelfth-century Gospels from St. Augustine's, Canterbury, has most of the first set of revisions, but none of the second set.

[47] The following is a list of unusual readings from Paris B.N. Lat. 261 occurring in the Gundulf Bible; see Köhler, 348-61:
Matthew 16:9 *quinque panum et quinque milia*
       16:26 *mundum universum*
       17:7 *surgite et nolite*
       21:27 *dico vobis*
       23:13 *sinitis intrare*
       24:2 *dixit illis*
       24:3 *discipuli eius*
       24:13 *perseveraverit*
Mark 16:14 *crediderunt*
       16:15 *eis*
Luke 6:4 *cum ipso*
       6:4 *licet*
       6:37 *dimittemini*
       6:46 *autem*
       6:49 *cecidit*

[48] Berger, 93-100; Fischer, *Bibeltext und Bibelreform*, 184. Also useful on this point is J. M. Harden, ed., *Psalterium Iuxta Hebraeos Hieronymi* (London, 1922), xiv. The Spanish element may be due ultimately to the revision of Maurdramnus, abbot of Corbie (772-81); see Raphael Loewe, "The Medieval History of the Latin Vulgate," in *The Cambridge History of the Bible*, ed. Geoffrey W. H. Lampe (Cambridge, 1969), 134.

Cavensis from ninth-century Spain.[49] The order of prefaces to the Gospels, along with the numbering and incipits of chapters, occurring in the Gundulf Bible are found in B.N. 261, mentioned above, one of a small group of related Gospel manuscripts copied from a Franco-Saxon exemplar in the ninth century at Tours.[50] The order of the Gospel prefaces is sufficiently unusual to indicate relationship: (1) the epistle of Jerome to Damasus (*Novum opus*), GB fol. 198v; (2) the prologue of Jerome (*Plures fuisse*), GB fol. 198v; (3) the letter of Eusebius to Carpianus (*Ammonius quidem*), GB fols. 198v-99r; (4) the spurious addition to Jerome's epistle to Damasus (*Sciendam etiam*), GB fol. 199r. The same is true of the chapters, which have been drawn in an uncommon arrangement from the Alcuin, Theodulf, and Spanish Bibles.[51]

Despite its affinities with B.N. 261, the Gundulf Bible probably has not descended from a Tours manuscript. The evidence available suggests that only Franco-Saxon Gospel texts were produced at Tours, yet the Bible shows the influence throughout. In fact, the Bible shares a number of distinctive readings with two ninth-century Vulgates from Northern France, Paris MS. B.N. Lat. 11532-11533 from Corbie and B.N. Lat. 45-93 from St. Riquier.[52] The Gundulf Bible is so different from these books in other respects, however, that a Northern French origin must be ruled out as well. Not only is the selection of prologues and chapters in the Northern French Bibles quite different from the Gundulf Bible, but also the Hebrew Psalter is used

---

[49] Checked against variants listed in Henri Quentin, *Mémoire sur l'Etablissement du Texte de la Vulgate*, Ière Partie, Octateuque (Rome, 1922), 350-51, and the textual notes to *Novum Testamentum Latine*, ed. John Wordsworth and Henry White, pt. 1, *Gospels* (Oxford, 1889), hereafter referred to as *NTL*, 1. Variants of the chapters to Matthew and Luke are given in *NTL*, 1: 18-38 and 274-306.

[50] Köhler, 320-30.

[51] See Berger, 356, sec. III. 2, where Vulgate manuscripts sharing chapters with the Gundulf Bible are listed.

[52] The development of the text posited here is reflected in the chart of Vulgate history in Loewe, 104-105. The following readings reflected in the Gundulf Bible are cited in Berger. I have verified them from the Corbie and St. Riquier MSS. in question:

Leviticus 11:2 after *Israel: custodite omnia quae scripsi vobis ut sim vester dominus* (B.N. 45), p. 199. Added to B.N. 11532.
John 5:4 *detinebatur infirmitate* (B.N. 93), p. 230.
Acts 5:36 *Theodas, dicens se esse aliquem magnum* (B.N. 93), p. 161; *magnum* added to B.N. 11533.
14:2 *Dominus autem dedit cito pacem* (B.N. 93), p. 162.
18:2 *et salutavit eos* (B.N. 93), p. 96.
18:21 after *et dicens: Oportet me sollempnen diem advenientem facere ierosolymis* (B.N. 93), p. 162.
19:11 *non modicas* (B.N. 93), p. 162.
28:16 *sibimet foris extra castra* (B.N. 93), p. 162.
Genesis 16:15 omit *Agar* (B.N. 11532), p. 165. *Agar* is erased in B.N. 45.
I Chronicles 27:3 *principes cunctorum principum* (B.N. 11532), p. 230.
Acts 11:17 in margin: *ne daret illis Spiritum sanctum credentibus* (B.N. 11533), p. 161.
Galatians 3:1 *non credere veritati* (B.N. 11533), p. 159.

The examples cited here are fairly rare; they form a pattern with a host of more common readings found in the Franco-Saxon texts to indicate the heritage of the Gundulf Bible.

in B.N. 93.⁵³ Instead, the text may have reached southern England via St.-Germain-des-Prés. The Northern French manuscripts mentioned above were brought by monks to the Benedictine house of St.-Germain-des-Prés near Paris during the Viking invasions of the ninth and tenth centuries, where they were studied and reproduced.⁵⁴ This line of transmission may be evidenced in the Gundulf Bible by certain readings characteristic of texts that were emended after they came into the possession of St.-Germain-des-Prés.

Since most of the St.-Germain interpolations are Spanish, it can be difficult to know whether a particular reading came from that French textual tradition or another Spanish-influenced source. For example, three unusual readings from St.-Germain Bibles described by Berger are found in the Gundulf Bible and in B.N. 93 from St. Riquier, a Northern French text.⁵⁵ There are at least three other significant readings, however, in which the Gundulf Bible agrees with the St.-Germain text against the Northern French tradition:

Luke 7:39 after *mulier: esset*⁵⁶
Acts 2:7 *ad invicem dicentes*⁵⁷
II Peter 3:10 *terra autem et quae in ipsa sunt opera exurentur.*⁵⁸

More importantly, the Gundulf Bible incorporates the following reading from the St.-Germain tradition into Proverbs 13:13, whereas the reading has been *added* by the second corrector in Paris, B.N. Lat. 11505, a Corbie Bible taken to St.-Germain-des-Prés, where presumably the addition was made:

Proverbs 13:13 *Filio doloso nichil erit boni; servo autem sapienti prosperi erunt actus et dirigetur via eius.*⁵⁹

The greatest proportion of St.-Germain readings, however, is not found in the Gundulf Bible. Therefore, an emended Northern French text similar to that of the Corbie Bible probably was its continental ancestor. Given the date of the closely related MSS. Royal I E. VII-VIII, the Gundulf Bible probably descends from a Carolingian text imported to Canterbury during the Bene-

---

⁵³ The Hebrew Psalter also occurs in another Corbie Bible, Paris MS. B.N. 11505. B.N. 11533 lacks a Psalter.

⁵⁴ Even when a group of monks decided to return to rebuild their monastery, as did those from Croix St.-Ouen near Evreux, they had to leave behind all that they had brought with them to St.-Germain-des-Prés; see François R. Dumas, *Histoire de St.-Germain-des-Prés* (Evreux, 1958), 42-43.

⁵⁵ II Kings 22:28 *et populum pauperem* (#77 in Delisle).
Acts 18:10 *et nullus tibi nocere poterit et nemo apponetur tibi ut noceat te* (Berger, 70).
Acts 23:18 *Paulus vocans rogavit me* (Berger, 70).

⁵⁶ Paris, MS. B.N. Lat. 11553, ninth century, second half of a Bible from St.-Germain-des-Prés, *NTL*, 1. This reading is not found in B.N. 93, but it does occur in two Corbie Bibles, B.N. 11505 and B.N. 11533.

⁵⁷ Berger, 70, n. 2

⁵⁸ Paris, MS. B.N. Lat. 11553, noted in *NTL*, 1. This reading is in B.N. 93, but not B.N. 11533. It has been added to B.N. 11505, a Corbie Bible taken to St.-Germain-des-Prés.

⁵⁹ Berger, 66, n. 3. This addition occurs in neither B.N. 93 nor B.N. 11533.

dictine Revival and copied there almost a century later for the refounded cathedral priory at Rochester.

The more individual characteristics of the Gundulf Bible, namely the order of the books and the types of materials added to it, tend to support copying for use at Rochester, though this cannot be proven definitely. As observed throughout the present study, Rochester books often demonstrate remarkable freedom in the selection and arrangement of traditional materials. In this context, we note that the order of books in the Gundulf Bible seems to be unique. No similar order is recorded by Berger nor found in any descriptions of the medieval Vulgate consulted in the course of this study.[60] Volume I has the Octateuch, Psalms, books of Wisdom, I-II Chronicles, Esdras, Nehemiah, and the Gospels. Volume II opens with I-IV Kings, followed by Job, Tobias, Esther, Judith, I-II Maccabees, the Prophets, Acts, Catholic Epistles, Apocalypse, Pauline Epistles. The collation indicates that I-IV Kings (volume II, quires 1-7, fols. 1-57) was copied separately from the rest of that volume, in 7 quires of 8 leaves each; an extra leaf (fol. 57) was added to the seventh quire to complete the text, and it was bound with the remainder of volume II possibly to equalize the length of the two volumes. This arrangement, it will be recalled, had been made by the time of the earliest catalogue description of the Bible.

As a rule, however, succeeding books and their prefaces follow one upon the other and were not susceptible to rearrangement. A case in point is Apocalypse, mistakenly recorded in the first catalogue description as the last book in Volume II. Apocalypse can never have been last because the prologues to the Pauline Epistles follow its explicit on the same page (fol. 228r).[61] The order of the Epistles is that of the second revision of the Alcuin Bible with the addition of Laodiceans.[62] Berger lists thirty-two manuscripts having the Pauline Epistles follow Apocalypse; in at least three of these, the Epistles themselves follow the order of the second Alcuinian revision, but the manuscripts show no clear pattern of relationship among each other.[63] Among contemporary Vulgates produced in England, Durham Cathedral MS. A II. 4 (Durham, late eleventh century) and Cambridge MS. Trinity College 148 (Lincoln, late eleventh century), have Apocalypse preceding the Pauline Epistles, but neither of these is related in textual type to the Gundulf Bible.

The Gundulf Bible is so closely related to MSS. Royal 1 E. VII-VIII, arranged in traditional order, that its unique presentation of the books must be

---

[60] Berger, 331-42.

[61] The quire arrangement also supports the original order of Apocalypse—Pauline Epistles. Fol. 228r occurs within the 29th quire.

[62] *Vetus Latina* 24/2, *Epistulae ad Phillipenses et ad Colossenses*, ed. Hermann J. Frede (Freiburg, 1966), 302.

[63] Berger, 339. The MSS. in question are Paris B.N. Lat. 4, a Theodulf Bible from Le Puy; B.N. Lat. 11553, a mixed text from St.-Germain-des-Prés; and St. Gall 75, an Alcuin Bible, now heavily corrected, produced at Tours. Rand, 374, states that the order of the latter is idiosyncratic.

deliberate. That is, despite evidence of the Northern French textual type in southeastern England, there is no indication that a Vulgate with a similar arrangement of books existed anywhere in England or Western Europe. Moreover, the Gundulf Bible probably has not been assembled from a variety of sources, a circumstance that might have led to the unusual order of the books. The consistency of textual type, and close relationship throughout to the older MSS. Royal I E. VII-VIII, weigh against multiple sources unless these were closely related. Instead, it seems that we must look for more practical reasons behind the anomaly. The Benedictine monks may have felt an urgent need for a Gospel text suitable for the new foundation, hence the inclusion of the Gospels in volume I. Alternatively, the aim of the arrangement might have been to separate the Gospels from the Epistles for easier reference in liturgical readings during the Mass, though admittedly the volumes still would have been awkward to handle.[64] Whatever the circumstances, it is clear that the text borrowed from Canterbury did not extend to the order of books in a given version.

Twelfth-century additions to the Bible made in the distinctive Rochester hand reflect pedagogical concerns and a certain freedom from convention. Dedicatory verses by Alcuin and Theodulf are copied at the end of the first volume—a real curiosity. Normally found in ninth-century Bibles from Tours and Orléans respectively, they represent rival traditions and never occur together elsewhere.[65] They are rare in Insular Bibles; Alcuin's verses appear in one twelfth-century Irish text,[66] while Theodulf's do not occur in any other known Bible of English provenance. In the Gundulf Bible, Alcuin's poem is a reduced version of eighteen lines found also in several continental manuscripts, including Paris MSS. B.N. Lat. 11504-11505, the Corbie Bible taken to St.-Germain-des-Prés. This provides another, independent link to the Northern French tradition through St.-Germain-des-Prés. Theodulf's poem, on the other hand, has been edited uniquely here to omit the last four lines, which traditionally form a kind of envoy. Neither poet is named in the Gundulf Bible, and since the order of the books cited in the verses does not reflect the peculiar arrangement of the Bible, the poems cannot have been meant to serve as indices, their original purpose. The verses, then, probably were copied for their pedagogical usefulness; they are handy mnemonic devices for learning the books of the Bible. Theodulf's list even provides brief commentary on the books. At the end of Theodulf's poem in the Gundulf Bible are six lines of Anglo-Norman verse copied later, the opening to some forgotten *chanson de geste*.[67] Appended to the second volume of the

---

[64] I am indebted to Professor John Benton, late of the California Institute of Technology, for this suggestion.

[65] *Biblia Sacra*, v. 1, *Librum Genesis*, ed. Henri Quentin (Rome, 1926), 51-60. Alcuin's verses are in Ernest Dümmler, *Poetae Latini aevi Carolini*, Monumenta Germaniae Historica (Berlin, 1881), 1:287-88; for Theodulf's verses, see 1:532-38.

[66] BL MS. Harley 1023.

[67] Printed in S. Harrison Thompson, "Oor Escutez Seinurs . . .," *Modern Language Notes*, 46 (1931): 368-69.

Bible in a twelfth-century hand are the prologue and text to the apocryphal Book of Baruch, followed by the letter of Jeremiah, in the Old Latin version *a* identified by Kneucker.[68] This version represents the first Latin translation from the Greek, and is found in early Italian and Spanish Bibles. There is no clue as to where the scribe located this text, but Canterbury is an obvious possibility because of its rich continental resources.

For at least fifty years prior to the introduction of another Bible worthy to be included in the Rochester library catalogues, the Gundulf Bible preserved the Vulgate text seemingly adopted by Rochester from Christ Church, Canterbury. Meanwhile, of course, a supply of patristic texts was copied for the priory and a monastic library was established. By 1125, however, a new, multi-volume Bible was in production, evidenced by entries in the first inventory of the Rochester library. Two volumes of that set remain today, the New Testament (Baltimore, Walters Art Gallery MS. W. 18) and Joshua-Judges-Ruth-Kings (BL MS. Royal 1 C. VII).[69] Both are decorated, and their text is virtually identical to that in the Gundulf Bible. Hence it appears that Rochester *maintained* the borrowed Vulgate text, possibly as a "use," throughout the twelfth century. Coincidentally, the two volumes have been influenced paleographically by Christ Church, Canterbury, which suggests the involvement of Bishop John I (1124-37), a former archdeacon of Canterbury and the first post-Conquest bishop of Rochester not a monk. Having come from a see noted for its richly decorated manuscripts, and lacking the ascetic tastes of the former monk-bishops, John may well have commissioned a decorated Bible when he found there was none at Rochester and have drawn on the resources of Canterbury to get the project underway. These are conjectures, however; the best evidence for the origin of the Bible rests in the medieval catalogues and in the physical and textual features of the books themselves.

In the inventory of 1124, references to portions of a multi-volume Vulgate indicate that these volumes were newer than most of the other books described. On fol. 226r of the *Textus Roffensis*, near the end of Jerome's list, the following entries occur in the main hand (Table 1, items 32 and 33):

(32) Item quinque libros moysi in uno volumine novo.
(33) Iesum nave. Iudicum. et Ruth. in uno volumine novo.

Two further references are added in a slightly later hand at the end of the catalogue (Table 1, items 94 and 97):

(94) Novum testamentum in uno volumine.
(97) Quinque libri moysi. et iosue et iudicum in uno volumine.

---

[68] J. J. Kneucker, *Das Buch Baruch* (Leipzig, 1879), 141-51.
[69] Claus M. Kauffmann, *Romanesque Manuscripts 1066-1190, A Survey of Manuscripts Illuminated in the British Isles*, 3 (London, 1975): #45, 81; Mary P. Richards, "A Decorated Vulgate Set from 12th-century Rochester, England," *The Journal of the Walters Art Gallery*, 39 (1981): 66.

Like entries 32 and 33, entries 94 and 97 probably refer to recent acquisitions, because they are part of an effort to keep the catalogue up to date. The question is whether one or more Vulgate sets is implied by the four entries. A definite answer is not possible, but the testimony of the second catalogue made in 1202 on fols. 2r-3r of BL MS. Royal 5 B. XII indicates that only one set was completed:

Pentateuchi moysi. In volumine Novo. Item Iosue. Iudicum. Regum. iiii. In alio Novo. Tercia pars incipiens a salomone cum multis aliis. in alio volumine. novo. De est ad huc quarta pars veteris testamentum. hoc est. xvi prophete et paralipomena. Item novum testamentum in volumine. Novo.

No other unglossed portions of the Vulgate are listed in the 1202 inventory. Further, the separate catalogue of books connected with Alexander the precentor in BL MS. Royal 10 A. XII describes an identical set said to be stored in the *armarium*:

i pars est Genesis. ii Iosue Iudicium Regem. iii predictus liber continens libros salomone. Iob. Iudith. Hester. Esdras. Machabeorum adhuc deest autem iiii pars est xvi prophete et paralipomena.

On the basis of the descriptions in the three catalogues, and a comparison of the two extant manuscripts that can be associated with the volumes described, the probability is that items 32, 33, 94, and 97 refer only to one Vulgate set in progress c. 1125. That set then is complete and fully catalogued in the 1202 list.

As stated above, two volumes remaining today can be associated with the set described in the medieval catalogues, and these volumes reflect a continuing link with Canterbury in the production of Bibles for Rochester. The first, Walters Art Gallery MS. W. 18, is a twelfth-century New Testament that seems to be a joint production of Christ Church, Canterbury, and Rochester.[70] Dodwell believes that the book was written in the Canterbury script style, but illuminated at Rochester.[71] Ker assigns Rochester ownership of the volume.[72] Since only one New Testament is mentioned in each of the catalogues, and since the Walters manuscript is the only such volume extant that has been connected with Rochester, it is probable that the Walters volume is the one referred to. The script style of the Walters New Testament is, in fact, hard to place. The extensive use of hairlines and the pronounced angularity of minuscule *c, d, e,* and *o* are the features that suggest the "prickly" Christ Church, Canterbury, script most strongly.[73] Further, the scribe avoids round *r,* commonly used in Rochester manuscripts. But the scribe also follows certain patterns found in the group of Rochester manuscripts copied 1108-23 as identified by Waller, namely, the distinction be-

---

[70] De Ricci, 1:766. See also Walters Art Gallery, *2,000 Years of Calligraphy* (Baltimore, 1965; rpt. 1972), 39-40.
[71] Dodwell, *The Canterbury School of Illumination,* 119.
[72] Ker, *MLGB,* 160.
[73] Ker, *English Manuscripts in the Century after the Norman Conquest,* 27.

tween ligatures for *ae* and *oe*, avoidance of round-backed *d,* and the use of suprascript letters.[74] Thus, although the scribe seems to have been trained at Canterbury, he has adopted enough of the Rochester practices from the era in which he was working to indicate that he could have copied the New Testament at Rochester. Perhaps he accompanied Bishop John I in the move from Canterbury, to return after the decorated Bible project was well underway. Interestingly, the New Testament is the only volume in the Rochester set *not* connected with Alexander the precentor in his list quoted above.

The second volume remaining from the new Vulgate set, BL MS. Royal 1 C. VII, is strictly a Rochester production, though its text is linked to Canterbury. Waller classifies this volume in a group of manuscripts produced after 1122-23, evidence that it may be slightly later than the Walters New Testament.[75] Both script and illumination indicate a Rochester origin of c. 1125.[76] This volume contains the books of Joshua, Judges, Ruth, and I-IV Kings. At one time, however, Kings may have existed separately, for an historiated initial opens Joshua, but three other such initials occur at I, II, and IV Kings. I Kings also begins a new quire. If the manuscript is to be identified with entry 33 and/or 97 in the first catalogue (see above), we must assume that the books of Kings were in fact added to the volume sometime after the entries were written. It is possible, though by no means certain, that the new Pentateuch (entry 32) and the new volume containing Joshua-Judges-Ruth (entry 33) were combined temporarily into a single volume entered as item 97 by a later cataloguer. As evidence, this cataloguer does not express the awareness that he is dealing with a Heptateuch, which might have been intended to stand alone. If indeed the texts had been combined, he could easily have missed the short book of Ruth while making his description. Later, as the set was completed, item 97 would have been subdivided and the second portion combined with Kings in order to form volumes of roughly equal length. We noted a similar situation regarding Kings in the Gundulf Bible, where it had been copied separately and subsequently added to the opening of volume II.

Despite the uncertainty of the references in the first catalogue, there is little doubt MS. Royal 1 C. VII is the referent of the volume described

Item Iosue. Iudicum. Regum. iiii. In alio Novo,

item 113 in the catalogue of 1202. Compared with the Gundulf Bible, the only other Vulgate recorded in the catalogue, the five-part set was new. The omission of Ruth in the entry is not a major concern, for, since it is mentioned nowhere else in the description of the set, it probably was missed by a cataloguer glancing through the volume. We can conclude, then, that a

---

[74] Waller, 112-14.
[75] Waller, 127.
[76] On the decorative motifs and initials, see Dodwell, *The Canterbury School of Illumination,* 76-77; Claus M. Kauffmann, "The Bury Bible," *Journal of the Warburg and Courtauld Institutes,* 29 (1966): 78-79; Kauffmann, *Romanesque Manuscripts,* 81; and Thomas S. R. Boase, *English Art 1100-1216* (Oxford, 1953), 64-65.

Vulgate set containing volumes like the Walters New Testament and MS. Royal 1 C. VII had been completed by 1202. Since these volumes are connected with Rochester, and are roughly contemporary with the additions made to the earlier catalogue that indicated a set in progress, they are likely candidates for a set described in both catalogues.

Physically, the Walters New Testament and MS. Royal 1 C. VII resemble each other in detail. They are nearly identical in size, format, and style of decoration. Both are arranged in quires of eight leaves, ruled in dry point and lead. They differ in script, as mentioned above, the placement of quire signatures, and the extent of decoration. The gatherings of MS. Royal 1 C. VII are numbered in bold Roman numerals with one or two dots on the last verso. Quires II-XII and XXIX of the Walters New Testament are marked identically in smaller Roman numerals, while XIII-XXVIII are so numbered on the recto of the first leaf. Quires 30-33 have been numbered later on the recto of the first leaf. Since Rochester manuscripts c. 1120-30 normally have quire signatures on the last verso, the variation in style in the New Testament could be further evidence that the scribe had been trained elsewhere, perhaps in an earlier era. The Gundulf Bible, for instance, which seems to have been copied at Canterbury some fifty years before, has quire numbers on the first recto. Although the two later manuscripts share a number of decorative motifs, such as the human-profile terminal, flowers, fruit, and griffins, MS. Royal 1 C. VII has, in addition, four colored historiated initials at the openings of Joshua, I, II, and IV Kings as mentioned above. Space for one such initial has been left at the opening to Matthew in the Walters New Testament, but it was never filled.

Although the two parts of the Vulgate set are close in date, the Walters New Testament seems to have been produced first.[77] A Canterbury scribe more likely would have been used to get the project underway than to contribute to a work already in progress. Further, the script style and the appearance of signatures on the first recto of certain quires reflect older practices associated with Canterbury that were declining when the New Testament was copied. The entries in the first catalogue are ambiguous on the matter of the Vulgate set, and their order could be used to argue that the New Testament was the later of the two volumes. Paleographic evidence should, however, take precedence over the uncertainty of the catalogue additions, and this evidence favors a date earlier than that of MS. Royal 1 C. VII.

The textual relationship between the two volumes confirms that they formed parts of the same set, for it reflects the distinctive textual type traced in MSS. Royal 1 E. VII-VIII and the Gundulf Bible. As regards prefaces and chapters, the Walters New Testament is missing quire 1 and whatever prefaces to the Gospels it contained. Further, there are no prologues or chapters

---

[77] In a private communication, T. A. (Sandy) Heslop has argued for an earlier date for MS. Royal 1 C. VII by comparing its decoration to that of MS. Royal 5 D. VII, presumably part of the first item in the inventory of 1124.

to the individual Gospels. In subsequent books, however, the prefatory materials are identical to those found in MS. Royal 1 E. VIII and the Gundulf Bible, including the lengthy series preceding Romans. By comparison, the portion of the Old Testament, MS. Royal 1 C. VII, has the chapters to Joshua and the preface to Judges found in the Canterbury Bible, MS. Royal 1 E. VII, and the preface to Kings found in both earlier Bibles, but lacks chapters to Kings.[78]

Each of the two portions of the Vulgate has unique readings, but most readings are characteristic of the text shared by Christ Church, Canterbury and Rochester. MS. Walters 18 shares a number of unusual readings with the two earlier Bibles,[79] MS. Royal 1 E. VIII and the Gundulf Bible, and approximately equal numbers of readings with one against the other.[80] Although they do not reveal a clear-cut pattern, the independent readings in the Walters text generally reflect an older tradition, Italian, Irish, and Spanish.[81] The Irish influence is the most marked, as in

---

[78] Joshua and Judges: Berger, *Histoire*, 346, Josue et Juges I. I-II Kings: Stegmüller, 323.

[79] Readings such as the following occur in the Walters New Testament, MS. Royal 1 E. VIII, and the Gundulf Bible:
Matthew 16:9 *quinque panum et quinque milia*
18:9 *unum oculum habentem*
24:42 *duo in lecto unus assumetur et alter relinquetur*
27:43 *liberet eum nunc si vult*
Mark 6:3 *Nonne iste est faber*
Luke 11:8 *et ille perseveraverit pulsans*
John 16:23 *interrogabitis*
Acts 2:7 *ad invicem dicentes*
3:11 *tenerent*
5:36 *Theodas dicens esse se aliquem magnum* (B.N. 93)
18:2 *et salutavit eos* (B.N. 93)
18:10 *et nullus tibi nocere poterit et nemo apponetur tibi ut noceat te*
23:18 *Paulus vocans rogavit me*
James 1:2 *temptationes varias*
II Peter 3:10 *Terra autem et quae in ipsa sunt opera exurentur* (B.N. 11553)
I Corinthians 11:24 om. *accipite et manducate*

[80] Readings shared by Walters 18 with only one of the two earlier Bibles, MS. Royal 1 E. VIII or the Gundulf Bible:
Matthew 16:10 *quattuor* (Royal 1. E. VIII); *quatuor* (GB)
Mark 11:32 *timebant* (Royal 1 E. VIII); *timemus* (GB)
5:35 *archisynagogum* (Royal 1 E. VIII); *archysinagogum* (GB)
Luke 10:30 *suspiciens* (Royal 1 E. VIII); *suscipiens* (GB)
Acts 13:2 *separate* (GB); *segregate* (Royal 1 E. VIII)
I James 5:12 *iuramentum vestrum* (GB); *iuramentum* (Royal 1 E. VIII)
I Peter 3:18 *mortificatos . . . vivificatos* (GB); *mortificatus . . . vivificatus* (Royal 1 E. VIII)
4:8 *vobismet ipsis* (GB); *vobismet ipsos* (Royal 1 E. VIII)
I Corinthians 10:17 *et de uno calice* (Royal 1 E. VIII); om. (GB)
I Timothy 5:16 *si qua fidelis* (Royal 1 E. VIII); *si quis fidelis* (GB)
Apocalypse 1:13 *zona aurea* (GB); *zona auream* (Royal 1 E. VIII)
1:15 *auricalco* (GB); *oricalco* (Royal 1 E. VIII).

[81] Independent readings in Walters 18:
Matthew 18:26 *rogabat; orabat* (Royal 1 E. VIII, GB)
19:20 *a iuventute mea;* om. (Royal 1 E. VIII, GB)
23:25 *pleni estis; pleni sunt* (Royal 1 E. VIII, GB)
24:44 *qua hora; quia qua nescitis hora* (Royal 1 E. VIII, GB)
27:32 no addition; *venientem obviam sibi* (Royal 1 E. VIII; *venientum* GB).

Luke 11:2 *Fiat voluntas tua sicut in caelo et in terra*
    11:3 *hodie*

neither of which occurs in the earlier Bibles. Because of this influence, the Gospels in the Walters New Testament shares a few distinctive readings with Goda's Gospels, perhaps a sign of the latter's influence on Rochester books after its arrival early in the twelfth century.

MS. Royal 1 C. VII (Joshua, Judges, Ruth, I-IV Kings) bears the same close relationship with the earlier Bibles as does MS. Walters 18, but it has fewer independent readings.[82] This situation is not surprising, for the Irish influence was strongest on the New Testament, particularly the Gospels, in England. Generally speaking, however, the two Vulgate portions are so close to the Bibles from Canterbury, and Rochester, that they must have been copied from a nearly identical text. Taken together with the paleographic evidence, the textual affinity of MSS. Walters 18 and Royal 1 C. VII confirms that they once formed part of a five-volume Vulgate set at Rochester. Our best evidence indicates that this set remained the sole decorated Bible in the Rochester library for at least a century, until the production of Oxford MS. St. John's College 4 in the late thirteenth century, a Vulgate book that departs from the distinctive text described here.

---

[82] Most of the characteristic readings found in Royal 1 E. VII and the Gundulf Bible occur in this newer text, for example:
  Joshua 2:16 *diebus tribus*
         3:1 *per tres dies*
  Judges 1:3 *in sorte mea . . . sorte tua*
         2:19 *multa maiora faciebant quam . . . et servientes*
         2:23 *in manibus*
         20:22 *Rursumque*
  Ruth 2:1 *vir*
       2:11 *dereliqueris*
       2:16 *corripiat*
       2:19 *esset*
  I Kings 10:24 *non sit ei similis . . . cunctus populus*
          18:30 *agebat*
          20:3 *in conspectu tuo*
          20:9 *Absit hoc a me*
          21:7 *Hic pascebat mulas Saul*
          25:44 *alio viro*
  II Kings 12:7 *qui fecisti hanc rem*
           15:34 *patere me vivere*
           17:14 *et ut videretur esse consilium chusai bonum coram absalon*
           22:28 *et populum pauperem*
  III Kings 1:8 *semei et cerethi*
However, MS. Royal 1 C. VII shares a few individual readings with only one of the two Bibles:
  Judges 21:5 *grandi* (Royal 1 E. VII); *grande* (GB)
  II Kings 13:32 *in die* (Royal 1 E. VII); *ex die* (GB)
            16:1 *onusti* (Royal 1 E. VII); *honusti* (GB)
  I Kings 18:13 *et ingrediebatur* (GB); *egrediebatur* (Royal 1 E. VII).
In most cases where the later text agrees with the Canterbury Bible against the Gundulf Bible, the Canterbury Bible has been corrected to the reading reflected in MS. Royal 1 C. VII. In a few cases, however, the Old Testament portion agrees with neither of the earlier texts:
  Judges 5:1 *barach; barac* (Royal 1 E. VII, GB)
         16:31 *asthahol; asthaol* (Royal 1 E. VII, GB)
         17:5 *edeculam; ediculam* (Royal 1 E. VII, GB)
  Ruth 1:2 *filiis; liberiis* (Royal 1 E. VII); *liberis* (GB)
       1:6 *coedo; cedo* (Royal 1 E. VII, GB).

One final witness to the Vulgate text adopted at Rochester from Christ Church, Canterbury, is the so-called "Dover Bible," Cambridge MS. Corpus Christi College 3-4, produced in the mid-twelfth century at Canterbury and sent to its cell at Dover in the fourteenth century.[83] Although it has illuminated initials and canon tables decorated in gold and therefore is a more elaborate production than the earlier books, this Bible has identical prefaces and chapters to MSS. Royal 1 E. VII-VIII, the tenth-century Vulgate from Canterbury, and shares all of the characteristic readings of that text and the Gundulf Bible.[84] In cases where the Canterbury and Rochester versions of the text differ, the Dover Bible, not surprisingly, conforms to the Canterbury text. The main copyist, however, includes the alternate readings found in both earlier manuscripts, usually with an insert above the word in question. This shows that the Vulgate texts were indeed compared with one another, and that the development of related materials was a conscious process at the two leading Benedictine foundations in Kent.

Several important conclusions emerge from an intensive study of the textual tradition that influenced Vulgates produced at Rochester before the middle of the twelfth century. The tradition is continental, having been brought to Christ Church, Canterbury, by the end of the tenth century. It seems to have persevered through the middle of the twelfth century. More remarkably, it demonstrates a continuing process of interchange well after Rochester had acquired a copy of this shared Vulgate text in the Gundulf Bible. Despite a certain rivalry for properties and influence felt, we can be sure, more strongly by the monks of Rochester, they clearly were allied in matters of book production and textual transmission with their brethren at Canterbury. Moreover, the shared Vulgate text is distinct from those produced elsewhere in England during the post-Conquest periods. On the basis of the type and order of prefatory materials and individual readings provided by Glunz, we can distinguish the group of texts produced at Canterbury and Rochester from those at Lincoln (Lincoln Cathedral MS. 1 and Cambridge MS. Trinity College B.5.2. [148], late eleventh century);[85] Durham (Durham Cathedral MS. A. II. 4, late eleventh century);[86] Bury St. Edmunds (Cambridge, Corpus Christi College, MS. 2, twelfth century);[87] St. Albans (Cambridge, Corpus Christi College, MS. 48, twelfth century);[88] and Winchester (Winchester Cathedral MS. 17, twelfth century).[89] If MSS.

---

[83] Dodwell, *The Canterbury School of Illumination*, 48; James, *Descriptive Catalogue of Manuscripts in the Library of Corpus Christi College, Cambridge*, 1:8-14; Kauffmann, #69, 97-98.

[84] Don Denny states incorrectly that the prefatory materials in the Dover Bible match those in MS. Royal 1 C. VII. This is not quite accurate: the latter lacks chapters to I-II and III-IV Kings found in the Dover Bible. See "Notes on the Lambeth Bible," *Gesta*, 16 (1977): 52.

[85] Ker, *MLGB*, 116, n. 8; Kauffmann, #13, 59-60. Described in Reginald M. Woolley, *Catalogue of the Manuscripts of Lincoln Cathedral Chapter Library* (Oxford, 1927), 1-2, and Montague R. James, *The Western Manuscripts in the Library of Trinity College, Cambridge*, 1:174-81.

[86] Mynors, 33 and pl. 16-18; Glunz, 192.

[87] James, *Corpus Christi College, Cambridge*, 1:3-8; Kauffmann, #56, 88-91.

[88] Ibid., 1:94-96; Kauffmann, #91, 115. Rodney Thomson defines a larger family of post-Conquest Bibles and New Testaments from St. Albans in *Manuscripts from St. Albans Abbey 1066-1235* (Bury St. Edmunds, 1982), 1:32.

[89] Larry M. Ayres, "Studies in the Winchester Bible" (Harvard Univ. dissertation, 1970), 14-18; Glunz, 183; Kauffman, #83, 108-11.

London, Lambeth Palace 3 and Maidstone Museum 1, two parts of a twelfth-century Bible, are indeed from St. Augustine's, Canterbury, we can tentatively eliminate that foundation as well and focus the southeastern textual tradition of Northern French origin more narrowly at the Benedictine houses of Christ Church, Canterbury, and Rochester.[90]

Can we say that certain features of this tradition are strictly Kentish? The order and type of prefatory materials to Romans may be unique. They and the chapters to Numbers seem to be known only in Insular Bibles produced in Kent, but they may well have had continental antecedents. The distinctive readings provided in note 79 are useful for comparison within England, though again they could have been adopted from an imported text. In short, we can specify these and other features as being characteristic of Bibles produced in Kent, with the important exclusion of St. Augustine's, but their origin cannot be ascertained at present.

The evidence for a common "use" at Canterbury and Rochester resides then in the shared Vulgate text maintained over a century and a half. Obviously the text was important to both foundations since they seemed to have owned duplicate copies. In this area particularly, scholarly and spiritual concerns met, and provided compelling motivation to produce unified materials. For Rochester, such a text would have had greater authority than anything remaining from the Anglo-Saxon foundation, and the traditional association with Gundulf could have sustained the borrowed text easily through the twelfth century. Canterbury, on the other hand, may have been pleased to "improve" a text connected with Dunstan's era rather than to seek a newer version of its established text. Documenting the text does more, however, than remind us again of the close relationship between the two sees. Developments took place there independently of influences and styles in other parts of the country. The Christ Church, Canterbury-Rochester axis in southeastern England was responsible for distinctive, even innovative, manuscript productions whose significance as a body of related works is just now becoming appreciated. It is not surprising, then, to learn that the relationships of both vernacular and Latin materials extend beyond a shared Anglo-Saxon heritage and Vulgate text to a wide array of homiletic and liturgical materials.

---

[90] Ker, *MLGB*, 45, and notes 7-8; Kauffmann, #70, 99-100. The Lambeth Palace MS. is described in Montague R. James and Claude Jenkins, *A Descriptive Catalogue of the Manuscripts in the Library of Lambeth Palace* (Cambridge, 1930), 1:2-6. See also Eric G. Millar, "Les Principaux Manuscrits à Peintures," *Bulletin de la Société Française de Reproductions de Manuscrits à Peintures* (Paris, 1924), 8:15-21. Thomson rules out a Bury St. Edmunds origin for the Lambeth Bible, and proposes St. Augustine's, Canterbury and St. Albans as more probable alternatives in *Manuscripts from St. Albans Abbey*, 1:33.

IV. THE MEDIEVAL HOMILIARY AT ROCHESTER

As we have seen, one important link to the continent and the Carolingian reforms of the eighth and ninth centuries existed in the great Bibles produced at Canterbury and Rochester. Through their revisions, Alcuin and Theodulf had attempted to provide a better text of Jerome's translation than was available after centuries of transmission. These revisions then formed the basis of Vulgate texts copied in Northern France and taken to Kent in the tenth century. Another substantial link to Charlemagne's reforms occurs in the homiletic manuscripts surviving from Canterbury and Rochester. The Latin homiliaries reflect the types of monastic compilations commissioned by the emperor, while the more popular Old English sermon materials find their sources in these and other collections from the Carolingian period.[1] As with the Bibles, the probable line of transmission leads from the continent to Canterbury, and finally to Rochester.

Our situation again is one where basic monastic texts have survived from Rochester in greater numbers than from more prominent local foundations, so that textual relationships can be difficult to trace. But in contrast to the affinity among the great Bibles in Kent, which suggested that Rochester and Christ Church had a mutual text not shared with other foundations from which evidence survives, the homiliaries appear to have an affiliation with St. Augustine's, Canterbury, as well as with Christ Church. This affiliation seems clearest, as we will see, in the vernacular collections, which presumably did not relate as directly to the life of a Benedictine priory as did its Bibles. In addition, St. Augustine's owned a version of Paul the Deacon's homiliary very close to one from Rochester, hence it appears that homiletic materials generally were shared more widely than Vulgate texts among the various religious houses in Kent.

Compared with other English foundations, Rochester has an impressive number of homiliaries surviving from which to assemble a picture of its textual resources and activity. The medieval inventories of the library record certain items: two Latin homiliaries of two volumes each, a two-volume homiliary in English, another volume described "Alfricus I," a cycle of Latin

---

[1] For a brief overview of Carolingian reforms related to homiletic and sermon materials, see Thomas L. Amos, *The Origin and Nature of the Carolingian Sermon* (Michigan State Univ. dissertation, [1983], 196-99. On the connection to the Benedictine Revival, see Clare A. Lees, "The Dissemination of Alcuin's *De Virtutibus et Vitiis Liber* in Old English: A Preliminary Survey," in *Leeds Studies in English*, N.S. 16 (1985): 174. Mary Clayton describes the influence of Carolingian homiliaries on Anglo-Saxon homiletic collections in "Homiliaries and Preaching in Anglo-Saxon England," *Peritia*, 4 (1985): 207-42.

sermons, and assorted sermons and homilies in miscellaneous codices. But, as a study of the extant books will show, these lists specify only a portion of the homiletic collections that were available at the priory for use during the night office, mealtimes, catechetical occasions, and periods of individual study. In sum, four extensive Old English homiliaries associated with Rochester have survived, two of these being pre-Conquest products of the early eleventh century, while three Latin homiliaries remain, all post-Conquest in origin. The Anglo-Saxon canons at Rochester must have acquired the vernacular series almost a century before refoundation in order to assist in learning and teaching. Yet the interest in English homiletic materials persisted at Rochester well into the twelfth century as it did elsewhere in Norman England.[2] The Latin homiliaries, on the other hand, are typical of collections needed for a monastic priory. Together, these groups of texts provide an extensive view of the sources and range of homiletic materials available at Rochester and further evidence of the kinds of texts circulating in Kent during the pre- and post-Conquest eras.

Since they are the earlier group, we will begin with the Old English homiletic collections associated with Rochester. All are Ælfrician in nature, and range from early cycles very close to Ælfric's original compilations to late, freely edited assemblages. The four collections provide no direct evidence that Wulfstan's works were available at Rochester, though a number of anonymous homilies from the Vercelli Book, particularly for Rogationtide and other occasions not covered by Ælfric, occur even in the earliest manuscripts.[3] These Ælfrician collections have been studied in detail, most recently by Scragg, Godden, Pope, and Handley.[4] Our purpose here is not to duplicate their fine textual and paleographical work, but rather to examine the collections in the context of the medieval library and scriptorium at Rochester. Obviously they attest to a thriving vernacular prose tradition in southeastern England. More specifically, the collections probably descended from Canterbury originals, if they were not actually copied there. As we have seen in our examination of the lists and legal materials in the *Textus Roffensis*, sources for Old English texts at Rochester seem usually to have come from Christ Church, Canterbury. But in the case of the homiletic

---

[2] R. W. Chambers, *On the Continuity of English Prose from Alfred to More and his School*, EETS. Original Series 191a (rpt. 1957), XC-XCIV.

[3] The distribution of the Vercelli homilies in the manuscripts associated with Rochester and Canterbury is one of the main pieces of evidence leading to Donald G. Scragg's conclusion that the Vercelli Book was compiled in Kent, in "The compilation of the Vercelli Book," *Anglo-Saxon England*, 2 (1973): 189-207. Evidence for Rochester origin is provided in Margaret Martin, "A Note on Marginalia in 'The Vercelli Book,'" *Notes and Queries*, 223 (1978): 485-86. For matters of terminology in this chapter, I have relied heavily on Andrew Hughes, *Medieval Manuscripts for Mass and Office* (Toronto, 1982). Also indispensable is Milton McC. Gatch, *Preaching and Theology in Anglo-Saxon England* (Toronto, 1977).

[4] See Donald G. Scragg, "The corpus of vernacular homilies and prose saints' lives before Ælfric," *Anglo-Saxon England*, 8 (1979): 223-69; Malcolm R. Godden, *Ælfric's Catholic Homilies, The Second Series, Text* (EETS Supplementary Series 5, London, 1979); John C. Pope, *Homilies of Ælfric*, 2 vol. (EETS Original Series 259, 260, London, 1967-68); Rima Handley, "British Museum MS. Cotton Vespasian D. XIV," *Notes and Queries*, 21 (1974): 243-50.

collections, there is some reason to think that the ultimate source for these materials was St. Augustine's. Certain modifications may have been made, however, to reflect the particular interests of Rochester.

The one English homiliary listed in the catalogue of 1124 (Table 1, item 83), a two-volume work, is mentioned again in 1202. This entry almost certainly refers to the two-volume collection in Oxford MSS. Bodley 340 and 342, an early eleventh-century collection owned, and possibly produced, by Rochester. An early fourteenth-century inscription on the flyleaf of the second volume, "Sermones anglici," echoes the entries "Sermonalia anglica" in the first catalogue, and "Omeliaria anglica" in the later catalogue of 1202. The 1202 catalogue also contains the entry, "Alfricus I," which may refer to a second Ælfrician homiliary, although the specific book in question cannot be identified. As is well known, MSS. Bodley 340 and 342 represent an early version of Ælfric's two series of homilies combined into a single annual cycle from Nativity through Advent.[5] Ælfric's work is supplemented with eleven anonymous pieces, including five known from the collection in the Vercelli Book, used mainly for occasions omitted, or incompletely covered, by Ælfric.[6] Three items added at the end of Bodley 342 indicate Rochester provenance. On the last page is a portion of a narrative concerning Paulinus, the first bishop of Rochester, copied in the early eleventh-century hand of the principal corrector, that uses "her" in referring to that foundation as the place where he was invested, later buried, and continues to rest.[7] Then on two added quires occur Ælfric's homilies for St. Andrew, the patron of Rochester. The last items are in a different, but roughly contemporary, hand as compared with that of the main scribe of the two volumes, and they are modeled in format after those in the main collection, from the rubrics to the form of the letters used in the closing "Amen."[8]

In short, MSS. Bodley 340 and 342 are a complete Old English homiliary with materials added specifically for Rochester. The volumes are not lavish, but they are written in a good hand of square Anglo-Saxon minuscule and decorated sufficiently, with titles in red, to highlight the individual pieces. Each volume opens with an intricate initial, and each piece thereafter begins with a colored, less decorated initial. There are a few differences between the two volumes. More pericopes are included in MS. 342, nineteen as opposed to four in MS. 340. The absence of pericopes in the first volume possibly led to the designation "sermonalia" in the first catalogue entry of c. 1124. Secondly, certain initials in MS. 342 have motifs not found in MS. 340. The most striking of these are two where the body of the letter is an animal figure: on fol. 21r, an S is formed from a two-headed beast with wings; on

---

[5] Kenneth Sisam, "MSS. Bodley 340 and 342: Ælfric's *Catholic Homilies,*" rpt. in his *Studies in the History of Old English Literature* (Oxford, 1953), 148-98 and Ker, *Catalogue,* 361-67.

[6] Scragg, "The corpus of vernacular homilies," 238-40.

[7] Ker quotes the passage in his *Catalogue,* 367.

[8] For a close analysis of these MSS. see N. R. Ker, *A Study of the Additions and Alterations in MSS. Bodley 340-42* (Oxford B. Litt. thesis, 1934).

fol. 110v, a *D* is made by a snake. A *D* on fol. 127v is decorated in a different style with items including a flower bloom, a butterfly, and a crown, and these motifs are repeated several times on *D*s later in the manuscript. It appears that, wherever this collection was produced, there was more than one artist available to help with the colored initials. Based on similarities in script and decoration, Ker, following Pächt, indicates a possible St. Augustine's origin for MSS. 340 and 342.[9] The suggestion has merit, for St. Augustine's seems to have helped revitalize the scriptorium and library at Christ Church during the period when the MSS. were produced.[10]

The Bodley MSS. suggest that through its proximity to Canterbury, the Anglo-Saxon foundation at Rochester was the beneficiary of certain developments in learning and the dissemination of texts, namely, those directed toward the unlearned clergy and the laity, resulting from the Benedictine Revival of the tenth century.[11] Older collections, such as one from which the Vercelli homilies were drawn, obviously preceded the present homiliary, but in MSS. Bodley 340 and 342 we have the first surviving example of Canterbury texts being copied and modified specifically for Rochester. Given what we know about the state of the pre-Conquest priory at Rochester, it may be more than coincidence that this Old English compilation is one of very few books surviving from that period. The Bodley collection probably suited the needs of the Anglo-Saxon canons very well. Further, relations with St. Augustine's may have been strong at this point in Rochester's history before it became a Norman Benedictine cathedral priory closely allied with Christ Church.

A second, contemporary witness to this conjectural relationship between Rochester and St. Augustine's is another Old English homiliary composed primarily of Ælfrician texts, Cambridge MS. Corpus Christi College 162.[12] In its present state, this MS. contains eight general pieces followed by the Temporale from Epiphany to Advent.[13] Twelve of the fifty-five pieces are anonymous, where once again non-Ælfrician sources have been tapped for Rogationtide and other occasions covered insufficiently in Ælfric's two series.[14] According to Godden, this collection is very closely related to that in MSS. Bodley 340 and 342, and probably shares a common ancestor with it.[15] The homiliary in MS. 162 is distinct, however, not only in its principle of

---

[9] Ker, *Catalogue*, 56 and n. 1.
[10] Brooks, *The Early History of the Church at Canterbury*, 278.
[11] Ælfric obviously was a key figure in the transmission of continental learning, as emerges for example in Cyril Smetana's articles, "Ælfric and the Early Medieval Homiliary," *Traditio*, 15 (1959): 163-204 and "Ælfric and the Homiliary of Haymo of Halberstadt," *Traditio*, 17 (1961): 457-69. See also James E. Cross, "Ælfric and the Medieval Homiliary—Objection and Contribution," *Scripta Minora Regiae Societatis Humaniorum Litterarum Lundensis* (1961-62); Joseph B. Trahern, Jr., "Caesarius of Arles and Old English literature: some contributions and a recapitulation," *Anglo-Saxon England*, 5 (1976): 105-19; and Gatch, 40-55.
[12] Ker, *Catalogue*, 51-56.
[13] Godden, xxxi-iii.
[14] Scragg, "The corpus of vernacular homilies," 242, and Pope 1:23.
[15] Godden, xxxiii.

organization, but also because it has seven anonymous pieces and certain slightly later works by Ælfric not found in the Bodley collection.

On the basis of paleographic as well as textual evidence, the two collections seem to have been produced at the same center.[16] Script, decoration, and textual type indicate that the two MSS. are very close in date and origin. They are similar in script, an Anglo-Saxon minuscule, and layout. Colored, decorated initials of related style open each piece. MS. Corpus Christi College 162 is less handsome in every respect, however, as can be seen in the handling of rubrics. Like Bodley 340 and 342, the Cambridge MS. has rubrics in rustic capitals preceding each piece. But whereas these are given ample space and usually their own line preceding one or more lines for the pericope in MSS. 340 and 342, in MS. 162 they are often crowded in at the end of the preceding piece or around the pericope. Further, MS. 162 is more heavily corrected, with extensive erasures, interlineations, and marginal additions conveying the impression of ongoing revision. Although the two collections have not been copied directly one from the other, Godden has shown that, in a number of cases, they were corrected to agree with each other in the mid-eleventh century.[17]

Because of their close relationship and evidence that MSS. Bodley 340 and 342 were in Rochester by the mid-eleventh century, Godden, Scragg and Pope agree that Rochester was the likely provenance (but not necessarily the origin) for these two Old English homiletic collections. A sermon for St. Augustine, founder of Canterbury, is added to the end of MS. Corpus Christi College 162 in another early eleventh century hand. This anonymous piece is copied only to the bottom of the last recto, p. 563; yet, as was the case with the pieces for St. Andrew added to Bodley 340 and 342, its format, rubrics, and colored initial are in the style of the main collection. Although Augustine was specially venerated in Canterbury, he was instrumental, too, in the founding of Rochester and consecrated Justus, its first bishop.[18] Continued evidence of Rochester's interest in Augustine can be seen a century later in BL MS. Harley 3680, an early twelfth-century Rochester copy of Bede's *Historia Ecclesiastica*, where the passage describing Augustine's arrival in Kent is marked into eight lections by a contemporary hand.[19] Thus, it would have been entirely appropriate for a sermon on St. Augustine to be added to the present collection parallel to the additions for Paulinus and St. Andrew made in MSS. Bodley 340 and 342, and such a sermon certainly would have been available at St. Augustine's.

It seems likely, then, that in the early eleventh century Rochester acquired at least two Old English homiliaries from a southeastern source, possibly St.

---

[16] Ker notes that the initials are similar to those in BL MS. Royal 6 C. I, a later eleventh-century manuscript from St. Augustine's, Canterbury, as well as to those in MSS. Bodley 340 and 342, in *Catalogue*, 56.
[17] Godden, xxxii.
[18] *Bede's Ecclesiastical History*, ed. Colgrave and Mynors, 2:3, 142.
[19] Bede 1:23-26, on fols. 20v-23v.

Augustine's, Canterbury. The works of Ælfric, as Chambers observed, continued to be extremely popular in this period, and they must have helped to advance the aims of the Benedictine Revival. Apparently they were so useful that the canons housed at Rochester took whatever steps were required to obtain some texts of their own.[20] Secular canons may not have participated fully in the revived interest in continental texts and Latin learning, but they certainly were involved in the dissemination of Old English texts. The continuing popularity of these materials at Rochester is proven by the fact that three post-Conquest Ælfrician collections also remain from that house. As examination of these later materials will show, the Benedictine monks not only found them useful, but reworked them much as they had done the Old English laws in the *Textus Roffensis*.

First is an extensive collection in Cambridge MS. Corpus Christi College 303 (first half of the twelfth century) containing pieces for the Temporale from the second Sunday after Epiphany to Easter, and from Rogationtide to the twenty-first Sunday after Pentecost, divided by a Sanctorale from 3 May to 6 December. The collection is now incomplete, with forty-four leaves (by the medieval foliation) missing from the beginning.[21] These probably contained the first part of the Sanctorale and the missing portion of the Temporale. Sixty-one of the seventy-three articles listed by Ker were written by Ælfric, and the remaining twelve pieces are anonymous, composed in the tenth and eleventh centuries.[22] Among the latter group, one is assigned to Easter week, three to Rogationtide, and three are unique saints' homilies not included in Ælfric's work: for SS. Margaret, Giles, and Nicholas. The remaining anonymous pieces are a second homily for Easter Sunday, a substitute homily for the Invention of the Cross, and a homily on virgins followed by a short narrative that fills out the end of the quire.

MS. Corpus Christi College 303 gives evidence of Rochester origin in its script style (the so-called "prickly" type) and its close relationship to the two pre-Conquest collections described above.[23] Although work continues to be done on the problem, it now seems that three pieces, including those known more commonly as Vercelli Homilies XIX and XX for Rogationtide, derive from a tradition in common with the earlier MS. Corpus Christi College 162.[24] Further, Ælfric's homilies in the last portion of the Temporale (Rogationtide through the twenty-first Sunday after Pentecost) descend from an archetype of the collection in MSS. Bodley 340 and 342.[25] Additional evi-

---

[20] Two eleventh-century vernacular collections also survive from Exeter, which was refounded as a secular cathedral in 1050, and these might attest to interests similar to those at Rochester. See Ker, *MLGB*, 82-83 and nn. 2,3, and Scragg, "The corpus of vernacular homilies," 249-53, 255-56.
[21] Ker, *Catalogue*, 99-105, and Godden, xxxvi-vii.
[22] Scragg, "The corpus of vernacular homilies," 243.
[23] Ker, *Catalogue*, 105.
[24] Paul E. Szarmach, "Vercelli Homily XX," *Mediaeval Studies*, 35 (1973): 4-5; Godden, xxxv, and n. 3.
[25] Godden, xxxvi, and Scragg, "The corpus of vernacular homilies," 243, n. 4.

dence of Rochester origin possibly appears in the forms of excommunication in Latin and Old English found among the miscellaneous items at the end of the collection in MS. Corpus Christi College 303.[26] Forms of excommunication normally occur in collections of legal or ritual materials, but the English version of the present text has been made to fit its manuscript context by the addition of a homiletic opening: "Men þa leofestan gehera phwæt þeos boc seg ." In the English version, as opposed to the Latin preceding it, two saints not traditionally called upon to witness the excommunication are named, Nicholas and Augustine. With Andrew, the patron saint of Rochester, included in the apostles who are cited just previous to these saints, the author has added a saint having an important altar for the laity at Rochester Cathedral (Nicholas) and a founder of the see (Augustine).[27] Further, this use of parallel texts in Latin and Old English is reminiscent of the practice observed in the contemporary *Textus Roffensis*, though the terms of excommunication included there are entirely in Latin. On the question of origin, it is worth noting, too, that two of the three unique pieces for saints' days added to Ælfric's materials in MS. Corpus Christi College 303 are related directly to Rochester, those for Margaret and Nicholas. Margaret was the patron of a local church owned by the priory.[28] The third saint, Giles, was generally venerated in England.

In appearance, MS. 303 is an extremely plain, but clearly written book. Rubrics are in minuscule in a relatively poor hand, and are crowded into small spaces to the right of each selection. In this feature, the present homiliary resembles Latin homiletic collections produced in the post-Conquest era at Rochester. In fact, our rubricator seems to have forgotten temporarily the kind of collection he was annotating, for, to the usual title of Ælfric's homily "In Natale Sanctorum Apostolorum Petri et Pauli" he adds the following phrases unique to this version of the text: "Lectio Sancti Evangelii Secundum Matheum. Omelia venerabilis bede presbiteri de eadem lectione." These are the usual rubrics for Bede's homily on the same pericope for the same occasion, as included in Paul the Deacon's Latin homiliary.[29] A copy of this type of homiliary including Bede's work was made in the late eleventh century at Rochester (BL MS. Royal 2 C. III), and it could have intruded on our scribe's consciousness as he worked on the later vernacular homiliary, though whether or not he knew the particular volume is impossible to say. In addition to rather homely rubrics, MS. 303 has large red initials opening the pericopes and the homilies, and occasional large red initials and black initials highlighted in red within the selections. In terms of appearance, then, the present codex is inferior to the pre-Conquest collections despite the

---

[26] Printed in Liebermann, *Die Gesetze*, 1:438-39.
[27] Oakley, 50, 56-57.
[28] Oakley, 49-50.
[29] Grégoire 2: II, 52. The rubrics in MS. Royal 2 C. III, fol. 58v, are identical to those copied inadvertently into MS. Corpus Christi College Cambridge 303, p. 307. Although the homiliary attributed to Paul the Deacon appears in a variety of forms, the reference throughout the present study is to the homiliary in the "original" form reconstructed by Grégoire.

fact that it was produced when the post-Conquest monastic scriptorium was in its greatest phase of activity. Old English homiletic materials no doubt were of secondary importance to the refounded priory.

But MS. Corpus Christi College 303 gives us important information about the history of the vernacular homiliary at Rochester. First, the post-Conquest compiler was content to draw upon readily available materials for his volume. There is evidence of this not only in the close relationship between MS. 303 and the pre-Conquest collections at Rochester, but also in the fact that MS. 303 contains earlier works of Ælfric supplemented by other early pieces.[30] Further indication of St. Augustine's possible role in providing these materials can be seen in the fact that Augustine's name is added to the English form of excommunication in our MS. Secondly, it is an anachronistic volume in yet another sense, for the scribe obviously is struggling with the language of the texts he copies.[31] Thirdly, the state of the texts in MS. 303 implies the existence of a pool of such collections at the priory, although only one of these definitely is mentioned in the medieval catalogues of the library. The finest Ælfrician collection, in MSS. Bodley 340 and 342, seems to have been part of the catalogued library, but others must have been scattered in the refectory, the classroom, and elsewhere, perhaps even near the altar of St. Nicholas where the laity came to worship. Clearly there was need well into the twelfth century at Rochester for catechetical materials in Old English, and this need seems to have been filled by drawing on the resources at hand.[32]

A continuing demand for such texts accounts for the compilation of the remaining post-Conquest collections associated with Rochester and preserved now in BL MSS. Cotton Vespasian D. XIV and A. XXII. The earlier MS. Vespasian D. XIV is an unusual collection from the mid-twelfth century that has been the subject of debate in recent years regarding its origin and purpose.[33] Thirty-three of its fifty-three pieces are Ælfrician, though in some cases the works have been edited heavily. In addition to selections from the First and Second Series of Catholic Homilies, three of Ælfric's letters, a translation of his *De duodecim abusivis,* and one selection from his *Lives of Saints* appear in this collection. Since two of the letters quoted are Ælfric's first and second English letters to Wulfstan, the compiler must have had access to a group of Ælfric's later works not reflected in the homiliaries

---

[30] Scragg, "The corpus of vernacular homilies," 243. According to a recent private communication from Dr. Scragg, there is evidence to suggest that the compiler of MS. 303 had access to two of the Vercelli Book's sources.

[31] Pope, 1:20.

[32] Chambers, XCIV.

[33] Ker, *Catalogue,* 271-77, Handley's article cited above; and Viktor Schmetterer, *Drei Altenglische Religiöse Texte aus der Handschrift Cotton Vespasianus D. XIV* (Wien, 1981), 3-53, provide the most recent descriptions of MS. Cotton Vespasian D. XIV. Still valuable is Max Förster, "Der Inhalt der Altenglischen Handschrift Vespasianus D. XIV," *Englische Studien,* 54 (1920): 46-68.

previously discussed.³⁴ The non-Ælfrician materials, too, have been drawn from wider sources. The pieces possibly of eleventh-century date are Old English translations of the Gospel of Nicodemus, the *Vindicta Salvatoris* (Embassy of Nathan), Alcuin's *De Virtutibus et Vitiis*, and four sermons, including those for SS. James and Neot.³⁵ In addition, at least three pieces were written and translated in the twelfth century: a sermon on St. Mary by Ralph d'Escures and two portions of the *Elucidarius* by Honorius Augustodunensis. The latter was an extremely popular catechetical handbook written about 1100.³⁶ Other non-Ælfrician works of indeterminant date include pieces on Antichrist, on the fifteen days before Doomsday, a translation of John 14:1-13, a rendering of the Latin *Trinubium Annae*, the Old English homily on the phoenix, and short items such as weather prognostications used to fill out the quires.

From the survey of contents, it will be obvious that MS. Cotton Vespasian D. XIV is not a homiliary, strictly speaking. However, pieces for the Temporale and for fixed feasts are in rough calendar order, characteristic of homiletic collections intended for pious reading. The editing and arrangement of texts in the MS., together with paleographic features, indicate a more specific catechetical function for this collection. Pieces have been edited and summarized so as to avoid doctrinal complexity and legendary accretions.³⁷ The emphasis in the collection is on basic precepts, the fundamentals of Christian faith, and pious narratives, together developing an eschatological theme. Large colored initials within certain pieces mark off aphoristic statements, and rubrics in minuscule are used sparingly.³⁸ Clearly this is a simplified collection intended for instruction. As further evidence of this, the third piece in the MS. as it now stands is an English adaptation of the *Distichs* of Cato, a basic elementary teaching text in the Middle Ages. But the collection is unusual in that it is so carefully focused. It draws on traditional homiletic materials, and uses them in a new way.

The origin of MS. Vespasian D. XIV (fols. 4-169) has been debated in recent years, but the weight of evidence now is in favor of Rochester. First there is the matter of textual relationships. Although not related directly to MS. Corpus Christi College 303, the present collection draws on textual traditions for Ælfric's First and Second Series shared with the pre-Conquest homiliaries owned by Rochester, MSS. Bodley 340 and 342 and Corpus

---

[34] Godden, xli. The texts are printed in Rubie D-N. Warner, *Early English Homilies*, EETS Original Series 152 (London, 1917).

[35] Scragg, "The corpus of vernacular homilies," 261.

[36] Valerie I. J. Flint, "The 'Elucidarius' of Honorius Augustodunensis and Reform in Late Eleventh Century England," *Revue Bénédictine*, 85 (1975): 178-89.

[37] Handley, 244-47, and Malcolm Godden, "Ælfric and the Vernacular Prose Tradition," in *The Old English Homily and its Backgrounds*, ed. Paul E. Szarmach and Bernard F. Huppé (Albany, NY, 1978), 112-13.

[38] An example of the way these initials are used in the MS. is described in Mary P. Richards, "Innovations in Ælfrician Homiletic Manuscripts at Rochester," *Annuale Mediaevale*, 19 (1979): 22.

Christi College 162.³⁹ Further, certain dialect features link it to the Rochester area.⁴⁰ Beyond text and language, the evidence is ambiguous and could apply equally to Christ Church, Canterbury, or to Rochester. This would include the "prickly" script style and the inclusion of certain supplementary texts, such as the sermon by Ralph d'Escures who, it will be recalled, served both as bishop of Rochester and archbishop of Canterbury, and the unique piece on St. Neot. Although Neot was celebrated in the post-Conquest calendar at Canterbury, he was known, too, at Rochester. Through Gundulf, the connection with Bec, which held a dependency at St. Neot's in Huntingdonshire, was almost as strong at Rochester as at Canterbury. Anselm named Gundulf one of four trustees of the priory at St. Neot's, and the Rochester foundation held property in Huntingdonshire roughly ten miles from St. Neot's.⁴¹

The collection in MS. Vespasian D. XIV, then, is a unique, late witness to the perseverance of the Old English homiletic tradition in southeastern England. Although the MS. may have originated at Rochester, it draws on materials available at Canterbury. The careful manner in which texts have been edited and assembled, however, shows a need for teaching materials different from the ordinary homiliary, yet closely related. A similarly edited, though far shorter, group of homiletic selections occurs in yet a later Rochester manuscript, BL MS. Cotton Vespasian A. XXII (fols. 54r-57v), dating from the late twelfth or early thirteenth century.⁴² Two of the four pieces are Ælfrician, and the group as a whole demonstrates the continuing usefulness of simplified vernacular homiletic materials almost two centuries after the production of MSS. Bodley 340 and 342. Always strong in Kent, the Old English homiletic tradition obviously continued to flourish long after the area came under Norman domination. With regard to Rochester in particular, it may be useful to link the interest in revitalizing older homiletic materials with the parallel efforts underlying the contemporary production of the *Textus Roffensis*. At Rochester, preservation of its Anglo-Saxon heritage was important to a sense of identity and this factor, together with an established need for Old English teaching, must have motivated the kinds of post-Conquest collections that survive.

The Latin homiliaries surviving from Rochester reflect, on the other hand, the kinds of learning appropriate to the Benedictine monks who were installed there soon after the Conquest. These books are much closer to one

---

³⁹ Godden, xli-ii.
⁴⁰ Richards, "On the Date and Provenance of MS Cotton Vespasian D. XIV, ff. 4-169," 31-35.
⁴¹ Gibson, 176. Æthelred II gave Bishop Godwine of Rochester an estate at Fen Stanton and Hilton, Hunts., in 1012 according to a charter copied into the *Textus Roffensis*, fols. 159v-62. These lands are omitted, however, from the Domesday account of the Rochester fief, and there is uncertainty as to exactly how long they remained in Rochester's ownership; Campbell, xvii, xix, and 45-47. See also the communication from Charles S. Perceval in the *Proceedings of the Society of Antiquaries*, 2nd ser., 3 (1865): 47-50.
⁴² Mary P. Richards, "MS Cotton Vespasian A. XXII: The Vespasian Homilies," *Manuscripta*, 22 (1978): 97-103.

another in date than are the Old English collections, since they were produced for the new monastic library, but they still display considerable variety in sources and relationships. In chronological order, these are BL MS. Royal 2 C. III (late eleventh century), containing homilies and sermons for Septuagesima through Good Friday, followed by pieces for saints' days from Stephen through Andrew and for the Common of Saints;[43] Edinburgh National Library MS. Adv. 18.2.4 (early twelfth century), with homilies from Holy Saturday through the fourth Sunday after Epiphany;[44] and Vatican MS. Lat. 4951 (twelfth century), with sermons from the Nativity through Trinity Sunday followed by pieces for saints' days from St. Vincent through the Decollation of St. John and for the Common of Saints.[45] All three books contain convincing evidence of Rochester provenance. The Royal and Vatican manuscripts have the usual Rochester *ex libris* and anathema at the foot of the flyleaf. An *ex libris* has been cut from the bottom of fol. 1r of the Edinburgh MS., but certain records relating directly to Rochester are copied on fol. 198v.[46]

Two entries in the medieval inventories of the Rochester library relate to these extant volumes. The first, made c. 1124 (Table 1, item 84),

Sermones diversarum solennitatum diversorumque auctorum in i volumine

probably is amplified as follows in the catalogue of 1202:

Leo ad flavianum, et sermones annui diversorum auctorum in i volumine.

This set of entries could refer to Vatican MS. Lat. 4951, or a copy of a similar collection, for the Vatican MS. opens with the letter from Pope Leo to Flavius, bishop of Constantinople, *De Incarnatione Verbi*, and also fits the remainder of the description. The second set of entries,

Omelaria duo in duobus voluminibus. Unum de dominicis, aliud de sanctis.

from the 1124 catalogue (Table 1, item 85), and simply "Omelaria II" in 1202, indicates that there were two additional Latin homiliaries each separated into a Temporale and a Sanctorale in the Rochester library. Only the Edinburgh MS. Adv. 18.2.4 is a candidate for one of these sets, as it is a collection for Sundays and other movable feasts. The Temporale and Sanctorale in MS. Royal 2 C. III are joined together in the middle of the fifth quire in such a way that they can never have formed separate volumes.

It is worthwhile to describe the three extant Rochester collections in detail and to determine relationships among them because the survival of a group of such texts from one medieval library is relatively unusual. Although homiliaries were basic to the religious life of any monastic foundation,

---

[43] *Catalogue of Western Manuscripts in the Old Royal and King's Collections*, 1:51.
[44] *Summary Catalogue of the Advocates' Manuscripts* (Edinburgh, 1971), 100.
[45] Pierre Salmon, *Les Manuscrits Liturgiques Latins de la Bibliothèque Vaticane*, Studi e Testi 267, v. 4 (Città del Vaticano, 1971): 58.
[46] These are described below on 104.

relatively few of these books remain. Neither their plain appearance nor their subject matter was sufficiently attractive to merit preservation in great numbers after the Dissolution. To illustrate, only two fragmentary homiliaries have been assigned by Ker to Christ Church, Canterbury, and another is attributed to St. Augustine's.[47] By comparison, Durham Cathedral, with a great number of its books intact today in the cathedral library, preserves three Latin homiliaries, two from the eleventh and one from the fourteenth centuries.[48]

More importantly, the Rochester homiliaries provide evidence for the circulation of certain post-Conquest Latin homiletic texts and traditions in southeastern England. MSS. Royal 2 C. III and Edinburgh N. L. Adv. 18.2.4 are two of fifteen surviving manuscripts produced in England in the eleventh and twelfth centuries bearing a relatively close relationship to the continental version of Paul the Deacon's homiliary.[49] In addition to Rochester, the provenance is known for twelve of the volumes, two each from Durham, Bury St. Edmunds, Norwich, and Salisbury, and one each from Christ Church and St. Augustine's, Canterbury, Windsor (St. George's Chapel), and Worcester. The third Rochester homiliary, MS. Vatican Lat. 4951, is closer to the earlier Roman homiliary attributed to Alan of Farfa than to Paul the Deacon's Carolingian compilation, though it is the latest, paleographically speaking, of the three manuscripts.[50] Although MS. Vatican Lat. 4951 preserves the most comprehensive of the three collections, there is very little duplication of materials between it and the others. It shares 13 of the 117 pieces found in the earlier MS. Royal 2 C. III, and has no pieces in common with the Edinburgh collection. Thus, at least two separate types of the Latin homiliary were represented at Rochester, one drawing on Roman tradition, and the other Carolingian in origin. These particular manuscripts have never been fully inventoried, and published descriptions of them often have been in error.

To begin with the earliest Rochester collection, MS. Royal 2 C. III preserves the homiliary on the first 169 folios in quires of varying sizes numbered at the foot of the last verso. The pages measure approximately 321 x 241 mm. and are ruled in double columns. The works have been copied in two main hands, English followed by Norman, the second taking over at fol. 106.[51] Rubrics in rustic capitals are red, and the opening words of each text are highlighted in red. Large initials open the first homily (for Septuagesima), the fourth (for Quadragesima), the sixteenth (for Easter), the

---

[47] Ker, *MLGB*, 40-47, and *Medieval Manuscripts in British Libraries* II. Abbotsford-Keele (Oxford, 1977), 315-17. London MS. BL Harley 652, late eleventh or early twelfth century, preserves the homiliary from St. Augustine's.
[48] Ker, *MLGB*, 61-76: MSS. A.III.29, B.II.2, B.II.31.
[49] Cyril L. Smetana, "Paul the Deacon's Patristic Anthology," in *The Old English Homily and its Backgrounds*, 86-87. MS. Lincoln Cathedral 158 is the only one from the group having no known provenance.
[50] On the differences between the Roman and Carolingian homiliaries, see below 117-18.
[51] Waller, 273.

twenty-eighth (for the nativity of St. Stephen), the thirty-third (for the Purification of St. Mary), and the thirty-eighth (for the Annunciation). With the change of hands in item 79, the use of these large capitals ceases. Item 89, for the nativity of St. Andrew, the patron of Rochester, has a decorated capital, but this is a fairly regular feature of the openings to texts in the second part of the collection. Item 88, for the vigil of St. Andrew, is not distinguished in any way. From these observations it seems clear that this is a standard monastic collection, not one that has been modified for Rochester in any visible way. The usual distinction between sermon and homily is made in the rubrics, though occasionally a Gospel pericope is followed by a *sermo*.

In its selection and ordering of materials, MS. Royal 2 C. III is almost identical to two contemporary homiliaries, Lincoln Cathedral MS. 158 (provenance unknown) and Cambridge University Library MS. Kk IV. 13 (Norwich).[52] A chart comparing their contents is found in Table 2. Although Lincoln 158 begins and ends imperfectly, it is otherwise identical to the collection from Norwich. The two collections share only one piece, a homily for the Saturday before Easter, not found in Royal 2 C. III. A space was left at the corresponding point (fols. 44v-45r) in the latter MS., and it was filled with three additional lections (vii-ix) from another, unknown source in a twelfth-century Rochester hand. The rubrics are not uniform in the three collections. Lincoln 158 often fails to mention the occasion of the text, while Royal 2 C. III shows confusion in homilies for Quadragesima such that the whole series becomes reassigned by one week.

Aside from minor differences, however, the three homiliaries are in close agreement. In fact, Royal 2 C. III and Lincoln 158 seem to have been corrected to agree with each other (or with a common text) in late eleventh/early twelfth-century hands, though later glosses added to Lincoln 158 do not correspond to anything in Royal 2 C. III. Together, this group of three homiliaries constitutes one version of Paul the Deacon's collection that circulated in England soon after the Conquest. Other versions became available shortly thereafter, but the present one could have originated in Kent, as we will see. The evidence shows that, as a newly founded Benedictine priory, Rochester quickly became linked to the network of texts circulating in southeastern England, and made its own copy of this and other materials key to the spiritual life of the foundation. What, then, are the significant features of this important collection?

Although 70 of the 117 pieces in Royal 2 C. III, and seventy-one of 118 in Camb. U. L. Kk IV. 13, occur in the continental version of Paul the Deacon's homiliary, their arrangement differs in the English collections. Homilies rarely are assigned to an occasion other than that for which they were intended originally, but multiple texts for a single occasion occur in a new

---

[52] Woolley, 119-23; and Charles Hardwick and H.R. Luard, *A Catalogue of the Manuscripts preserved in the Library of the University of Cambridge* (Cambridge, 1858; rpt. 1980), 3:658-63.

TABLE 2

		Royal 2 C. III	Lincoln Cath. 158	Camb. U.L. Kk. IV. 13
In Septuages.	I, 69—Gregory[1]	x		x
In Sexages.	I, 71—Gregory	x		x
In Quinquag.	I, 73—Gregory	x		x
In Quadrag.	I, 78—Leo	x		x
In Quadrag.	I, 76—Gregory	x	x	x
In Quadrag.	I, 74—Leo	x	x	x
In Quadrag.	I, 77—Leo	x	x	x
In Quadrag.	I, 79—Leo	x	x	x
Dom. I Qdg.	I, 86—Leo	x	x	x
Dom. II Qdg.	PL102:130-2—Smaragdus	x	x	x
Dom. III Qdg.	I, 90—Bede	x	x	x
Oct. Assump. Mariae	PL94:421-2—Bede	x	x	x
Dom. IV Qdg.	I, 92—Bede	x	x	x
Dom. V Qdg.	I, 94—Gregory	x	x	x
Dom. Palmarum	I, 97—Bede	x	x	x
Fer. II	I, 98—Leo	x	x	x
Fer. III	I, 100—Leo	x	x	x
Fer. III	I, 101—Leo	x	x	x
Fer. IV	I, 102—Leo	x	x	x
Fer. IV	I, 103—Leo	x	x	x
Fer. V	Grenoble 32, 19a-c	x	x	x
Fer. V	I, 105—Bede	x	x	x
In Cena Domini	I, 104—Leo	x	x	x
Fer. VI	Grenoble 32, 20a-c	x	x	x
In Parasceve	I, 106—Leo	x	x	x
In Parasceve	I, 107—Leo	x	x	x
Sabb.	Grenoble, 32, 21a-c	x	x	x
Sabb.	II, 1—Jerome		x	x
S. Stephani	AF I, 21a—Ps. Aug.	x	x	x
S. Stephani	PL38:1431-4—Aug.	x	x	x
S. Stephani	AF I, 17—Aug. ?	x	x	x
In Conversione S. Pauli	Rd'A I, 98—Ps. Aug.	x	x	x
S. Pauli	II, 54—Jerome	x	x	x
In Purificat. S. Marie	PL89:1291-1304-Amb. Autp.[2]	x	x	x
In Purificat. S. Marie	I, 67—Bede	x	x	x
In Cathedra S. Petri	PL95:1463-5—Unknown	x	x	x
In Cathedra S. Petri	II, 52—Bede	x	x	x
In Cathedra S. Petri	PL38:791-6—Aug.	x	x	x

[1]References of the type I, 69 refer to Paul the Deacon's reconstructed homiliary as described in Grégoire 2.
[2]CCCM 27, 985-1002.

TABLE 2 *(Continued)*

		Royal 2 C. III	Lincoln Cath. 158	Camb. U.L. Kk. IV. 13
S. Marie	AF II, 65—Ps. Aug.	x	x	x
S. Marie	PL118:31-6—Bede[1]	x	x	x
S. Marci	III, 100—Aug.	x	x	x
SS. Philippi et Jacobi	II, 23—Aug.	x	x	x
Inv. S. Crucis	Barré It. 46—Aug.	x	x	x
Vig. S. Iohannis Bapt.	II, 40—Bede	x	x	x
S. Iohannis Bapt.	Fleury 67—Caesarius	x	x	x
S. Iohannis Bapt.	II, 44—Bede	x	x	x
S. Iohannis Bapt.	II, 42—Ps. Max.	x	x	x
S. Iohannis Bapt.	II, 43—Ps. Max.	x	x	x
S. Iohannis Bapt.	II, 41—Ps. Max.	x	x	x
S. Iohannis Bapt.	CCSL 120:27,l.306-28, l.377—Bede	x	x	x
Vig. S. Petri	II, 45—Bede	x	x	x
SS. Petri et Pauli	II, 46—Leo	x	x	x
SS. Petri et Pauli	Rd'A I, 81—Ps. Aug.	x	x	x
SS. Petri et Pauli	Rd'A I, 83—Ps. Aug.	x	x	x
SS. Petri et Pauli	Rd'A I, 92—Ps. Aug.	x	x	x
SS. Petri et Pauli	II, 47—Ps. Max.	x	x	x
S. Pauli	Rd'A I, 99—Aug.	x	x	x
Oct. S. Iohannis Bapt.	AF II, 37—Ps. Aug.	x	x	x
S. Pauli	PG13:994-1000—Origen	x	x	x
S. Pauli	PG13:1314-20—Origen	x	x	x
SS. Petri et Pauli	II, 48—Ps. Max.	x	x	x
SS. Petri et Pauli	II, 49—Ps. Max.	x	x	x
SS. Petri et Pauli	II, 50—Ps. Max.	x	x	x
Oct. Petri et Pauli	II, 51—Maximus	x	x	x
Oct. Petri et Pauli	AF II, 47—Ps. Aug.	x	x	x
Oct. Petri et Pauli	PL39:1884-6—Aug.	x	x	x
S. Iacobi	Haerent sibi divinae lectionis . . . iam vultus exaltari.	x	x	x
S. Petri ad vinculam	PL94:498—Bede	x	x	x
S. Petri ad vinculam	Rd'A I, 94—Leo	x	x	x
Vig. S. Laurentii	CCSL 120:202, l.1407-204, l.1489—Bede	x	x	x
S. Laurentii	II, 68—Aug.	x	x	x
S. Laurentii	II, 65—Ps. Max.	x	x	x
S. Laurentii	II, 66—Ps. Max.	x	x	x
S. Laurentii	II, 67—Ps. Max.	x	x	x

[1]Also CCSL 120:30, l.425-35, l.631.

TABLE 2 *(Continued)*

		Royal 2 C. III	Lincoln Cath. 158	Camb. U.L. Kk. IV. 13
Assump. Mariae	Rd'A II, 20—Aug.	x	x	x
Oct. Assump. Mariae	II, 70—Bede	x	x	x
S. Augustini	Sal appellantur apostoli quia . . . factores legis iustificabuntur.	x	x	x
Decollatio Iohannis bapt.	PL110:444-6—Rab. Maur.[1]	x	x	x
S. Marie	CCSL 77:7, l.1-10, l.71—Jerome	x	x	x
Exaltatione S. Crucis	CCSL 36:448-51—Aug.	x	x	x
Vig. S. Matthaei	PL94:419-20—Bede	x	x	x
S. Matthaei	PL76:806-8—Gregory	x	x	x
S. Matthaei	II, 99—Bede	x	x	x
S. Michaelis	PL95:1525-30—Haymo	x	x	x
S. Luci	PL76:814-17—Gregory	x	x	x
S. Luci	PL76:1139-49—Gregory	x	x	x
Omnium Sanctorum	PL94:452-5—Ps. Bede[2]	x	x	x
Omnium Sanctorum	PL94:450-2—Ps. Bede[3]	x	x	x
Vig. S. Andreae	II, 97—Bede	x	x	x
S. Andreae	II, 98—Gregory	x	x	x
In Nat. Apost.	III, 101—Gregory	x	x	x
In Nat. Apost.	III, 102—Aug.	x	x	x
In Nat. Apost.	CCSL 36:544, l.38-545, l.14—Aug.[4]	x	x	x
In Nat. Apost.	PL94:423-5—Bede	x	x	x
In Nat. Mart.	III, 110—Jerome	x	x	x
In Nat. Mart.	III, 112—Gregory	x	x	x
In Nat. Mart.	III, 111—Jerome	x	x	x
In Nat. Mart.	III, 118—Gregory	x	x	x
In Nat. Mart.	CCSL 120:336, l.1635-341, l.1836—Bede	x	x	x
In Nat. pl. Mart.	III, 113—Aug.	x	x	x
In Nat. pl. Mart.	PL94:447-50—Bede	x	x	x
In Nat. pl. Mart.	III, 119—Leo	x	x	x
In Nat. pl. Mart.	III, 120—J. Chrysostom	x	x	x
In Nat. pl. Mart.	III, 116—Gregory	x	x	x
In Nat. pl. Mart.	III, 117—Ps. Max.	x	x	x
In Nat. pl. Mart.	CCSL 120:595, l.1-597, l.105—Bede	x	x	x

[1] Plus one paragraph, ends . . . aecclesiasticae librum.
[2] Edited fully by J. E. Cross in "'Legimus in Ecclesiasticus Historii': A Sermon for All Saints, and its Use in Old English Prose," *Traditio*, 33 (1911): 101-35.
[3] See Grégoire 2: 67.
[4] Followed by other, unidentified material; ends . . . quia ipse erat in omnibus omnia.

TABLE 2 *(Continued)*

		Royal 2 C. III	Lincoln Cath. 158	Camb. U.L. Kk. IV. 13
In Nat. Conf.	III, 108—Fulgentius	x	x	x
In Nat. Conf.	PL94:470	x	x	x
In Nat. Conf.	III, 106—Ps. Max.	x	x	x
In Nat. Conf.	III, 104—Gregory	x	x	x
In Nat. Conf.	III, 107—Bede	x	x	x
In Nat. Conf.	CCSL 120: 603, l.331-604, l.366—Bede	x	x	x
In Nat. pl. Conf.	III, 109—Gregory	x	x	x
In Nat. Virg.	III, 122—Gregory	x	x	x
In Nat. Virg.	III, 121—Aug.	x	x	x
In Nat. Virg.	III, 123—Gregory	x		x
Dedic. eccles.	III, 127—Caesarius	x		x
Dedic. eccles.	III, 129—Bede	x		x

order, and texts from the continental Temporale and the Common of Saints appear in the English Sanctorale. The five pieces for Quadragesima illustrate the manner in which the English group differs from the continental scheme. As listed in Grégoire 2, items 74-84 in Paul the Deacon's Winter series cover Quadragesima, eleven in all; the English collections include only Grégoire items 78, 76, 74, 77, and 79 in that order. The entire Temporale in the English collections, however, encompasses only the first twenty-seven, or twenty-eight, of their items. Items 28-89, or 29-90, cover the Proper of Saints from St. Stephen through St. Andrew. The Sanctorale in the continental version of Paul the Deacon's homiliary thus is greatly augmented in the corresponding portion of the English version but, equally important, the organization of the continental homiliary has been vastly modified in the process.

As reconstructed by Grégoire, the collection of Paul the Deacon is arranged by the seasons, with only the *Commune Sanctorum* separated from the homilies for Sundays and feast days. If we focus on those pieces attributed to Paul's original homiliary, the extent of revision in our group of post-Conquest English MSS. is clear. First, the Western calendar dictates the order of all the materials in the English group excepting a misplaced selection in honor of John the Baptist.[53] Besides this fundamental adjustment, a selection to commemorate the nativity of St. Paul is used in the English Sanctorale to honor his Conversion. Similarly, a selection from the Common of Saints is used to honor St. Mark. The last group of texts in the English

---

[53] This Pseudo-Augustinian sermon on the Nativity of St. John the Baptist is II, 37 in Alan of Farfa's homiliary as described in Grégoire 1: 16-70. Although correctly rubricated for the feast it celebrates, the piece occurs in MS. Royal 2 C. III among texts for SS. Peter and Paul, many of which are not part of Paul the Deacon's homiliary.

collections is a fairly complete representation of the *Commune Sanctorum* in the continental homiliary. From the reconstructed series of thirty-four items, the English MSS. preserve twenty-one excluding the one reassigned to St. Mark, though again not in the original order.

As mentioned earlier, our group of English MSS. has forty-seven pieces drawn from sources outside Paul's reconstructed homiliary. Nine of these are traditionally associated with the continental homiliary, however, and are printed in the expanded version edited by Migne.[54] The nine include a homily for the Octave of the Assumption of Mary, the Purification of Mary, St. Peter's Chair, the Annunciation, the feast of St. James, the Vigil of St. Matthew, the feast of St. Michael, and All Saints (two). Additionally, our Temporale has one selection from Smaragdus and three pieces for Easter week found as well in the Carthusian homiliary, Grenoble MS. 32 (twelfth century), described by Etaix.[55] These are the lessons during nocturns for the last three days before Easter: a selection from the Lamentations of Jeremiah, followed by a portion of Augustine's commentary on Psalms, and closing with a few verses from the Pauline Epistles.[56] Our Sanctorale, however, draws from a greater variety of sources.

The most significant of these is the Roman homiliary of Alan of Farfa, from which appears a total of six sermons and homilies for five occasions: St. Stephen, the Annunciation, Peter and Paul, the Nativity of John the Baptist, and the Octave of Peter and Paul. Five pieces are found in another Roman homiliary attributed to Agimundus:[57] for the Conversion of St. Paul, SS. Peter and Paul, and the Assumption of Mary. Additional pieces in the Sanctorale come from a variety of collections, the most interesting being Rabanus Maurus for Bede's sermon on the Decollation of St. John; Gregory's Homilies in Ezekiel for the feasts of SS. Matthew and Luke; another homily by Gregory for St. Luke's day; a sermon by Caesarius and others on the Nativity of St. John, found in the homiliary of Fleury; and Augustine's homily for St. Stephen. The remaining selections are drawn primarily from commentaries on the Gospels by Leo, Jerome, Augustine, and Bede.

The most striking feature of the Sanctorale in the English homiliaries is the number of pieces commemorating SS. Peter and Paul, the early patrons of St. Augustine's, Canterbury, whose feast at 29 June had a secondary grading at Christ Church.[58] Altogether thirteen pieces are designated for this feast, from the vigil through the octave. The present group of MSS., there-

---

[54] PL 95:1159-92. For descriptions of the expanded version, see Smetana, "Paul the Deacon's Patristic Anthology," 87-89, and Grégoire 2: 426.

[55] Raymond Etaix, "L'Homéliaire Cartusien," *Sacris Erudiri*, 13 (1962): 67-112. These are items 19a-c, 20a-c, and 21a-c in MS. Grenoble 32 described in Etaix, 71-72.

[56] See Hughes, 61.

[57] Grégoire 2: 343-92.

[58] This was the highest grade assigned to a saint's day. See F. A. Gasquet and Edmund Bishop, *The Bosworth Psalter* (London, 1908), 72 and 94.

fore, might derive from a Canterbury original.[59] This would explain, perhaps, the lack of special emphasis on other patron saints in these collections. Worth noting, too, is the fact that our collections have been brought up to date with additional feasts for the Virgin, but no English saints have been added.

The Common of Saints shows further rearrangement of Paul's reconstructed collection. In our group of English MSS., as in the continental compilation, first place is given to commemorations for the apostles, but these are followed by an extensive group of materials for martyrs augmented by homilies drawn from Bede's commentaries. Our collection concludes then with Paul's materials for priests and confessors, which preceded those for martyrs in his own reconstructed scheme. Within the Common of Saints in the English MSS., Grégoire's item III, 107 for the Nativity of a Confessor is a variation of a text from one of the post-Carolingian homiliaries associated with Auxerre.[60] As this last example continues to demonstrate, the group of English MSS. to which the Rochester collection belongs has been influenced by continental texts outside the tradition of Paul the Deacon, and these external sources seem primarily to be Roman and French. Given the close ties among Canterbury, Rochester, and the Abbey of Bec in the decades after the Conquest, this type of homiliary might have been imported during that era, for in its continental influences it differs from certain other versions of Paul's homiliary found in England. But before exploring the question of relationships in further depth, we should examine the second remaining portion of Paul's homiliary as found in MSS. from Rochester, St. Augustine's, Canterbury, and Norwich set forth in Table 3.

The homiliary in Edinburgh N. L. MS. Adv. 18.2.4 from Rochester is copied on the first 198 folios of the codex in quires of 8 leaves now lacking signatures. It is followed on fol. 198r by verses on the utility of confession, and on fol. 198v by copies of two documents preserved in the *Textus Roffensis*, an account of a dispute between Bishop Gundulf and one Pichot, and a list of William I's benefactions to Rochester. On fol. 199v is a list of churches in Rome to which forty days of prayer are owed. The main hand of the homiliary is in the distinctive Rochester style of the first quarter of the twelfth century.[61] At 293 x 203 mm., the pages are smaller than those of MS. Royal 2 C. III, but the original volumes may have been similar in size, for the Edinburgh MS. has been cut down considerably in height as well as width. Contemporary entries in the top margins, for example, are often damaged

---

[59] Peter and Paul were heavily commemorated elsewhere in England, however. Thomas Rud's description of Durham Cathedral MS. A. III. 29, an eleventh-century version of Paul the Deacon's homiliary, lists a total of eleven pieces including two for the octave. See *Codicum Manuscriptorum Ecclesiae Cathedralis Dunelmensis Catalogus Classicus* (Durham, 1825), 46-56.

[60] Barré, 194.

[61] Among the features of the main hand are short, barely split ascenders and minims, and *g* with an angular tail balancing the body of the letter; Ker, *English Manuscripts in the Century after the Norman Conquest*, 32.

TABLE 3

		Harley 652	Camb. U.L. Ii. II. 19	Edinburgh NL Adv.18.24
Sabbato Sancto	II, 2—Bede	x	x	x
Sabbato Sancto	I, 108—Leo	x	x	
In die Paschae	II, 5—Gregory	x	x	x
In die Paschae	II, 3—Maximus	x	x	
In die Paschae	II, 4—Maximus	x	x	
In die Paschae	II, 6—Eusebius	x	x	
In die Paschae	AF II, 2—Ps. Aug.	x	x	
Fer. II	AF II, 3—Ps. Aug.	x		
Fer. II	AF II, 4—Ps. Aug.	x		
Fer. II	AF II, 5b—Eusebius	x		
Fer. II	PL47:1155-6—Ps. Aug.	x		
Oct. Paschae	AF II, 6—Caesarius	x		
Fer. II	AF II, 8—Ps. Max.	x		
Fer. II	PL38:1130-3—Aug.	x		
Fer. III	PL38:1133-8—Aug.	x		
Fer. III	II, 9—Gregory	x	x	x
Fer. III	II, 10—Bede	x	x	x
Fer. IV	II, 11—Gregory	x	x	x
Fer. V	II, 12—Gregory	x	x	x
Fer. VI	II, 13—Bede	x	x	x
Sabbato	PL76:1174-81—Gregory	x	x	x
Oct. Paschae	AF II, 5a—Jerome	x	x	
Dom. I post Paschae	II, 15—Gregory	x	x	x
Dom. I post Paschae	II, 20—Gregory	x	x	x
Dom. II	II, 21—Bede	x	x	x
Dom. III	II, 22—Bede	x	x	x
Dom. IV	II, 24—Bede	x	x	x
Fer. II in Roga.	II, 17—Maximus	x	x	
Fer. III	II, 19—Bede	x	x	x
Fer. IV	II, 18—Ps. Aug.	x	x	
Vig. Ascensionis	II, 25—Aug.	x	x	x
Ascension	II, 26—Leo	x	x	
Ascension	II, 27—Leo		x	
Ascension	II, 28—Gregory	x	x	x
Oct. Ascensionis	II, 29—Bede		x	x
Vig. Pentecostes	II, 30—Bede	x	x	x
Pentecost	II, 31—Leo	x	x	
Pentecost	II, 33—Gregory	x	x	x
Pentecost	II, 32—Leo		x	
Pentecost	II, 34—Leo	x	x	
Fer. II	CCSL 36:127, l.3-128, l.23—Aug.	x	x	x

TABLE 3 *(Continued)*

		Harley 652	Camb. U.L. Ii. II. 19	Edinburgh NL Adv.18.24
Fer. III	CCSL 36:390, l.15-392, l.2—Aug.	x	x	x
Fer. IV	CCSL 36:260, l.6-261, l.9—Aug.	x	x	x
Fer. V	PL110:271-3—Rab. Maur.	x	x	x
Fer. VI	II, 84—Bede	x	x	x
Sabbato	PL110:278-9—Rab. Maur.	x	x	x
Oct. Pentecostes	PL12:959-68—Eusebius	x	x	
Dom. I	II, 16—Bede	x		x
Dom. I	PL76:1301-12—Gregory	x	x	x
Dom. II	II, 38—Gregory	x	x	x
Dom. III	II, 39—Gregory	x	x	x
Dom. IV	PL102:368-70—Smaragdus	x	x	x
Dom. V	II, 57—Bede	x	x	x
Dom. VI	II, 58—Aug.	x	x	x
Dom. VII	II, 60—Bede	x	x	x
Dom. VIII	II, 61—Origen	x	x	x
Dom. IX	PL110:396-8—Rab. Maur.	x	x	x
Dom. X	PL76:1293-1301—Gregory	x	x	x
Dom. XI	II, 64—Bede	x	x	x
Dom. XII	II, 69—Bede	x	x	x
Nat. Domini	I, 20—Ps. Max.	x	x	
Nat. Domini	I, 21—Ps. Max.	x	x	
Nat. Domini	I, 10—Quoduultdeus	x	x	
Nat. Domini	I, 9—Ps. Aug.	x	x	
Nat. Domini	CCSL 77:7, l.1-9, l.38—Jerome	x	x	x
Nat. Domini	I, 24—Gregory	x	x	x
Nat. Domini	I, 25—Bede	x	x	x
Nat. Domini	I, 26—Bede	x	x	x
S. Stephani	I, 27—Fulgentius	x	x	
S. Stephani	I, 30—Jerome	x	x	x
S. Stephani	I, 28—Caesarius	x	x	
S. Iohannis ev.	I, 33—Bede	x	x	x
SS. Innoc.	I, 35—J. Chrysostom	x	x	
SS. Innoc.	I, 36—Bede	x	x	x
Oct. Nativ.	CCSL 120:44, l.1009-52, l.1328—Bede	x	x	x
Oct. Nativ.	CCSL 120:53, l.1332-56, l.1449—Bede	x	x	x
Oct. Nativ.	PL122:283-96—John Scotus	x	x	x
Dom. I post Oct.	I, 23—Ps. Max.	x	x	

by trimming. The MS. is more elaborately decorated than MS. Royal 2 C. III, with capitals in red, green, or purple beginning each piece, and one illuminated initial opening the collection on fol. 1r. This is a capital U decorated with men, fish, and birds. Extremely large initials with minor decoration occur at a few key points in the collection: Easter (fol. 4r), Advent (fols. 124v and 126v), and the Nativity (fols. 145v and 148r). Rubrics to individual pieces are in red rustic capitals. Because the Edinburgh MS. differs significantly from the other remaining English examples of the summer portion of Paul the Deacon's homiliary, its description will precede comparison with the related collections from St. Augustine's, Canterbury, and Norwich.

In the proportion of pieces drawn from Paul's reconstructed collection, and in their order of presentation, the homiliary in the Edinburgh MS. is actually closer to this continental tradition than is the one preserved in the Royal MS. Some fifty-nine of the eighty selections are from the collection as described in Grégoire 2. Two changes in organization are worth noting. Bede's homily for *Feria VI mensis septimi*, the Ember days in Trinity, is moved to the week following Pentecost, where the Edinburgh collection departs substantially from Paul in any event, with six of its ten pieces drawn from other sources, including two from Rabanus Maurus.[62] Also in this group, a homily from Bede traditionally assigned to the Octave of Easter serves for the Octave of Pentecost. The most obvious difference in our collection, as compared with Paul's and that in MS. Royal 2 C. III, is that each piece is preceded by a Gospel pericope. The terminology is not absolutely consistent, but most of the pieces are labeled *omelia*.

Although they are complementary in coverage of the liturgical calendar, the two Rochester collections are linked physically only by a series of marginal markings, black apostrophes, found frequently in the Edinburgh MS., and in MS. Royal 2 C. III at pieces for the vigil of St. Andrew and the nativity of martyrs. In the Royal MS. the marks serve to indicate the words of Christ, but they do not seem to have a consistent function in the later collection. The types of materials used to supplement or replace those attributed to Paul the Deacon also differ from those in the Royal collection. The present homiliary draws on the collections of Rabanus Maurus and Smaragdus for seven additional works, while only one piece, a homily by Gregory for Saturday of Easter week, occurs in the expanded version of Paul's homiliary printed by Migne. There are four additional selections from Gregory's homilies on the Gospels, as well as pieces drawn from Jerome's and Bede's commentaries on the Gospels.[63] The range of materials is narrower in the Edinburgh MS., then, and this collection lacks familiarity with the more recent continental collections associated with Auxerre, for exam-

---

[62] Three pieces are from Augustine's Commentary on John 3:16, 10:1, and 6:44. The two from Rabanus Maurus are PL 110:271-73 and 278-79, and the last, a selection from Eusebius (PL 12:959-68), is attributed in the MS. to Gregory.

[63] Gregory PL 76:1293-1301, 1239-46, 1282-93, 1211-13; Jerome CCSL 77:7-9:1-38; Bede CCSL 120:44-52:1019-1328, 53-56:1332-1449, 67-71:1905-2037.

TABLE 3 (Continued)

		Harley 652	Camb. U.L. Ii. II. 19	Edinburgh NL Adv.18.24
Dom. I post Oct.	CCSL 120:67, l.1905-71, l.2037—Bede	x	x	x
Circumcisione	CCSL 120:56, l.1452, excerpted—Bede	x	x	
Circumcisione	I, 40—Bede	x	x	x
Circumcisione	I, 37—Ps. Max.	x	x	
Vig. Epiphaniae	PL102:52-5—Smaragdus	x	x	x
Epiphania	Rd'A I, 34—Isaiah	x		
Epiphania	I, 42—Leo	x	x	
Epiphania	I, 48—Gregory	x	x	x
Epiphania	I, 43—Leo	x	x	
Dom. XIII	II, 63—Bede	x	x	x
Dom. XIV	II, 74—Bede	x	x	x
Dom. XV	II, 75—Bede	x	x	x
Dom. XVI	II, 76—Bede	x	x	x
Dom. XVII	II, 80—Bede	x	x	x
In ieiunio mensis VII	II, 82—Bede	x	x	x
In ieiunio mensis VII	II, 81—Leo	x	x	
In ieiunio mensis VII	II, 83—Leo	x	x	
In ieiunio mensis VII	II, 85—Leo	x	x	
Fer. VI	PL76:1239-46—Gregory	x	x	x
Sabbato	II, 86—Gregory	x	x	x
Dom. XVIII	Ostenditur ex hac interrogatione . . . sed difficile conquiescere.	x	x	x
Dom. XIX	II, 89—P. Chrysologus	x	x	x
Dom. XX	PL76:1282-93—Gregory	x	x	x
Dom. XXI	PL76:1211-13—Gregory	x	x	x
Dom. XXII	II, 94a—Jerome	x	x	x
Dom. XXIII	PL102:504-5—Smaragdus	x	x	x
Dom. XXIV	PL118:736-41—Haymo	x		
Dom. ante Adventum	I, 1—Aug.	x	x	x
Dom. II	I, 3—Gregory	x	x	x
Dom. III	I, 5—Gregory	x	x	x
Dom. III	I, 11—Bede	x	x	x
Dom. III	I, 12—Bede	x	x	x
Dom. III	I, 13—Gregory	x	x	x
Dom. IV	I, 8—Gregory	x	x	x
Vig. Nativitatis	I, 15—Ps. Origen	x	x	x
Nat. Domini	I, 16—Isidore	x	x	
Nat. Domini	I, 18—Leo	x	x	
Nat. Domini	AF II, 89—Leo	x		

TABLE 3 *(Continued)*

		Harley 652	Camb. U.L. Ii. II. 19	Edinburgh NL Adv.18.24
Nat. Domini	I, 17—Leo	x	x	
Nat. Domini	I, 19—Fulgentius	x	x	
Epiphania	I, 56—Leo	x	x	
Epiphania	I, 57—Leo	x	x	
Epiphania	I, 47—Fulgentius	x	x	
Epiphania	I, 45—Ps. Max.		x	
Epiphania	I, 53—Ps. Max.	x	x	
Epiphania	I, 46—Ps. Max.	x	x	
Epiphania	I, 50—Ps. Max.	x	x	
Epiphania	I, 51—Ps. Max.	x	x	
Epiphania	I, 52—Ps. Max.	x	x	
Epiphania	I, 54—Ps. Max.	x	x	
Epiphania	I, 44—Leo	x	x	
Epiphania	I, 58—Bede	x	x	x
Oct. Epiphaniae	I, 49—Bede	x	x	x
Dom. I	I, 59—Bede	x	x	x
Dom. II	I, 60—Bede	x	x	x
Dom. II	I, 61—Origen	x	x	x
Dom. II	I, 64—Origen	x	x	x

ple, on the one hand, and the Roman collections on the other, found in MS. Royal 2 C. III. Aside from the group of pieces substituted during the Ember fast following Pentecost, the greater number of additions occurs at the Octave of the Holy Innocents, where three new items are included for ferias of the octave.

As stated previously, there is little evidence beyond their complementary coverage of the liturgical year and certain marginal markings to suggest that the two Rochester portions of Paul the Deacon's homiliary are related directly. Likely, therefore, they represent two separate cycles. There is, in fact, paleographic evidence of different purposes for these collections. The pieces in MS. Royal 2 C. III usually are marked for lections. Beginning with the Gospel pericope when one is present, pieces are marked viiii-xii or, less frequently, i-viii, and even i-iii and i-xii, suitable for the divine office.[64] Again, these pieces vary in length, and a number do not have Gospel readings preceding them. By comparison, the collection in Edinburgh N. L. MS. Adv. 18.2.4 has no lections marked, has a Gospel pericope before each piece, and is generally regular in appearance and presentation of materials. The front page, however, is stained and rubbed, an indication that the MS. was exposed, perhaps even unbound for a time, as it might have been in the

---

[64] Hughes, 61-62.

cloister. Without lections, it would have been an appropriate volume for individual reading and study, though of course not precluded from use in services or other oral settings. Numerous marginal markings highlight passages for special attention, perhaps much as pointing fingers would do at a later date.

In BL MS. Harley 652 from St. Augustine's, Canterbury (late eleventh or early twelfth century), is a collection very closely related to that in MS. Edinburgh N. L. Adv. 18.2.4. MS. Harley 652 covers the same portion of the year but has 118 pieces as opposed to 59 in the Edinburgh MS. The difference in length is misleading, however, for the two collections share several runs of texts in identical order, the longest composed of 19 pieces from the first Sunday after the Octave of Pentecost through Feria IV of the Ember fast in Trinity. This group of texts includes the rearrangements in Paul's reconstructed order described previously; the interpolated selections from Gregory, Smaragdus, and Rabanus Maurus; and an unusual version of Bede's homily for the Ember fast in Trinity.[65]

It is possible that the collection in Edinburgh 18.2.4 was edited from a larger one such as is found in Harley 652. Another related collection intermediate between these, as shown in Table 3, occurs in Cambridge University Library MS. Ii. II. 19, a contemporary homiliary from Norwich.[66] Our homiliary from Rochester, however, is sufficiently different to prevent grouping it with the other two collections as an example of a distinctive English tradition. Although Cambridge U. L. Ii. II. 19 would have made a full companion volume to MS. Kk. IV. 13 from Norwich, described above, the Rochester volume probably did not serve such a function, as we have seen. A similar, but not identical, condensation of the summer portion of Paul's homiliary occurs in MS. Bodley 267, third quarter of the twelfth century, from Windsor,[67] which breaks off after the nineteenth Sunday after Pentecost. The existence of this volume is further indication that MS. Edinburgh N. L. 18.2.4. derives from a textual tradition separate from that found in MS. Royal 2 C. III, but again underlines the richness of the materials remaining from Rochester, where a remarkable range of texts has been preserved.

Contemporary homiliaries from other areas of England are more distantly related to the Rochester books. For example, Cambridge MSS. Pembroke College 23 and 24 are companion volumes from Bury St. Edmunds, copied in the eleventh century, that correspond roughly in coverage to the Rochester MSS. Royal 2 C. III and Edinburgh N. L. Adv. 18.2.4.[68] The Sanctorale in MS. Royal 2 C. III compares to Pembroke 24, which is entirely a collection of materials for the Proper and Common of Saints. Both follow Paul's reconstructed order closely with some rearrangement, particularly in

---

[65] "Loca rebus congruunt" as in MS. Vatican Lat. 8563, cited in Grégoire 2: 468.
[66] *Catalogue . . . University of Cambridge*, 3:388-93.
[67] Ker, *MLGB*, 203.
[68] Descriptions in M. R. James, *A Descriptive Catalogue of Manuscripts in the Library of Pembroke College, Cambridge* (Cambridge, 1905), 20-25.

the Common of Saints. The major difference between them is that MS. Royal 2 C. III contains additional selections for certain feasts, most notably for SS. Peter and Paul, drawn from a variety of continental sources, while the Pembroke MS. expands the number of feasts *per se*, with selections for SS. Nereus, Basilides, Gervasius, and others from the Roman calendar. Thus, in terms of coverage of the calendar of fixed feasts, the Bury Sanctorale is far more complete than either the reconstructed continental collection or the version of Paul's compilation found in MS. Royal 2 C. III. The portions of the Temporale found in the Edinburgh MS. and Pembroke 23, however, are more similar. Both MSS. include the summer portion of Paul's homiliary from Easter week to Advent, with at least nine identical supplementary pieces. For the Saturday after Easter, for example, both have Gregory's homily for that occasion as found in Migne's expanded version of Paul's work, and the two share a run of three homilies drawn from Bede's commentary on Luke for the Ember fast after Pentecost.

Another collection in Durham Cathedral MS. A.III.29, copied at Durham in the eleventh century, covers the same period of the year as MSS. Edinburgh NL. Adv. 18.2.4, Camb. U. L. Ii. II.19, Harley 652, and Pembroke College 23.[69] It is divided into a Temporale supplemented with the homilies of Gregory and a Sanctorale expanded with selections for Roman martyrs and English saints. No doubt there are other copies of collections representing the English tradition of Paul the Deacon's homiliary still to be identified, but again, only two fragmentary MSS. have been linked directly to Christ Church, Canterbury. It is clear from the collections attributed to Rochester, St. Augustine's, Canterbury, and Windsor, however, that two versions of Paul the Deacon's homiliary, one full and the other condensed, circulated in southeastern England, and that the full tradition was known at least as far as Norwich.

The third extant collection from Rochester is quite a different matter. This set of texts, preserved in Vatican MS. Lat. 4951, is a series of sermons for the Temporale (188), Sanctorale (16), and Common of Saints (18), arranged according to the calendar but not prefaced by Gospel pericopes. Physically this is the largest book of the three, now measuring some 334 x 251 mm. and containing 222 sermons on 217 folios. The MS. is quired in eights with signatures in small Roman numerals at the foot of the last verso, typical of Rochester work in the first decades of the twelfth century. It is copied throughout by one scribe, whose hand resembles closely that of the so-called partner of the *Textus Roffensis* scribe sometimes identified as Humphrey the precentor. Our scribe differs mainly in his lack of distinction between tailed *a* and *o*. He no doubt was part of the cadre, numbering at least a dozen according to Waller, who worked c. 1107-23 at Rochester.[70]

---

[69] The most complete description of Durham Cathedral MS. A.III.29 is in Rud, 46-56. See also Mynors, *Durham Cathedral Manuscripts*, 43.
[70] Waller, 84-126.

Contrary to published description, MS. Vatican Lat. 4951 cannot be termed a version of Paul the Deacon's homiliary (Table 4).[71] Of the 221 sermons in the collection, only 57 are connected with Paul's reconstructed homiliary, as opposed to 78 with Alan of Farfa's Roman homiliary.[72] Twenty-four pieces in our collection occur in both of these early homiliaries. To confirm the Roman influence, there are fifteen additional pieces characteristic of the Roman homiliary of Agimundus. This is not to say, however, that the Rochester collection is a copy of an ancient homiliary supplemented with later works. If so, it would resemble the two Rochester homiliaries described above, where an overall structure is followed in temporal order with occasional rearrangement, substitution, and augmentation of texts. In MS. Vatican Lat. 4951, to the contrary, blocks of sermons have been lifted from various collections including, besides Paul, Alan, and Agimundus, the homilies of Augustine, Pseudo-Augustine, and Caesarius of Arles. It seems that for each occasion the original compiler turned to sources at hand and copied a range of appropriate materials.

According to its rubrics, the Temporale in MS. Vatican Lat. 4951 is organized around major feast days and seasons; no Sundays or ferias are indicated. Extensive titles are given only for pieces on specific topics, such as Caesarius on the Ten Commandments and Ten Plagues, that do not fit in the temporal scheme and have not been drawn from the reconstructed collections of Paul the Deacon or Alan of Farfa. As evidence of the emphasis given to major feasts, twenty-two pieces are intended for the Nativity, including a block of seven from Paul, and blocks of three and four from Alan. Twenty-two pieces celebrate Epiphany, including thirteen from Paul and five from Alan, again drawn in blocks. Lesser homiliaries, too, contribute materials in groups. Following the selections for Lent is a group of materials on Old Testament and general subjects formerly attributed to Augustine, but now thought to be mainly the work of Caesarius. A group of four sermons from Augustine's Temporale is found amidst selections for Easter. Even pieces drawn from the Roman homiliary of Agimundus tend to occur together or in close proximity within the larger cycle. A group of four pieces, for example, is included under the general rubric for Pentecost.

The Sanctorale seems to have been compiled similarly, but since it contains only sixteen pieces, the pattern is less developed. A block of six pieces covering John the Baptist, Peter and Paul, and Laurence is drawn from the homiliary attributed to Alan of Farfa, but the piece for John is actually the last in a series of three for the saint in our Rochester collection. It seems as if the compiler turned to a homiliary based on Alan's work for a selection on St. John, and then continued on with the materials he found there. On the

---

[71] Salmon, 58, states the following: "Type anglais, Paul Diacre complété, entre autre, par une collection de Césaire d'Arles."

[72] For background to Alan of Farfa's collection, see Edoardo Hosp, "Il Sermonario di Alano di Farfa," *Ephemerides Liturgicae*, 50 (1936): 375-83, and 51 (1937): 210-41, and Grégoire 1: 17-70.

TABLE 4

Vatican Lat. 4951	
De Incarnatione Verbi	AF II, 89—Leo
Nat. Domini	I, 17—Leo
Nat. Domini	I, 19—Fulgentius
Nat. Domini	I, 20—Ps. Max.
Nat. Domini	I, 21—Ps. Max.
Nat. Domini	I, 16—Isidore
Nat. Domini	I, 18—Leo
Nat. Domini	I, 9—Ps. Aug.
Nat. Domini	AF I, 2a—Ps. Aug.
Nat. Domini	AF I, 4a—Aug.
Nat. Domini	AF I, 7—Ps. Aug.
Nat. Domini	PL39:1992—Ps. Aug.
Nat. Domini	Ottobeuren 15—Ps. Aug.
Nat. Domini	PL38:1009-11—Aug.
Nat. Domini	CCSL 101:15-20—Eusebius Gall.
Nat. Domini	AF I, 10e—Ps. Aug.
Nat. Domini	AF I, 10b—Aug.
Nat. Domini	AF I, 10d—Aug.
Nat. Domini	AF I, 10a—Aug.
Nat. Domini	AF I, 5—Ps. Aug.
Nat. Domini	CCSL 138:102-8—Leo
Nat. Domini	I, 23—Ps. Max.
Nat. Domini	I, 22—Ps. Aug.
S. Stephani	I, 27—Fulgentius
S. Stephani	I, 28—Caesarius
S. Stephani	AF I, 21a—Ps. Aug.
S. Stephani	PL38:1431-4—Aug.
S. Stephani	AF I, 17—Aug. ?
Nat. Innocentium	AF I, 27—Caesarius
Nat. Innocentium	AF I, 28—Ps. Aug.
Nat. Innocentium	AF I, 29—Ps. Aug.
Nat. Innocentium	AF I, 30a—Ps. Max.
Nat. Innocentium	I, 35—J. Chrysostom
De kal. ianuarii	Ottobeuren 23—Caesarius
De kal. ianuarii	Ottobeuren 24—Caesarius
De circumcisione dom.	I, 37—Ps. Max.
In epiphania dom.	I, 42—Leo
In epiphania dom.	I, 43—Leo
In epiphania dom.	I, 56—Leo
In epiphania dom.	I, 57—Leo
In epiphania dom.	I, 44—Leo
In epiphania dom.	I, 47—Fulgentius

TABLE 4 *(Continued)*

Vatican Lat. 4951	
In epiphania dom.	I, 45—Ps. Max.
In epiphania dom.	PL57:289-92—Maximus
In epiphania dom.	I, 46—Ps. Max.
In epiphania dom.	I, 50—Ps. Max.
In epiphania dom.	I, 51—Ps. Max.
In epiphania dom.	I, 52—Ps. Max.
In epiphania dom.	I, 54—Ps. Max.
In epiphania dom.	I, 55—Ps. Max.
In epiphania dom.	CCSL 104:786-8—Caesarius[1]
In epiphania dom.	AF I, 40—Aug.
In epiphania dom.	Fleury 29—Ps. Aug.
In epiphania dom.	AF I, 37—Aug.
In epiphania dom.	AF I, 39—Aug.
In epiphania dom.	AF I, 41—Aug.
In epiphania dom.	AF I, 42a—Ps. Aug.
In epiphania dom.	Toledo Add. 4—unknown
In Quadrag.	I, 74—Leo
In Quadrag.	I, 77—Leo
In Quadrag.	I, 79—Leo
In Quadrag.	I, 78—Leo
In Quadrag.	AF I, 70—Caesarius
In Quadrag.	PL38:1044-6—Aug.
In Quadrag.	AF I, 54—Ps. Aug.
In Quadrag.	AF I, 55—Maximus
In Quadrag.	CCSL 104:641-5—Caesarius
In Quadrag.	AF I, 52—Caesarius
In Quadrag.	AF I, 67—Jerome
In Quadrag.	AF I, 68—Ps. Aug.
In Quadrag.	PL38:1046-7—Aug.
In Quadrag.	PL39:2029-30—Ps. Aug.
In Quadrag.	AF I, 69—Ps. Leo
In Quadrag.	PLS 2:1190-1—Ps. Aug.
De muliere chananaea	Wilmart 19—J. Chrysostom
De iacob et ioseph	CCSL 103:365-9—Caesarius
De ioseph	PL39:1770-3—Ps. Aug.
De dec. verbis legis et dec. plagis	CCSL 103:407-13—Caesarius
De S. Gedeone	CCSL 103:487-91—Caesarius
De Heliseo	CCSL 103:535-8—Caesarius
De conpetentibus	CCSL 104:807-12—Caesarius[2]
De symbolo	PL39:2191-3—Caesarius

[1] Toledo Add. 5.
[2] Toledo Add. 10a.

TABLE 4 *(Continued)*

Vatican Lat. 4951	
De oratione dom.	CCSL 104:602-4—Caesarius
In passione dom.	I, 98—Leo
In passione dom.	I, 100—Leo
In passione dom.	I, 101—Leo
In passione dom.	I, 102—Leo
In passione dom.	I, 103—Leo
In passione dom.	I, 106—Leo
In passione dom.	I, 107—Leo
In passione dom.	PLS 2:1191-3—Ps. Aug.
In passione dom.	PL57:343-7—Maximus
In passione dom.	PL39:2053-5—Ps. Aug.
In passione dom.	Fleury 41—Severinus
In passione dom.	I, 89—Maximus
In cena dom.	Fleury 38—Caesarius
In cena dom.	I, 104—Leo
In passione dom. Feria VI	AF I, 91—J. Chrysostom
De sepultura dom.	PL39:2204-6—Ps. Aug.
In sabbato sancto	I, 108—Leo
In die Paschae	II, 3—Maximus
In die Paschae	II, 4—Maximus
In die Paschae	II, 6—Eusebius
In die Paschae	AF II, 2—Ps. Aug.
In die Paschae	AF II, 3—Ps. Aug.
In die Paschae	AF II, 4—Ps. Aug.
In die Paschae	AF II, 5b—Eusebius
In die Paschae	PL47:1155-6—Ps. Aug.
In die Paschae	AF II, 5a—Jerome
In die Paschae	AF II, 6—Caesarius
In die Paschae	AF II, 7a—Caesarius
In die Paschae	AF II, 8—Ps. Max.
In die Paschae	PL38:1130-3—Aug.
In die Paschae	PL38:1133-8—Aug.
In die Paschae	Wolfenbüttel 44—Aug.
In die Paschae	PL38:1171-9—Aug.
In die Paschae	AF II, 9—Aug.
In die Paschae	AF II, 11—Aug.
In die Paschae	PLS 2:475-8—Aug.
In die Paschae	PLS 2:478-80—Aug.
In die Paschae	Vienne 25—Aug. ?
In die Paschae	PLS 2:1195-6—Ps. Aug.
In die Paschae	PLS 2:558-62—Aug.
In die Paschae	Rd'A I, 37—Aug.

TABLE 4 (Continued)

Vatican Lat. 4951	
In die Paschae	Rd'A I, 40—Aug.
In die Paschae	Rd'A I, 41—Aug.
Ad. nov. baptizatos	Wolfenbüttel 27—Aug.
Ad. nov. baptizatos	Rd'A I, 65—Aug.
Ad. nov. baptizatos	PL46:827-8—Aug.
Ad. nov. baptizatos	Wolfenbüttel 53—Aug.
Ad. nov. baptizatos	PLS 2:481-2—Aug.
Ad. nov. baptizatos	PL39:1560-5—Aug.
Ad. nov. baptizatos	Rd'A I, 35—Aug.
Ad. nov. baptizatos	Quod lectum est de sancto evangelio commendat . . .
De Pascha	PL39:1851-3—Aug.
De Pascha	PLS 2:1196-8—Ps. Aug.
Resurrectio dom.	Mai 1:174-7—Aug.
Resurrectio dom.	PLS 2:482-3—Aug.
Resurrectio dom.	Rd'A I, 42—Aug.
Resurrectio dom.	PLS 2:1201-5—Ps. Aug.
Resurrectio dom.	Rd'A I, 38—Ps. Leo
Resurrectio dom.	Deus rex noster ante . . . partem habere cum Christo.
Nat. Petri et Pauli	Rd'A I, 80—Aug.
Nat. Petri et Pauli	PL38:799-800—Aug.
Ad. nov. baptizatos	Nemo nas faciamur acturi . . .
Oct. Paschae	AF II, 12—Eusebius
Oct. Paschae	AF II, 14—Ps. Aug.
Oct. Paschae	Rd'A I, 46—Ps. Aug.
Oct. Paschae	Toledo 30—Ildefonse
Oct. Paschae	PLS 2:483-8—Aug.
Oct. Paschae	Rd'A I, 45—Aug.
Oct. Paschae	PLS 2:489-94—Aug.
Oct. Paschae	Rd'A I, 47—Ps. Aug.
Oct. Paschae	CCSL 103:421-24—Caesarius
Oct. Paschae	Ecce karissimi fratres dies sanctificaties ac venerabilis . . .
Oct. Paschae	CCSL 104:828-31—Caesarius[1]
Oct. Paschae	PL39:1851-3—Ps. Aug.
Oct. Paschae	AF II, 18—Caesarius
Oct. Paschae	AF II, 19—Caesarius
Oct. Paschae	CCSL 103:588-9—Caesarius
In Rogationibus	II, 17—Maximus
De ieiunio	II, 18—Ps. Aug.
De Ascensione dom.	II, 26—Leo
De Ascensione dom.	II, 27—Leo
De Ascensione dom.	AF II, 23—Eusebius

[1]Toledo 43.

TABLE 4 *(Continued)*

Vatican Lat. 4951	
De Ascensione dom.	AF II, 21—Aug.
De Ascensione dom.	PLS 2:494-7—Aug.
De Ascensione dom.	PLS 2:527-31 and 704-8—Aug.
De Ascensione dom.	Fleury 58—Aug.
De Pentecoste	Rd'A I, 62—Aug.
De Pentecoste	Rd'A I, 60—Ps. Aug.
De Pentecoste	Rd'A I, 61—Aug.
De Pentecoste	Rd'A I, 64—Aug.
De Pentecoste	Clavis 233—Ps. Aug.
De Pentecoste	Ad id quid scriptus est in evangelio . . .
De Pentecoste	PL38:1229-31—Aug.
De medio Pentecostes	Clavis 234—Ps. Aug.
In die Pentecostes	AF II, 36—Ps. Aug.
In die Pentecostes	Scientate vestrae . . .
In die Pentecostes	AF II, 32—Ps. Aug.
In die Pentecostes	II, 31—Leo
In die Pentecostes	II, 32—Leo
In die Pentecostes	II, 34—Leo
De S. Trinitate	PL12:959-68—Eusebius
De ieiunio vii mensis	II, 81—Leo
De ieiunio vii mensis	II, 83—Leo
De ieiunio vii mensis	II, 85—Leo
S. Vincent	PL38:1255-7—Aug.
S. Vincent	PL39:2095-8—Ps. Aug.
S. Vincent	PL38:1257-68—Aug.
Conv. Pauli	AF II, 58—Ps. Aug
S. Iohannis bapt.	CCSL 103:143-7—Caesarius[1]
S. Iohannis bapt.	PLS 2:496-9—Aug.
S. Iohannis bapt.	AF II, 37—Ps. Aug.
SS. Petri et Pauli	AF II, 51—Maximus
SS. Petri et Pauli	AF II, 52—Maximus
S. Laurentii	AF II, 63—Maximus
S. Laurentii	AF II, 59—Leo
S. Laurentii	AF II, 60—Ps. Aug.
Assump. Mariae	PL30:122-42—Ps. Jerome[2]
Decollatio Iohannis bapt.	PL38:1406-7—Aug.
Decollatio Iohannis bapt.	II, 71—P. Chrysologus
Decollatio Iohannis bapt.	II, 72—J. Chrysostom
Nat. Martyrorum	AF II, 93—Maximus

[1] Toledo Add. 19.
[2] Actually Paschasius Radbertus; see Albert Ripberger, *Der Pseudo-Hieronymus-Brief IX "Cogitis Me," Spicilegium Friburgense*, v. 9 (Freiburg, 1962).

TABLE 4 *(Continued)*

Vatican Lat. 4951	
Nat. Martyrorum	PL57:705-8—Maximus
De martyribus et inimicis diligendis	AF II, 94—Caesarius
De diligendis inimicis	CCSL 104:873-7—Caesarius[1]
Nat. conf. et episc.	Gaudete dilectissimi fratres in domino . . .
Nat. conf. et episc.	II, 103—Ps. Max.
In Nat. pl. conf.	AF II, 104—Ps. Max.
Ordinatio episc.	CCSL 104:911-13—Caesarius
Ordinatio episc.	CCSL 104:918-21—Caesarius
Decem virgines	PL38:573-80—Aug.
Quales sint Christiani boni . . .	CCSL 103:76-8—Caesarius[2]
De expetenda magis . . .	CCSL 103:224-7—Caesarius[3]
Sermo ad eos qui in festivitatie	CCSL 103:240-4—Caesarius
Sermo ad eos qui auguria . . .	CCSL 103:235-9—Caesarius
Sermo ad eos qui defectum . . .	Ipsi videtes fratres karissimi quod mea non cessat . . .[4]
Sermo de castitate . . .	CCSL 103:195-200—Caesarius
Sermo de martyrio . . .	CCSL 103:179-84—Caesarius
Dedic. eccles.	II, 127—Caesarius

[1]Toledo 8.
[2]Toledo 63.
[3]Toledo 65.
[4]Attributed to Augustine in the MS.

other hand, he drew two of three pieces for the Decollation of John from Paul the Deacon. The pieces for the Common of Saints come primarily from Caesarius of Arles, eleven of the eighteen, with additional selections from the homiliary of Alan of Farfa, from Augustine, and from Maximus of Turin.

In MS. Vatican Lat. 4951, then, we have a composite cycle of sermons, heavily indebted to Roman homiliaries, yet influenced considerably by other important collections. There are, however, no pieces from the expanded version of Paul the Deacon, nor any from the homiliaries of Haymo, Rabanus or Smaragdus. Further, there are no selections included from Bede or Gregory the Great. In this last feature our collection again shows an affinity with the earlier homiliary of Alan of Farfa, where Bede and Gregory are included only once, and the favored authors are Augustine, Pseudo-Augustine, and Caesarius. Given the traditions behind it, MS. Vatican Lat. 4951 must be a twelfth-century copy incorporating a much older continental sermon collection. It has not undergone detectable localizing influence, however, nor is it possible to trace a relationship to Bec, from which no homiliaries survive. Even its intended use is questionable. Only two pieces are marked for lections, a sermon for Trinity Sunday drawn from a letter of Eusebius (six lections) and a lengthy piece for the Assumption of Mary divided into seven series of three lections each followed by two series of eight. The source of the latter piece is the spurious letter of Jerome to Paul and Eustochius, now attributed to Paschasius Radbertus. These materials for Trinity and the Assumption of Mary are marked initially with a large colored and decorated capital, but they share this feature with certain other pieces for important occasions so marked within the codex. The most impressive of these capitals signals the beginning of the Sanctorale on fol. 173v, at the opening of Augustine's sermon for the nativity of St. Vincent.

Similar to the homiliary in the earlier MS. Royal 2 C. III, the collection in the Vatican MS. is divided into a Temporale and a Sanctorale such that it never was a two-volume set comparable to those described in the medieval catalogues of Rochester Priory. As different as they are in the sources and presentation of their materials, the two collections share certain blocks of texts, as well as three isolated ones, that suggest a distant relationship between them. All but one of the thirteen shared items are found in the homiliary of Alan of Farfa, and seven of these are used also by Paul the Deacon. These same seven occur together in the largest block, sermons by Leo for Passion Week, copied in identical order in our two MSS. as follows: I, 74a; I, 74b; I, 75b; I, 73; I, 76 in Alan of Farfa's homiliary as described in Grégoire 1. In MS. Royal 2 C. III, four pieces intervene, and the block continues with I, 77b and I, 77c. The run of seven is uninterrupted in MS. Vatican Lat. 4951, and they are all grouped under one rubric for Leo on the Passion, whereas a rubric "De Passione Domini" is repeated four times in MS. Royal 2 C. III. These pieces by Leo must have been traditional for Passion Week in England. But the texts of the pieces, when compared, do not seem to have been copied one from another. The later MS. 4951 has better readings in certain instances than does Royal 2 C. III and in places they seem to have been corrected to agree with each other (or a common tradition).

There is better evidence of relationship, limited in scope, in a block of three pieces for St. Stephen—I, 21a and I, 17 from Alan of Farfa separated by a sermon from Augustine—that occurs in both Rochester collections. The most striking feature about this block of materials is its setting in the different MSS. It opens the Sanctorale in MS. Royal 2 C. III, a version of Paul the Deacon, and is followed by no further materials for the saint. In MS. Vatican Lat. 4951, on the other hand, the block occurs in the Temporale, and follows two pieces on St. Stephen from Paul's reconstructed homiliary. When we recall the general method behind the compilation of the collection found in Vatican Lat. 4951, that is, groups of sermons drawn from a variety of sources for specified occasions, we must speculate whether the three items for Stephen were drawn from MS. Royal 2 C. III or from a related source. The latter seems more likely, because again Vatican Lat. 4951 shows readings superior to the earlier texts. Indeed, it can be said of all thirteen texts shared by the two Rochester collections that the better version normally is the later, so direct copying cannot have taken place.

The source of the collection in MS. Vatican Lat. 4951 remains a mystery. The materials are so unusual, yet so well preserved, that Mai, Morin, and other editors have often drawn on it for their editions of Augustine, Pseudo-Augustine, and Caesarius. There appears to be no comparable collection surviving in England, nor is there any particular indication that the materials were compiled there. The tenuous connection between this MS. and English versions of Paul the Deacon's homiliary could, in fact, have continental origins. That is, both traditions may derive from continental collections such that their commonalities are simply coincidental. If so, the excellent state of the texts in Vatican Lat. 4951 may attest to its being a relatively recent import, as yet uncorrupted by successive recopying. Alternatively, the collection could be copied from a well-preserved book at a neighboring foundation, perhaps in Canterbury, where continental connections remained strong and a variety of resources was available through the twelfth century.

Despite the unavoidable need to conjecture about sources and origins, one feature is clear: the Latin homiliaries acquired by and for Rochester do not show the same type of localizing influence as do the Old English collections. These homiliaries have not been altered in any detectable manner to suit Rochester observances or any other identifiable needs, other than a possible emphasis on SS. Peter and Paul. They are simply a selection of basic monastic texts to cover the feasts of the Western calendar. The contrast between the two groups of homiliaries, Latin and Old English, thus could hardly be more striking. We must imagine a community of monks whose lives centered on rituals supported by reading and study of Latin texts, yet who found need for vastly simplified teaching materials in the language of the laity. A cathedral priory serving also as the parish church must have had obligations requiring both types of materials. Although it is doubtful that the monks had direct contact with the laity, the Old English collections could have served a variety of purposes, from preaching to the instruction of young students. The presence of localized materials underlines the immediacy of the contexts for which they were intended, and the understanding that the intended audience had needs quite different from the monks. From all indications, Rochester was not unusual in preserving Old English homiletic texts for such purposes in the decades after the Conquest. Christ Church, Canterbury, certainly did so, and St. Augustine's had the resources to meet whatever needs it had in this area.

From the surviving books, it appears that Rochester was particularly adept at balancing an Anglo-Saxon heritage and all that it implied, with the need to acquire continental texts in support of its Benedictine affiliation. The monks used Old English materials as reminders of Rochester's glorious past at the same time that they secured a monastic library for their foundation and pursued the life of a monastic priory. The paradox of independence and conformity seems to have energized the monks of St. Andrew's in several spheres of activity, most obviously the production and acquisition of books. Now, however, the Rochester manuscripts provide most of the evidence for the traditions and relationships which once sustained its scriptorium and library.

V. CONCLUSION

One of the most dramatic events in post-Conquest monasticism is celebrated by the monk Eadmer in his biography of St. Anselm.[1] There Eadmer relates the skepticism of Archbishop Lanfranc and other Norman clergy toward local saints venerated by the English, and cites in particular an incident where Lanfranc expressed doubts about the martyrdom of St. Elphege of Canterbury. Lanfranc drew a distinction between dying in the name of Christ and choosing death over enforced penury to one's followers as Elphege did. In response, Anselm defended Elphege so successfully that, soon thereafter, Lanfranc commissioned a hymn in celebration of Canterbury's martyr to the Vikings. The hymn and a later *Life* and *Translation* of St. Elphege were written by Osbern (d. 1093), a monk of Christ Church, marking the beginning of post-Conquest Canterbury hagiography.[2] Charming as it is, this story has direct implications for our understanding of developments in the scriptorium and library of Rochester Cathedral Priory.

Monks from the Norman Abbey of Bec arrived soon after the Conquest to establish the new Benedictine foundation at Rochester, beginning an era when its relationship to Christ Church was so close as to be symbiotic. Under the leadership of Bishop Gundulf, the monks borrowed essential books and otherwise followed the lead of Canterbury in developing their own scriptorium, library, and monastic community on the Norman model. By the early decades of the twelfth century, however, their successors were collecting and producing materials reflective of the Anglo-Saxon heritage of the see. They even produced a new copy of the Vulgate text adopted by the first Rochester monks from Christ Church, a text that had been available at Canterbury, as far as we know, from the late tenth century. Thus it seems that a transformation in attitude toward things Anglo-Saxon, parallel to that effected by Anselm at Canterbury, occurred at Rochester, and led to the production and acquisition of certain texts such as we have examined in the foregoing study. In broader context, Anselm was arguing that service to God in England reflected the particular nature of that country's history, and should be celebrated, not discredited, for its instructive value to those coming afterward and for its evidence of God's interest in the English nation. His ideas echo the theme of Bede's *Historia Ecclesiastica*, which the Norman monks certainly knew. Whether by a conscious effort or not, the monks of

---

[1] Ed. Southern, 51-53.
[2] R. W. Southern, *St. Anselm and His Biographer* (Cambridge, 1963), 250.

Rochester learned to appreciate, and hence to use, materials from the Anglo-Saxon period as they worked to establish an identity for their priory.

At Rochester such a task was especially difficult because there appears to have been so little continuity between the Anglo-Saxon and Norman foundations. Its Anglo-Saxon charters provided a sketchy endowment on which to build, but the major acquisitions of property, the buildings, and library resulted from the efforts of Gundulf and his immediate successors. The compilation of the *Textus Roffensis* indicates that the monks tried to anchor their foundation in the Anglo-Saxon past as a way of defining its identity. At the same time, they continued a close relationship to Christ Church through their Norman bishops. They adopted a common Vulgate text and shared in the circulation of Latin homiliaries from the area. In the process, they were able to develop essential resources such as the library and buildings in imitation of Canterbury while maintaining a certain independence in western Kent. The evidence for this independence appears not only in variations of Canterbury styles, but also in the locations of properties, and even in diocesan observances surviving into the fifteenth century. Calendars from that period indicate that two early Anglo-Saxon bishops of Rochester, Romanus and Ithamar, were commemorated exclusively in the Rochester diocese.[3]

Although its sources and styles usually were derivative of Christ Church, Canterbury, in particular, Rochester's scriptorium was capable of producing exceptionally fine books such as the early thirteenth-century illuminated bestiary in British Library MS. Royal 12 F. XIII. The independent spirit that continued to develop throughout the twelfth century was productive in other ways as well. Despite ongoing disputes with the bishops over monastic properties, and with the archbishop of Canterbury over the right to elect their own bishop, the monks of Rochester finally were able to win their cases and take control of the foundation in the early thirteenth century.[4] Quite simply, the monks had little capital other than the priory's Anglo-Saxon heritage and the legacy of Gundulf and his immediate successors. The monks seem to have felt their situation keenly, and to have bent every effort toward rendering the priory secure from threats to its independence.

At the height of its energy, the priory produced the *Textus Roffensis*, a document that illustrates its dependence on Canterbury for texts and materials concomitantly with a demonstration of its separate identity. There is no question that the foundation at Rochester was shaped by its neighbors to the south. But the evidence also shows that the lesser foundation was able to define itself in the process, much as a child, given the proper nurturing, develops independently of the parent. The delicacy of the situation cannot be overestimated, yet it illustrates again how valuable the surviving books from Rochester can be in reconstructing the sources and circulation of texts

---

[3] Mary P. Richards, "Some Fifteenth-Century Calendars for Rochester Diocese," *Archaeologia Cantiana*, 102 (1985): 71-85.
[4] Oakley, 50, 57.

in southeastern England. In examining the struggles of a rather poor and undistinguished cathedral priory, we can receive insights into English monastic life as it was experienced in the decades after the Conquest.

The foregoing chapters make clear that Rochester had relatively little in common with the great cathedral priories and monastic foundations outside Kent. Its library was built from local resources for the most part, and its properties were not far-flung. It did not have a distinguished ecclesiastical heritage to build on, as for instance did Winchester and Durham, nor did it have a celebrated saint other than Paulinus, whose major commemorations in any case were in the south of England, with the exception of York. It never approached Bury St. Edmunds in size or influence and, as we have seen, it even lagged behind the Christ Church cell at Dover in respect to the size of its library. Rochester had an active scriptorium in the twelfth century, but its books ordinarily were available in single copies, and its endowments could support only sixty monks at best. This situation surely caused Rochester to rely on local libraries for texts and, ultimately, enabled it to make modest contributions to the circulation of manuscripts in southeastern England.

A study of book production at Rochester, then, contributes most to an understanding of Kentish monasticism in the post-Conquest era. As we have seen, the books produced there have a distinct textual heritage limited, ordinarily, to the region. There is no question that the quality of texts was extremely important to Canterbury and Rochester, and that a significant effort was made to bring texts into agreement with each other. The monks at Rochester found ways to participate in the important intellectual and spiritual work of Christ Church, Canterbury, without being absorbed into the larger enterprise. The duality of their accomplishment continues to enlighten the present-day study of medieval monasticism.

INDEX

Ap, 51
Adam of Balsham, 17
Adam of Cobham, 17
Ælfred, king of Wessex (871-899), 1, 45
Ælfred-Ine, laws of, 45, 47-50
Ælfric, abbot of Eynsham (1005-c. 1010), 87-90, 92, 93, 94
Ælfstan, bishop of Rochester (964-965), 55
Æthelberht, king of Kent (560-616), ix, 45, 49, 53, 54, 57
Æthelberht, laws of, 45, 49
Æthelred I, king of Wessex (866-871), 54
Æthelred II, king of England (978-1016), 49, 55, 94
Æthelstan, laws of, 49-51
Æthelwulf, king of Wessex (839-855), 54, 55
Agimundus: Roman homiliary, 102
Ailred of Rievaulx, 19
Alan of Farfa's homiliary, 101, 102, 111, 117, 118
Alberic, 10
Alcuin, 71, 72, 76, 86
Alcuin Bible, 71, 75
Alcuin:
  De dialectica, 9, 10, 15
  De trinitate, 8
  De virtutibus et vitiis, 85, 93
Alexander the cantor, donor to the Rochester library, 17-19
Alexander of Hales: *Summa*, 20
Alexander the precentor, 13, 16, 19, 42, 78, 79
Amalarius: *De officiis divinis*, 9
Ambrose, 4, 7, 8, 14
Ambrose:
  De fide, 9
  De mysteriis, 9
  De officiis, 9
  Exposition of Luke, 9
  Hexameron, 9
  tracts on virginity, 9
Ambrosius Autpertus, 15
Ambrosius Autpertus: *De conflictu vitiorum atque virtutem*, 9
Anselm, archbishop of Canterbury (1093-1114), 8, 10, 20, 44, 58, 94, 121
Anselm:
  Cur Deus Homo, 10
  De conversatione monachorum, 8
  De eterna beatitudine, 8
Apollonius of Tyre, 17
Arator, 17
Aristotle, 20

Aristotle:
  Organon, 18
  Rhetorica ad herennium, 18
Arnost, bishop of Rochester (1175-1176), 3
Ascelin, bishop of Rochester (1142-1148), 17
Augustine of Hippo, 4, 7, 8, 13-15, 18, 19, 102, 117-20
Augustine:
  commentary on Genesis, 14
  commentary on I-II Corinthians, 14
  commentary on John, 14, 108
  commentary on Psalms, 12, 102
  commentary on Romans, 14
  Confessiones, 9
  Contra faustum manicheum, 12
  De civitate dei, 8
  De doctrina christiana, 8
  De trinitate, 12
  Homily for St. Stephen, 102
  monastic rule, 9
  Retractationes, 9
Auxerre, 103, 106

Baldwin, archbishop of Canterbury (1185-1192), 13
Bartholomeus: *Practica*, 18
Bec, Norman abbey of, 3, 4, 5, 7, 49, 69, 94, 103, 117, 121
Becwæp, 47, 49
Bede, 7, 10, 14, 15, 45, 103, 104, 107-109, 117
Bede:
  (ascribed) *Vita beati Fursei*, 19
  commentaries on Acts, Apocalypse, Mark, Nehemiah, Ezra, Tobias, 9
  De aequinoctio, 9
  De arte metrica, 9, 10
  De schematibus, 9, 10
  De tabernaculo Dei, 9
  De temporibus, 9, 10
  Historia Ecclesiastica, 9, 44, 45, 89, 121
  Martyrologium, 9
  metrical life of St. Cuthbert, 9
  Sermon on the Decollation of St. John, 102
Boethius, 17
Bromley, Kent, 56
Bull of Eugenius III, 59
Bury Bible, 79
Bury St. Edmunds, 84, 96, 109, 123

Caen, Norman abbey of, 3
Caesarius of Arles, 102, 117
Carilef Bible, 68

Cassiodorus:
  Collationes, 10
  Institutiones, 10
Cato, 17
Charlemagne, 85
Charles the Bald, 63
Christ Church, Canterbury, ix, x, 3-8, 10, 11, 21, 44, 47, 48, 56-59, 61-63, 66, 68, 70, 71, 77-78, 81, 83-85, 86, 88, 94-96, 102, 110, 119-23
Cicero: De officiis, 18
Cluny, 12
Cnut, laws of, 47, 48
Codex Cavensis, 73
Coenwulf, king of Mercia (796-821), 55
Constantine of Monte Cassino: Viaticus, 18
Corbie, Norman abbey of, 73, 74, 76
Coronation Charter of Henry I, 52
Cuthred, king of Kent (798-807), 55

Danelaw, 50
Dares: History of the Trojan Wars, 10, 19
De accusatoribus, 48, 49
Defensor: Liber Scintillarum, 9
De miraculis Britanniae, 19
Dioscorides, 18
Distichs of Cato, 94
Domesday, 57
Donatus, 17
Dover Priory, 7, 11, 21, 42, 48, 62, 68, 123
Durham, 69, 76, 84, 96, 123
Dynamides, 18

Eadgar, king of England (959-975), 55
Eadgar, laws of, 48
Eadmer:
  Life of Anselm, 20
  Life of Herlewin of Bec, 20
Eadmund I, king of Wessex (939-946), king of York (944-946), 54
Eadmund I, laws of, 51
Eadric, laws of, 49
Eadward, laws of, 49, 50
Eadward and Guthrum, laws of, 51
Ecgberht, king of Kent (765-780), 54
Ely, 12
Ephraim the Syrian: De compunctione cordis, 9
Episcopal lists, 47, 52
Ernulf, bishop of Rochester (1114-1124), 5, 7, 10, 11, 17, 43, 45, 58, 59
Ernulf: De incestis conjugibus, 19
Eusebius, 4, 10, 106, 116
Exeter, 3, 70, 90

Fawkham, Kent, 56
Felixstowe, Walton, Kent (cell of Rochester), 18, 42, 58
Flavius, bishop of Constantinople, 95

Gepyncpo, 51
Genealogies of English kings, 47

Gervase of Canterbury, 17
Gilbert Crispin, 19
Gilbert Foliot: Commentary on the Song of Solomon, 18
Gilbert Glanville, bishop of Rochester (1185-1214), 13, 16, 17
Gilbert of Porrée, 17
Goda, Countess, 58
Goda's Gospels (BL MS. Royal 1 D. III), 2, 45, 65, 66, 82
Godwin II, bishop of Rochester (c. 1050), 52
Godwine, bishop of Rochester (c. 995), 56
Gospel of Nicodemus, 93
Gregory the Great, 4, 7, 14, 19, 107-109, 117
Gregory:
  commentary on Ezekiel, 12
  Dialogi, 9, 19
  Homilies on Ezekiel, 9, 102
  homily for St. Luke's Day, 102
  letters, 9
  Liber Regulae Pastoralis, 1, 9, 14
  Moralia in Job, 9, 14
  Registrum, 9
  (attributed) Speculum, 9
Gregory of Tours, 17
Guillaume Perault: Summa de vitiis et virtutibus, 20
Guitmund of Aversa: De corpore et sanguine Domini, 20
Gundulf, bishop of Rochester (1077-1108), 3, 4, 9, 17, 43, 45, 54, 57-59, 68, 84, 94, 103, 121
Gundulf Bible, 62-65, 66-77, 79-84

Hadbot, 49, 51
Haymo, 100, 117
Hedenham, 57
Hegesippus, 10
Helyas, sacrist (c. 1203) then prior of Rochester (1214-1217?), 45
Henry I, king of England (1100-1135), 53, 57, 58
Henry II, king of England (1154-1189), 13
Heraclitus, 10
Hilary of Poitiers: Expositio Hymnorum, 19
Hlothhære, laws of, 49
Honorius of Autun, 20
Honorius: Elucidarius, 93
Horace, 17
Humphrey the precentor, 110
Hyginus: De spera mundi, 10
Hystoria Normannorum, 10

Imar of Tusculum, 11, 59
Instituta Cnuti, 47, 50, 51, 59
Isidore of Seville, 9, 15
Isidore:
  De summo bono, 16
  Etymologiae, 9, 15-17
  Synonyma, 16

Ithamar, bishop of Rochester (644-660), ix, 17, 122
Itineraria of Peter, 10
Iudicia Dei I-III, 52
Ivo of Chartres, 10
Ivo of Chartres: *Panormia*, 17

Jerome, 4, 7-9, 12, 14, 77, 87, 102, 107
Jerome:
  commentaries on Isaiah, Psalter, Ezekiel, Jeremiah, Ecclesiastes, Matthew, twelve prophets, Daniel, 9
  commentary on Philemon, 18
  commentary on Titus, 9, 18
  Interpretationes hebraicorum nominum, 9
  tract against Jovinian, 9
John Bromyard: *Summa predicantium*, 20
John Cassian, 9
John Chrysostom, 4, 100, 112-114, 114
John Chrysostom: *De reparatione lapsi*, 9
John I, bishop of Rochester (1124-1137), 11, 77, 79
John II of Séez, bishop of Rochester (1138-1142), 59
John of Cornwall: *Summa*, 18
John of Salisbury: *Policraticus*, 18
Jordanes, 10
Josephus, 10
Judith of Flanders, 66, 67
Julian of Toledo: *Prognosticon*, 9
Julius Valerius: translation of the *Gesta Alexandri*, 10
Justin's Abbreviation of Pompeius Trogus, 8, 10
Justus, bishop of Rochester (604-624), ix, 1
Juvenal: *Satires*, 2

Kent, 1, 44-46, 54, 57, 60, 61, 68, 83, 84, 85, 86, 122, 123

Lanfranc, archbishop of Canterbury (1070-1092), ix, 3, 4, 20, 49, 54, 57, 58, 63, 67
Lanfranc:
  Constitutiones, 10
  letters, 10
  treatise against Berengar of Tours, 10
Le Puy, 76
Leo, 102, 118
Leo: *De Incarnatione Verbi*, 95
Letbert, Abbot of Ruf, 18
Letbert: *Flores Psalterii*, 19
Letter of Alexander the Great to Aristotle, 10
Liber Temporalium (Rochester), 53-55
Liber Vitae of Durham, 46
Lincoln, 76, 84
Lisieux, 13
London, 6, 44, 54, 59
Lord Lumley's Catalogue (1611), 68
Lucan, 17

Macrobius, 17
Macrobius: *Somnium Scipionis*, 10
Malling, Kent, 18
Manumission, 46
MANUSCRIPTS
  Baltimore:
    MS. Walters Art Gallery W. 18, 32, 62, 77, 78-83
  Brussels:
    MS. Bibliothèque Royale de Belgique 1403, 19
  Cambridge:
    MS. Corpus Christi College 2, 83
    MSS. Corpus Christi College 3-4 (Dover Bible), 83
    MS. Corpus Christi College 48, 83
    MS. Corpus Christi College 62, fols. 49-208, 34; fols. 209-74, 37
    MS. Corpus Christi College 162, 2, 88-90, 93-94
    MS. Corpus Christi College 184, 29
    MS. Corpus Christi College 191, 70
    MS. Corpus Christi College 303, 20, 91-94
    MS. Corpus Christi College 318, 20
    MS. Corpus Christi College 332, 7, 25
    MS. Corpus Christi College 383, 47, 49, 51
    MS. Pembroke College 23, 109, 110
    MS. Pembroke College 24, 109
    MS. Trinity College B.4.27 [141], 9
    MS. Trinity College B.5.2 [148], 75, 83
    MS. Trinity College O.2.24 [1128], 30
    MS. Trinity College O.4.7 [1238], 26
    MS. University Library Ff.4.32, 24
    MS. University Library Ii.II.19, 104-5, 110, 111
    MS. University Library Kk.IV.13, 98-101, 110
  Durham:
    MS. Durham Cathedral A.II.4, 75, 83
    MS. Durham Cathedral A.III.29, 96, 103, 110
    MS. Durham Cathedral B.II.2, 96
    MS. Durham Cathedral B.II.31, 96
  Edinburgh:
    MS. Edinburgh National Library Adv. 18.2.4, 20, 95, 104-111
    MS. Edinburgh National Library Adv. 18.3.9, 29
  Eton:
    MS. Eton College 80, 26
  Fleury:
    MS. Fleury 29, 113
    MS. Fleury 38, 114
    MS. Fleury 41, 114
    MS. Fleury 58, 116
    MS. Fleury 67, 99, 102
  Grenoble:
    MS. Grenoble 32, 98, 102
  Lincoln:

INDEX

MS. Lincoln Cathedral 1, 83
MS. Lincoln Cathedral 158, 98-101
London, British Library:
  MS. Cotton Domitian A. X, 54
  MS. Cotton Otho A. XV, 36
  MS. Cotton Tiberius A. II, 66
  MS. Cotton Tiberius B. XI, 1
  MS. Cotton Vespasian A. XIII, 32
  MS. Cotton Vespasian A. XXII, 5, 13, 15, 17, 45, 54, 57, 69, 92, 94
  MS. Cotton Vespasian D. XIV, 19, 20, 86, 92-94
  MS. Cotton Vespasian D. XXI, fols. 1-17, 32
  MS. Harley 23, 35
  MS. Harley 261, 35
  MS. Harley 652, 96, 104-05, 109-10
  MS. Harley 1023, 76
  MS. Harley 3680, 30, 89
  MS. Royal 1 B. IV, 36
  MS. Royal 1 B. XI, 72
  MS. Royal 1 C. VII, 19, 27, 62, 77, 79-82
  MS. Royal 1 D. III, 45, 65
  MS. Royal 1 D. IX, 66, 67
  MS. Royal 1 E. VII, 63, 64, 68, 75, 80-83
  MS. Royal 1 E. VIII, 63, 64, 65, 68, 75, 80-83
  MS. Royal 2 C. I, 20
  MS. Royal 2 C. III, 20, 91, 95, 98-101, 103, 108-110, 118
  MS. Royal 2 D. VI, 19, 34
  MS. Royal 2 E. VII, 41
  MS. Royal 2 F. XI, 41
  MS. Royal 3 B. I, 18
  MS. Royal 3 C. IV, 29
  MS. Royal 3 C. VII, 41
  MS. Royal 3 C. IX, 33
  MS. Royal 3 C. X, 33
  MS. Royal 4 A. XVI, 36
  MS. Royal 4 B. I, 29
  MS. Royal 4 B. VII, 19
  MS. Royal 4 C. IV, 33
  MS. Royal 4 C. X, 35, 39
  MS. Royal 4 E. V, 20
  MS. Royal 5 A. IV, 54
  MS. Royal 5 A. VII, 19, 28
  MS. Royal 5 A. XV, 23
  MS. Royal 5 B. IV, 23
  MS. Royal 5 B. VI, 23
  MS. Royal 5 B. VII, 23
  MS. Royal 5 B. X, 23
  MS. Royal 5 B. XII, x, 23-41, 78
  MS. Royal 5 B. XIII, 24
  MS. Royal 5 B. XVI, 24
  MS. Royal 5 C. I, 33
  MS. Royal 5 C. VIII, 33
  MS. Royal 5 D. I, 23
  MS. Royal 5 D. II, 23
  MS. Royal 5 D. III, 23
  MS. Royal 5 D. VII, 80
  MS. Royal 5 D. IX, 23
  MS. Royal 5 E. I, 34
  MS. Royal 5 E. II, 29
  MS. Royal 5 E. X, 29
  MS. Royal 6 A. I, 28
  MS. Royal 6 A. IV, 28
  MS. Royal 6 A. XI, 35
  MS. Royal 6 A. XII, 29
  MS. Royal 6 B. II, 19, 29
  MS. Royal 6 B. VI, 28
  MS. Royal 6 C. I, 89
  MS. Royal 6 C. IV, 28
  MS. Royal 6 C. VI, 29
  MS. Royal 6 C. X, 29
  MS. Royal 6 D. II, 28
  MS. Royal 6 D. V, 34
  MS. Royal 7 A. XI, fols. 19-24, 28
  MS. Royal 7 C. XIII, 20
  MS. Royal 7 C. XIV, 20
  MS. Royal 7 E. IV, 20
  MS. Royal 7 E. VIII, 20
  MS. Royal 8 D. V*, 34
  MS. Royal 8 D. XVI, 31
  MS. Royal 9 C. IV, 20
  MS. Royal 9 E. XI, 20
  MS. Royal 10 A. XII, 13, 19, 27, 34, 35, 37, 41, 42, 78
  MS. Royal 10 A. XIV, 20
  MS. Royal 10 B. II, 20
  MS. Royal 10 C. IV, 41
  MS. Royal 10 C. XII, 20
  MS. Royal 11 B. XV, 20
  MS. Royal 11 C. I, 20
  MS. Royal 11 D. I, 20
  MS. Royal 12 C. I, 20, 31
  MS. Royal 12 C. IV, 31
  MS. Royal 12 D. XIV, 20
  MS. Royal 12 F. I, 20
  MS. Royal 12 F. VIII, 41
  MS. Royal 12 F. XIII, 20, 122
  MS. Royal 12 G. II, 20
  MS. Royal 12 G. III, 20
  MS. Royal 15 A. XIX, 20
  MS. Royal 15 A. XXII, 19, 32
  MS. Royal 15 B. XI, 19, 32
  MS. Royal 15 C. X, 2, 39
London, Lambeth Palace:
  MS. Lambeth Palace 3, 84
  MS. Lambeth Palace 76, fols. 1-147, 24
Maidstone, Kent:
  MS. Maidstone Museum 1, 84
New York:
  MS. Pierpont Morgan Library 708, 66
  MS. Pierpont Morgan Library 709, 66
Ottobeuren:
  MS. Ottobeuren 15, 112
  MS. Ottobeuren 23, 112
  MS. Ottobeuren 24, 112
Oxford:
  MS. Bodley 134, 25
  MS. Bodley 267, 109
  MSS. Bodley 340-342, 2, 32, 87-94

MS. Bodley 387, 27
MS. Bodley 535, 70
MS. Bodley 579, (Leofric Missal) 46
MS. Bodley Auct. D. Inf. 2.9, 70
MS. Bodley Digby 13, 48
MS. Bodley Laud misc. 40, 19
MS. Bodley Rawlinson C. 641, 47, 48, 52
MS. Bodley Wood B.3, 2
MS. St. John's College 4, 82
Paris:
  MS. B.N. Lat. 4, 76
  MSS. B.N. Lat. 45-92, 73
  MS. B.N. Lat. 93, 65, 74
  MS. B.N. Lat. 261, 66, 72, 73
  MS. B.N. Lat. 11504, 76
  MS. B.N. Lat. 11505, 74-76
  MS. B.N. Lat. 11532, 73, 74
  MS. B.N. Lat. 11533, 73-75
  MS. B.N. Lat. 11553, 74, 75
Pasadena, CA:
  MS. Huntington Library HM 62 (Gundulf Bible), 5, 26, 62-65, 67-77, 80-84
Rochester (Kent County Archives):
  MS. Rochester Cathedral DRc/Z18, 1-2, 11, 23, 24, 26, 27, 29-31, 33, 36, 37, 42
  Textus Roffensis, x, xi, 1, 2, 6-8, 10-13, 23-32, 43-60, 61, 78, 86, 90, 94, 103, 110, 122
St. Gall:
  MS. St. Gall, 75, 76
Toledo:
  MS. Toledo 8, 117
  MS. Toledo 30, 115
  MS. Toledo 43, 115
  MS. Toledo 63, 117
  MS. Toledo 65, 117
  MS. Toledo Add. 4, 113
  MS. Toledo Add. 5, 113
  MS. Toledo Add. 10a, 113
  MS. Toledo Add. 19, 116
Vatican:
  MS. Vatican Lat. 4951, 20, 32, 95, 96, 112-117
  MS. Vatican Lat. 8563, 110
  MS. Vatican Reg. lat. 646, fols. 1-48, 11, 31
  MS. Vatican Reg. lat. 458, fols. 1-36, 11, 31
  MS. Vatican Reg. lat. 598, fol. 8r, 11, 31
Vercelli:
  MS. Biblioteca Capitolare 117 (Vercelli Book), 86-88, 90
Vienne:
  MS. Vienne 25, 114
Winchester:
  MS. Winchester Cathedral 17, 83
Wolfenbüttel:
  MS. Wolfenbüttel 27, 115
  MS. Wolfenbüttel 44, 114
  MS. Wolfenbüttel 53, 115

Master Hamo, donor to Rochester library, 16-18
Master Robert, donor to Rochester library, 18
Maximus of Turin, 117
Mercia, 54
Mircna laga, 51

Nennius, 10
Nennius: *Historia Brittonum*, 19
New Minster, Winchester, 66
Norwich, 96, 97, 103, 106, 109, 110
Norþleod, 51

Odo of Bayeux, 57
Odo of Meung, 18
Offa, king of Mercia (757-796), 54
Omnibonus, 18
Ordal, 50
Oribasius, 18
Orléans, 72, 76
Orosius, 10
Osbern, monk of Christ Church, Canterbury (d. 1093), 121
Ovid, 17, 18

Palladius: *Paradysus*, 10
Paschasius Radbertus, 116, 118
Paschasius Radbertus: *De corpore et sanguine Domini*, 9
Paul the Deacon's homiliary, 10, 85, 91, 96, 97, 101, 103, 106-11, 117-19
Paulinus, bishop of Rochester (633-644), ix, 17, 58, 87, 89, 123
Pax, 50
Penenden Heath, 57, 58
Persius, 17
Peter Cantor: *Distinctiones*, 20
Peter Comestor, 16
Peter Comestor: *Historia scholastica*, 20
Peter Damian, 15, 20
Peter Helias: *Summa*, 20
Peter Lombard: *Sententiae*, 12, 16-18, 20
Peter of Cornwall: *Pantheologus*, 20
Peter Riga, 20
Peterborough, 6
Priscian, 17, 18
Priscian: *Periegesis of Dionysius*, 10
Prosper of Aquitaine/Julianus Pomerius: *De vita contemplativa et activa*, 9
Prudentius: *Psychomachia*, 17
Pseudo-Apuleius, 18
Pseudo-Augustine, 112-17
Pseudo-Seneca, 20
Pseudo-Turpin, 16
Publilius Syrus, 20

Quadripartitus, 46, 47, 49-52, 59
Quintus Serenus, 18

Rabanus Maurus, 102, 106, 109, 117

INDEX

Radulph de Frend, donor to Rochester library, 16
Ralph d'Escures, bishop of Rochester (1108-1114), 5, 43, 52, 93, 94
Ralph d'Escures: *De ratione et peccatore*, 10
Ralph of Battle: *Octo Puncta*, 10
Rathramnus of Corbie, 8
Razi, the Arab, 18
Reginald of Canterbury: *Vita Malchi*, 17
Remigius super Donatus, 17
Robert de Hecham, donor to Rochester library, 15, 17
Robert of Walton (Felixstowe), 18
Rochester Bridge, 56
Rochester Castle, 57
Roger Bigot, donor to Rochester, 58
Roger de Derteford, donor to Rochester library, 16
Romanus, bishop of Rochester (624-633), 122
Rufinus, 10

St. Æthelwold, 62
St. Albans, 84
St. Andrew, 87, 89, 91, 97, 106
St. Augustine of Canterbury, ix, 12, 89, 91, 92
St. Augustine's, Canterbury, ix, 6, 11, 21, 56, 63, 70, 84, 85, 87-90, 92, 96, 102, 103, 106
St. Benedict, rule of, 9
St. Bonaventure, 20
St. Brendan, 12
St. Dunstan, 10, 62, 85
St. Elphege, 10, 44, 121
St. Etheldreda, 12
St. Etheldritha, 17
St. Giles, 90, 91
St. James, 93
St. Margaret, 90, 91
St. Mildred, 17
St. Neot, 6, 93, 94
St. Nicholas, 90-91
St. Oswald, 62
St. Peter and St. Paul, 102, 110, 119
St. Riquier, abbey of, 73, 74
St. Sexburga, 12
St. Thomas à Becket: *Miracula*, 17
St. Thomas Aquinas: Commentary on book IV of Peter Lombard's *Sententiae*, 20
St. Witburga, 12
St. Wulfram, 17
St.-Germain-des-Prés, abbey of, 62, 64, 65, 74-76
Salisbury, 96
Sallust, 17
Seneca, 17
Sidonius Apollinaris, 17, 19
Sigered, king of Kent (c. 762), 54
Siward, bishop of Rochester (1058-1075), 3
Smaragdus, 102, 107, 109, 117
Smaragdus: *Diadema Monachorum*, 9
Snodland, Kent, 55, 56
Solinus, 4
Solinus: *De mirabilibus mundi*, 10, 19
Statius, 17
Statius: *Thebiad*, 2
Strood, Kent, 13
Suetonius, 18
Swerian, 51
Swipulf, bishop of Rochester (880?-896?), 1

Ten Articles of William I, 48, 49
Tenth sibyl's prophecy prefaced by Lactantius, 10, 19
Terence, 17
Theodulf of Orléans, 72, 73, 76, 85
Theodulf Bible, 71, 76
Tours, 71, 73, 76
Trinubium Annae, 93

Vercelli Book, 86-88, 90
Victor of Capua: *Diatessaron* of Tatian, 18
Vindicta Salvatoris, 93
Virgil, 17
Vita Gundulfi, x, 5, 58, 69
Volumen Parvum of the *Corpus Iuris Civilis*, 20

Waleran, bishop of Rochester (1182-1184), 17
Walreaf, 50
Wer, 51
West Saxon Genealogy, 52
Wibert, possibly prior of Christ Church, Canterbury (1152-1167), 18
Wif, 51
Wihtræd, laws of, 49
Willem de Bradest, donor to Rochester library, 17
William I, king of England (1066-1087), 52, 57, 58, 103
William I, laws of, 47
William II, king of England (1087-1100), 57, 58
William of Conches: *Philosophia*, 17
William of Malmesbury, 16
William of St. Carilef, bishop of Durham (1081-1096), 69
Winchester, ix, 70, 84, 123
Windsor (St. George's Chapel), 96, 109, 110
Worcester, 96
Wouldham, Kent, 55
Wulfstan, bishop of Worcester (1002-1016) and archbishop of York (1002-1023), 49, 51, 87, 92

Zacharias Chrysopolitanus: *In unum ex quatuor*, 18

PUBLICATIONS

OF

The American Philosophical Society

The publications of the American Philosophical Society consist of PROCEEDINGS, TRANSACTIONS, MEMOIRS, and YEAR BOOK.

THE PROCEEDINGS contains papers which have been read before the Society in addition to other papers which have been accepted for publication by the Committee on Publications. In accordance with the present policy one volume is issued each year, consisting of four quarterly numbers, and the price is $24.00 net per volume. Individual copies may be purchased at $10.00 per copy.

THE TRANSACTIONS, the oldest scholarly journal in America, was started in 1769. In accordance with the present policy each annual volume is a collection of monographs, each issued as a part. The current annual subscription price is $70.00 net per volume. Individual copies of the TRANSACTIONS are offered for sale.

Each volume of the MEMOIRS is published as a book. The titles cover the various fields of learning; most of the recent volumes have been historical. The price of each volume is determined by its size and character, but subscribers are offered a 20 per cent discount.

The YEAR BOOK is of considerable interest to scholars because of the reports on grants for research and to libraries for this reason and because of the section dealing with the acquisitions of the Library. In addition it contains the Charter and Laws, and lists of members, and reports of committees and meetings. The YEAR BOOK is published about April 1 for the preceding calendar year. The current price is $12.00. A separate volume of GRANTEES' REPORTS is published annually. The listed price is $10.00.

An author desiring to submit a manuscript for publication should send it to the Editor, American Philosophical Society, 104 South Fifth Street, Philadelphia, Pa. 19106.

www.ingramcontent.com/pod-product-compliance
Lightning Source LLC
Chambersburg PA
CBHW080801020526
44114CB00035B/3